The Understructure of Writing for Film and Television

The Understructure
of Writing for
Film & Television

BEN BRADY & LANCE LEE

University of Texas Press, Austin

LIBRARY OF CONGRESS CATALOGING-IN-PUBLICATION DATA

Brady, Ben.
   The understructure of writing for film and television.

   Includes index.
   1. Moving-picture authorship.   2. Television authorship.
3. Playwriting.   4. Drama—Technique.   I. Lee, Lance, 1942–
II. Title
PN1996.B715   1988   808.2′2   87-25508
ISBN 0-292-78514-3
ISBN 0-292-78515-1 (pbk.)

Contents

The Understructure of Writing for Film and Television

Preface

No one can teach another to write. Being able to write is a gift—you have it, or you don't. But creativity is much more widespread than generally thought. It can be guided. It can be provoked. It can be inspired. Students can be challenged to test their own resources as writers.

These thoughts have guided the development of the very successful writing program in the Radio, Television and Film Department at the State University of California at Northridge. Some semesters have seen more than three hundred students enrolled in sixteen sections of the beginning writing course for television and film and another seventy relegated to waiting lists.

The course takes the student over the ground of preparing and writing a half-hour television script. A textbook grew out of this practical experience, *The Keys to Writing for Television and Film*, now in its fourth edition and adopted by more than forty colleges and universities here and in Canada.

Nothing stands still. The continued growth and experience of the program at Northridge has led us to believe that students could use more writing experience than one introductory course offers before they go on to more ambitious projects. The professional staff that teaches this course has developed a more fundamental course that strengthens the excellent results already achieved.

We emphasize this emergent development so that you will see that this new text has grown out of the experience of teaching hundreds of students the fundamentals of writing for television and film. Our belief, already translated into practice at Northridge by instituting the new course this new text reflects, is that requiring students to write a variety of scenes leads to an ever-deepening awareness of the development of character and conflict, gives additional practice in using the screenplay format, and provides a much more substantial groundwork for developing longer scripts.

Any decent education of a writer has to insist on the sheer practice of writing. The principal objective of this text is to provide that necessary exercise through a progression of scenewriting assignments, culminating in the writing of a minidrama of 10–15 pages (longer if an instructor chooses). Our experience has been that beginning students clearly enjoy the greater freedom to test their wings as well as the challenge of dealing with multiple subjects in individual assignments.

Anything and everything a writer must accomplish in a long drama must also be accomplished in each of its scenes, namely, structuring beginning, middle, and end; introducing and developing character; establishing conflict and developing it to crisis; handling climax and resolution; coming to grips with elements of the back story; and using exposition in a dramatic way. Individual assignments emphasize each of these elements in turn. To illustrate these points, we have richly supplemented the text with sample scenes drawn from the screen repertoire. And since all plays—TV, film, and stage—have the same spine, an occasional notable example from the stage has been included.

Beginning writers would be ill educated were they not made aware of the common heritage playwrights share in the techniques that underlie the separate media for which a play can be written. There is a repertoire of dramatic techniques that go all the way back to the scenic spectaculars and costume shockers used by Aeschylus.

Although we concentrate on a *progression* of scenes, the book culminates with a simple explication of preparing and executing a miniscreenplay, taking the student through the necessary steps of developing a brief premise, a treatment, and a stepsheet.

When reading the analyses of the scenes included in the text, keep two points in mind: first, no two authors will write the same dramatic situation in the same way, and no author will write the same dramatic situation, like a love scene, in the same way twice; second, everyone is likely to have a different interpretation of the same material. Our analyses of the scenes included in the text are intended to provide the beginner with a model for an increasingly thorough analysis of dramatic structure, reality, and motivation. They also try to make clear why a given scene succeeds or is to some extent compromised. There is never the intention to imply that a scene can be written or interpreted in only one way. Yet scenes finally are written in one chosen way, the variants having been tried and sifted out by an author in the writing process, and those final choices are what we must examine. If an author succeeds, he imparts the feeling of a certain inevitability to a scene, and any analysis must deal with that inevitability. But it must be remembered the author has created that sense of inevitability as part of the illusion of reality he set out to create from his original, rough intentions. We hope when you differ with us you will do so with increasing confidence in using the analytic model we provide for your own creative ends.

Bear in mind that there are sophisticated variations to screenwriting as there are to other traditions. We have incorporated work from Aeschylus, Henrik Ibsen, and Ingmar Bergman in part for that reason. Drama and its cinematic variant are international. Dramatic fundamentals know no boundaries and must be dealt with whatever the writer's nationality, politics, or philosophy. Nonetheless, this text is meant as a practical introduction to American screenwriting traditions, to the world of professional practice prevalent in this country now. We believe that the student who masters its contents will be well positioned to tackle half-hour, hour, or full-length scripts for American markets with confidence and sophistication. But basics must come first, just as they have for other screenwriters.

Last, a word on language. The use of the pronoun *he* for both men and women in the body of the text is done so for the sake of brevity and simplicity of expression to support the learning process.

Acknowledgments

We gratefully acknowledge the following for permission to quote from their works: Columbia Pictures and Robert Benton for *Kramer vs. Kramer*, Larry Gelbart for *Tootsie*, John Huston for *The Treasure of the Sierra Madre*, New American Library for *A Doll House*, New Directions and the Tennessee Williams Foundation for *A Streetcar Named Desire*, Buck Henry for *The Graduate*, Pantheon Books for *Fanny and Alexander*, Paramount Pictures Corporation for *The Godfather*, Budd Schulberg for *On the Waterfront*, and Kendall/Hunt Publishing Company for *The Keys to Writing for Television and Film*, by Ben Brady.

Part One: Getting on Your Feet

1. Your Dramatic Heritage

When you sit down to write a screenplay, a teleplay, or a stage play, you are functioning as a playwright, as a dramatist. There are many differences in the possible treatment of a play because it is affected by (a) the type of theatre that is available for its production, (b) the use of a camera to make a film for theatrical release, or (c) the nature of a particular television show. Nonetheless, different though they may be in treatment, the underlying dramatic art of the play remains the same. Even the impulse to spectacular special effects, or spectacle, remains much the same, whether we are talking about the classics—plays written by eminently practical men of the theatre of their time—or contemporary achievements with the camera.

There is an immense gap in time between the opening of Aeschylus' *Agamemnon* 2,500 years ago and the filming of the long, full shots of wilderness that open Stanley Kubrick's modern science fiction classic *2001*. But the dramatic impulses in the ancient playwright and popular contemporary filmmaker are alike—the only difference is in dramatic structure and technology.

Take, for example, the opening of Aeschylus' play in which the Watchman is looking for a signal to indicate that Troy has at last fallen and the long Trojan war come to an end.

SCENE: Argos, before the palace of King Agamemnon. The Watchman is posted on the roof of the palace.

WATCHMAN
. . . Now let there be again redemption from distress,
the flare burning from the blackness in good augury.
(A light shows in the distance)

Oh hail, blaze of the darkness, harbinger of day's
shining, and processionals, and dance, and choirs
of multitudes in Argos for this day of grace.
Ahoy!
I cry the news aloud. . . .[1]

Aeschylus was the first master of special effects. Since his story was
staged outside and began at dawn, it is not inconceivable that "the flare"
turned out to be the rising sun. It is an effect we can still admire! Or
take Aeschylus' *Libation Bearers* in which he costumed the Greek cho-
rus with such reality as Furies, the ancient vengeful goddesses with
snakes in their hair, that his audience thought the real Furies had appeared, snakes and all, and recoiled in horror—just as we recoil today
when Willie, in Steven Spielberg's *Indiana Jones and the Temple of
Doom*, creeps across a bug-filled floor with insects in her hair to reach
into an insect-filled slimy crevice to release Indiana from the chamber
of descending knives. Today the camera brings us immediately and
closely in on the action, but the distance between the audience and the
event has always been defined less by technical resource than by emotion. In short, we the audience must have our emotions aroused in order
to be involved, something ancient and contemporary playwrights have
regarded as absolutely necessary for writing effective drama.

So as you begin to think dramatically, you will be learning an art that
was virtually created by Aeschylus, practiced by Shakespeare and the
polite dramatists of the eighteenth century, turned to his own use by
George Bernard Shaw, and redefined by Henrik Ibsen for the modern era.
Now that the art has been divided further by cinema and television, the
list of practitioners includes men like Alfred Hitchcock, Howard Hawks,
Ingmar Bergman, François Truffaut, Paddy Chayefsky, Robert Towne,
and your own particular favorite. In short, there is an immense repertoire of drama all written by practical men and women waiting for your
exploration, a body of work rich in precedent and full of suggestion for
you for almost any dramatic experiment you may want to try.

Now then, dwell for a moment on a word—*playwright*. It is an odd
word with that *wright* in it. A *wright* is a craftsman, someone who
makes and assembles things, a practical man par excellence. Drama has
always had to appeal to a wide taste, to please many different tastes at
one time. It is competitive. It has had to win prizes or celebrate divine
virtues to justify itself or to make money to support the companies

1. Aeschylus, *Agamemnon*, trans. Richmond Lattimore (New York: Modern
Library, 1942), p. 42.

creating it and the theatres displaying it. Even when patronized, it has had to be popularly successful. For thousands of years people have gathered to witness a play performed. They assembled in the open theatres of Greece and Elizabethan England, in the court theatres of baroque Europe, in the public theatres and first small experimental theatres in the nineteenth century, and now in our own modern theatres and cinemas. Television has expanded these audiences into the millions. So public and responsive an art must be practical; therefore, the playwright is the most practical artist within the great arts.

There is much to be said about the mechanics of the practical, down-to-earth nature of drama. Most of this text is largely devoted to that end. Never forget that drama happens before our eyes, on a stage or on a screen, as a visual, immediate, real experience, dependent on the presence of an audience whose attention it must hold and whose expenditure it must justify, or it is a failure as a drama.

That said, no playwright ever made his mark who was not also a man of vision. The central, most difficult lesson for a playwright to learn is how to embody his own vision in a practical play for stage or screen or television. Without such vision, there's not much reason to present or attend a play. This is true whether we are talking about a Saturday afternoon adventure flick or the premiere of a new drama on the stage of a resident theatre.

Consider the popular action-adventure science fiction *Star Wars* trilogy by George Lucas. He had a vision of what a film would look like, what new special effects could achieve, and he revolutionized the film industry by bringing it into the computer era. But such effects alone would not have held our attention through three films. Sooner or later we would have asked ourselves what they were all for, if they helped tell a story or just got in its way. Lucas knew this, and using computerized special effects and the disguise of a science fiction thriller, he presented in *Star Wars* a spectacular vision of failure and redemption in which an abandoned son redeems a fallen father.

2. What Is a Dramatic Conflict?

Drama comes from the Greek word *dran*, which means action. Our word *actor* literally means someone who carries out an action. *Agony* is derived from another Greek word, *agon*, which means contest. Plays are stories about people involved in a contest.

A dramatic story is an action. It is action on the part of your protagonist to overcome a difficult problem or go down swinging in the attempt. A dramatic story is a series of doings, of happenings, of events caused by the protagonist trying to solve his problem: it is not a thing of words, but behaviors. Dramatic action has a structure—a problem appears for the protagonist and worsens until a point of crisis is reached, which leads in turn to a climactic moment or sequence. The climax sees the ending of the problem for the protagonist one way or another.

You are going to construct a screenplay. That is, you are going to write a dramatic story for the screen structured in what is called a plot. You are not writing for a single individual next to a lamp with a book on his lap, but for people gathered together to see and hear your story. All you have is one and a half hours of their patience for the typical full-length screenplay.

It's not just filmed. It is enacted. It is lived. The audience will see people (your characters) going through actual experiences at the very moment they are having them. Your story will be made up of these immediate experiences. You will not only engage the conscious level of their identifications with your characters, but their unconscious mind, too, as it is affected by color, costume, scenery, sounds, movement, and spectacle as your characters attempt and succeed or fail to do something that they feel a great, immediate need to do and have a difficult time in actually doing because of some opposition to their needs. It is impossible to overemphasize this need for immediate, crucial action.

You will certainly want to entertain the audience, too. You won't have your characters doing familiar things in familiar ways. You will want to inform with original thought and ideas; you'll want to please by enlightening through the way your characters respond to their problems.

Since your story has a BEGINNING, MIDDLE, and END, it's not shapeless, not simply an accident or an incident like this:

Sally, a solid young woman of 28, an Olympic skier, crosses a street against the light and is hit by a car.

That's too bad, and it is a news story, but not a dramatic story. But look at it this way:

BEGINNING.   Sally, a 28-year-old Olympic skier, is hit by a car and taken to a hospital. She can't move her legs. Her physicians fear paralysis.

MIDDLE.   Sally refuses to accept paralysis. She works steadily in therapy, trying to regain sensation and movement. Even her parents think she is asking too much from herself. But Sally won't give up on herself and decides to go on trying to recover until something happens to make it appear hopeless.

END.   Unwilling to give up, she one day gets a twinge in a toe. Soon she is confounding everyone with her progress. She's a long way from being able to ski again but that, she asserts, as she takes her first free steps, is just a matter of time.

That's a dramatic story, though a very simple one. And it brings us face to face with the nature of dramatic conflict. Something happens to someone, to your main character, your protagonist. Sally is hurt. This is not just any kind of hurt, but one your protagonist needs to correct. It makes your protagonist do something in reaction. Here Sally struggles to regain her health. But your protagonist can't solve the problem easily, or the story is over immediately. So you have given Sally a problem that is very hard to solve and that requires a long struggle to overcome. And as Sally shows, your protagonist is a fighter. No matter how bad things get, she doesn't give up, even though her parents give up on her. Finally, your protagonist reaches some point of resolution. Sally makes it or fails to make it.

Your story has a build to it, then a moment of crisis when things seem hopeless, and finally a climactic moment or sequence of moments when a final effort is made to overcome the odds. In the example, Sally starts to get better.   ˙

So, what is a dramatic conflict? It is the motivation of the protagonist to cope with a problem of major proportions in a situation in which his attempt to resolve the problem encounters serious obstacles. That opposition can come from within the protagonist, it can come from others outside, or it can come from some sort of physical or natural obstacle. Those are the only three sources of conflict. Let's emphasize the idea of obstacle now. Sally is hurt: her obstacle is a physical one. She wants to ski again, but has to overcome paralysis.

Conflict in a good play is rarely as simple as Sally's. More often it will occur between people and require a good deal of their acting and reacting on one another before it comes clear. So let's reemphasize the protagonist's will to struggle with some opposing person (the antagonist) and think of conflict as a collision of wills. Your protagonist needs to do something in response to a problem. Someone (or something) else, your opposing force, won't let him have his way. The ensuing personal struggle is a dramatic conflict. This conflict is the action of the play.

Action causes a reaction that leads to new action that causes a chain of actions and reactions. This means that your play is made up of a series of minor conflicts. If there is no cause-and-effect struggle of this kind, nothing happens! Nothing arouses the audience's emotions. Nothing holds their attention. Nothing excites their imagination or provokes their thought. If the first obligation of good drama is to involve emotions, the second is to stimulate and increase anxiety as imagination and intellect are aroused.

3. What Is a Scene?

A *scene* could be a picture on a postcard. Imagine such a scene coming to life: the sun rises or sets, the wind blows, the leaves drift. Each moment affects the next so that no succeeding minute is exactly like the last. You can never go back to what used to be: it has been changed by time.

A postcard won't hold our attention beyond the moment we look at it. But put someone in a position in which he or she has to act, and our interest deepens. *A dramatic scene is the setting in which the protagonist tries to overcome the obstacle that stands in the way of his actual or imagined needs.* A dramatic scene is not a setting in which people merely say things, but where they *do* things. The scene is where the dramatic action happens. A scene is also a sequence of that action—appearance of the problem for the protagonist, his effort to solve that problem when he reaches a point of failure (crisis), and his final effort to resolve his problem (climax).

The Three Parts of a Scene

Let's look at the very simple but effective opening scene of Mario Puzo and Francis Ford Coppola's *The Godfather* in which we are introduced into an odd, extralegal world with its own rules of honor and its own resources in three pages of immediate conflict. We experience this world in action and not in any other way. See if you can determine where the BEGINNING, MIDDLE, and END are that we just said were essentials of scene structure. Ask yourself these simple questions, which you should be able to answer for any scene, including the scenes you will write later:

Who is the protagonist?

What problem has appeared in his life that he must act to solve immediately?

What obstacle—force or person—is opposing the action the protagonist takes to solve his problem? Who, in short, is the antagonist?

What does the protagonist do?

FADE IN:

INT.   DON CORLEONE'S OFFICE   (SUMMER 1945) (EST) DAY

The Paramount Logo is presented austerely over a black background. There is a moment's hesitation, and then the simple words in white lettering:

THE GODFATHER

While this remains, we hear: "I believe in America." Suddenly we are watching in CLOSE VIEW, AMERIGO BONASERA, a man of sixty, dressed in a black suit, on the verge of great emotion.

BONASERA
America has made my fortune.

As he speaks, THE VIEW imperceptibly begins to loosen.

BONASERA (CONT'D)

> I raised my daughter in the American
> fashion; I gave her freedom, but
> taught her never to dishonor her fam-
> ily. She found a boy friend, not an Ital-
> ian. She went to the movies with
> him, stayed out late. Two months ago
> he took her for a drive, with another
> boy friend. They made her drink
> whiskey and then they tried to take
> advantage of her. She resisted; she
> kept her honor. So they beat her like
> an animal. When I went to the hospi-
> tal her nose was broken, her jaw was
> shattered and held together by wire,
> and she could not even weep because
> of the pain.

He can barely speak; he is weeping now.

CONTINUED

CONTINUED

> BONASERA (CONT'D)
> I went to the police like a good
> American. These two boys were ar-
> rested and brought to trial. The judge
> sentenced them to three years in
> prison, and suspended the sentence.
> Suspended sentence! They went free
> that very day. I stood in the courtroom
> like a fool, and those bastards, they
> smiled at me. Then I said to my wife,
> for Justice, we must go to The
> Godfather.

By now, the VIEW is full, and we SEE Don Corleone's office in his
home. The blinds are closed, and so the room is dark, and with pat-
terned shadows. DON CORLEONE sits patiently behind his desk, TOM
HAGEN sits near a small table, examining some paperwork, and
SONNY CORLEONE stands impatiently by the window nearest his father, sipping from a glass of wine. We can HEAR music, and the
laughter and voices of many people outside.

> DON CORLEONE
> Bonasera, we know each other for
> years, but this is the first time you
> come to me for help. I don't remem-
> ber the last time you invited me to
> your house for coffee . . . even though
> our wives are friends.

> BONASERA
> What do you want of me? I'll give you
> anything you want, but do what I ask!

> DON CORLEONE
> And what is that, Bonasera?

BONASERA whispers into the Don's ear.

> DON CORLEONE
> No, you ask for too much.

> BONASERA
> I ask for Justice.

CONTINUED

CONTINUED

> DON CORLEONE
> The Court gave you justice.

> BONASERA
> An eye for an eye!

> DON CORLEONE
> But your daughter is still alive.

> BONASERA
> Then make them suffer as she suffers.
> How much shall I pay you?

Both Hagen and Sonny react.

> DON CORLEONE
> You never think to protect yourself
> with real friends. You think it's
> enough to be an American. All right,
> the Police protect you, there are
> Courts of Law, so you don't need a
> friend like me. But now you come to
> me and say Don Corleone, you must
> give me justice. And you don't ask in
> respect or friendship. And you don't
> think to call me Godfather; instead
> you come to my house on the day my
> daughter is to be married and you ask
> me to do murder . . . for money.

> BONASERA
> America has been good to me . . .

> DON CORLEONE
> Then take the justice from the judge,
> the bitter with the sweet, Bonasera.
> But if you come to me with your
> friendship, your loyalty, then your
> enemies become my enemies, and
> then, believe me, they would fear you.

Slowly, Bonasera bows his head and murmurs.

> BONASERA
> Be my friend.

CONTINUED

CONTINUED

> DON CORLEONE
> Good. From me you'll get justice.

> BONASERA
> Godfather . . .

> DON CORLEONE
> Some day, and that day may never
> come, I would like to call upon you to
> do me services in return.

> FADE OUT[1]

We are drawn into a dramatic situation immediately by Bonasera relating the beating of his daughter. Who is Bonasera? An elderly man, simply described, suffering from a typical miscarriage of justice. He wants something from Don Corleone—extralegal, illegal help—vengeance. He gives all this information to get the Godfather to do something for him.

We see Don Corleone with his adopted and eldest sons. What does Don Corleone do? He refuses help. Force opposes force—the obstacle has appeared. We are not receiving information as we would in a novel, calmly reading a passage of exposition for action still to happen: we are in the middle of an active reality, witnessing an immediate confrontation. Characters inform us as they inform each other of their need to get their way with each other. Thus, Bonasera, his first action—asking for help—failing, moves to a new action: he offers to buy help. But this, we discover with Bonasera, is an insult. Payment has to be in a future service. To get what he wants, Bonasera must pay a price, compromise his personal integrity, his freedom to do as he wishes, by agreeing to render Don Corleone a future service. When he asks the Godfather to be his friend, he makes this compromise. He is changed from what he was at the start.

We asked you to think where the BEGINNING, MIDDLE, and END were in this scene. Take a piece of paper and write those out for yourself before you read any farther. Do they correspond to what follows?

BEGINNING.   Bonasera tells his story and asks for help. There is something he wants badly, but he is refused. The protagonist's problem appears.

---

1. Mario Puzo and Francis Ford Coppola, *The Godfather* (unpublished third draft of manuscript, March 1971), pp. 1–3. Reproduced with permission from Paramount Pictures Corporation; copyright © 1988; all rights reserved.

MIDDLE.   Don Corleone, Bonasera's obstacle, his antagonist, forces
Bonasera to make a number of efforts to overcome his opposition.
Bonasera tries to buy him and fails, offending him. He has reached a
point of crisis.

Remember, the crisis in a scene is the point at which the protagonist's
efforts to solve his problem seem to be doomed.

END.   Bonasera gets his way, but only by agreeing to Don Corleone's
price, which draws him into the world of the Mafia. This is the climax, that point at which the protagonist's struggle succeeds or fails.

Inevitably, someone will want to know, "Why can't I write something
nice about nice people?" You can. But in drama even nice people have
problems they have to struggle to resolve, or you don't have a drama. Or,
"Why can't I write something just for laughter?" You can. But the problems for characters in a comedy or farce seem mountainous to them,
always just beyond their frantic efforts to solve. That is the fun of it!
Without the collision of wills or collision of your protagonist's will with
an opposing circumstance, there is simply nothing to laugh at, cry over,
or think about. So remember: the problem must always mean a great
deal to your protagonist, as much as you can make it mean! No half mea-
sures! Suppose when Don Corleone had reproached Bonasera for never
inviting him to his house, Bonasera had sagged, muttered something,
and left in embarrassment? His daughter couldn't have meant much to
him if that had been how the scene had gone. He couldn't have wanted
anything very much, if that had been how he had left! And he would
have left with empty hands.

   Obviously, a story can be contained in a single scene, and each significant scene does tell a story in the dramatic form indicated. Within a
longer piece, each scene continues to have the same struggle within it,
except that the climax is not yet final. Each scene is part of a sequence of
scenes delineating the protagonist's cumulative and failing effort to
reach a resolution satisfactory to him, until the crisis is reached, when
all seems lost. In a full-length screenplay, the crisis usually appears at
the end of the second act: the remainder of the screenplay is the climactic effort of the protagonist to resolve his problem.

   We repeat for emphasis that whether a scene is a story in itself or part
of a larger story, each scene

   is the setting for a dramatic action

   is a particular sequence of dramatic action: the introduction of the problem for the protagonist, his efforts to solve it failing (crisis), and a final effort to solve his problem (climax).

Two Scenes—Good, Better

This is a good place to review what we've learned. We can sum it up in three points:

1. A dramatic story is an action.

2. A dramatic action is a conflict generated by your protagonist who needs to solve a problem of great importance to him, but who meets an obstacle in the form of another person—an antagonist, like Don Corleone in the scene you just read—or in the form of circumstances—as in the case of the accident we imagined for Sally.

3. A scene is the setting for your action, both a place and a particular sequence of dramatic action. That sequence is the establishment of the protagonist with his problem (the BEGINNING); his attempt to solve that problem reaching a point of failure, the crisis, because of the antagonist or obstacle (the MIDDLE); and his final attempt to resolve his problem, the climax (the END).

Let's explore these three points further by looking at two scenes of increasing quality from contemporary films. We'll look first at an amusing romantic scene from the popular comedy *Tootsie* and end with the climactic scene from the first act of the more searching, award-winning *Kramer vs. Kramer.*

After you read each scene take out a piece of paper and jot down who you think the protagonist and antagonist (person or circumstance) are, what you think the obstacle is to the protagonist, and finally how you see the structure in terms of BEGINNING, MIDDLE, and END. Then compare your notes to those following each scene.

We will talk at greater length in Part 2 about the emotional realism of drama. But here, after each scene ask yourself: How did I feel about the emotional reality of what I read and imagined in my mind's eye? Did I question how these characters behaved? Or was I completely convinced?

For example, think of the love scene between Adrian and Rocky in the popular film *Rocky.* You may well have seen this box office smash that started the 'Rocky' phenomenon. Do you believe a badly inhibited woman of 30 would let herself be cornered in a battered boxer's messy room? Or that the boxer, removing her glasses, would discover she is pretty? Why is Rocky the first to see that, after all, Adrian is pretty? Or do you believe that, as he embraces her, she would give herself to him freely after having remained a spinster all her life? It's possible, of course: we know Adrian and Rocky are attracted to each other, and we want them to succeed individually and together, but these details do strain credulity and diminish our belief in these characters' emotional reality in this love scene.

Remember that your protagonist is the character who carries the action, from whose point of view we experience the entire story. He can be as likeable as Les in what follows, or as villainous as Salieri in *Amadeus* or Richard III in Shakespeare's play.

A "Love" Scene from Tootsie

You may remember *Tootsie* was an unusual comedy based on the premise of an out-of-work actor impersonating a woman and then enjoying great success—as an actress. It is both a comedy and an attempt to try and say something about the nature of sexual roles in our society. Michael is the actor who impersonates a woman, Dorothy, and as Dorothy he scores great success as an actress playing the role of Tootsie in a popular soap opera. But his life is complicated when, still impersonating a woman, he falls in love with Julie. Since this is a comedy and uses some very old comedic situations as well as its more unconventional elements, Julie, naturally, doesn't love Michael. Michael is Dorothy to her. Who falls in love with Michael while he is impersonating Dorothy? Les, Julie's father! Not only does he fall in love with Michael-as-Dorothy, he plans to propose to her! The scene we examine occurs just after Julie has warned Dorothy about her father's intentions and asked her to let her father, Les, down gently.

Now here's the scene.

FADE IN:

INT.   RAINBOW GRILL   (EST) NIGHT

DOROTHY and LES at a table, Les in his best. The BAND plays a romantic number.

>   LES
>   (to WAITER)
>   Two coffees. How about some brandy,
>   Dorothy?

CONTINUED

CONTINUED

> DOROTHY
> Just coffee for me. Well, perhaps a
> little brandy might be wise.

> WAITER
> Yes, Madam.

> LES
> Food wasn't bad, was it?

> DOROTHY
> No. Very fresh. Not overcooked.

> LES
> Fish wasn't frozen.
> (a pause)
> Potatoes were crisp.
> (beat)
> Would you like to dance?

> DOROTHY
> Dance?

He stands, takes her hand. His look makes it impossible for her to say no.

THE DANCE FLOOR

Les and Dorothy begin to dance, Dorothy finding it difficult to follow. A MIDDLE-AGED COUPLE recognizes her. [Remember she is Tootsie!] As they dance by

> MIDDLE-AGED MAN
> We love you. You're wonderful.

Dorothy smiles, is suddenly confused as Les executes a dazzling bit of footwork.

> LES
> My wife and I took a course.

They continue, Dorothy having a tough time.

> LES
> I'm sorry. I forget you're on your feet
> all day.

THEIR TABLE

Les holds her chair for her, then sits. Brandy is waiting. Dorothy
starts to drink hers.

                    LES
          I was sure happy you could come out
          tonight. I know you usually have a lot
          of lines to learn.

                  DOROTHY
                (after a breath)
          Les, I think there's something I better
          say.

                    LES
          There's something I want to say, too.
          Wouldn't it be funny if we both
          wanted to say the same thing?

                  DOROTHY
          I don't think what I have to say is
          what you have to say.

                    LES
          Mine's pretty simple. I'm not that
          good with words, anyway.
                (a beat)
          I'm not sure how to start . . . You ever
          buy a real good pair of boots?

                  DOROTHY
          Boots?

                    LES
          Work boots. If you get the right pair,
          and after you work them in real good,
          they feel just as much a part of you
          as your own feet, if you know what I
          mean. It's a lot like people, boots . . .
          You know, how comfortable they
          make you feel, how they hold up to
                  (MORE)

                                    CONTINUED

CONTINUED

>   LES (CONT'D)
> wear and tear over the years.
>   (stops, embarrassed)
> I don't know why I'm going on about
> shoes and feet.
>   (a beat)
> I only took two pictures in my whole
> life. My high school graduation and
> my wedding. My wife was standing
> next to me in both of them. I never
> thought I'd want anyone to fill her
> place. I never thought there could be
> another woman gave me the same
> feeling. That all changed last
> weekend.

>   DOROTHY
> Les—

>   LES
> Let me finish. I've got to do this in
> one go, or I'll never get through it.
>   (reaches into pocket)
> I know this is sorta quick but that's
> how I am. Never did believe in not
> gettin' down to it.
>   (then)
> I'd like you to be my wife.

He opens a ring box, revealing a small diamond ring.

>   LES (CONT'D)
>   (quickly)
> Don't say anything now! I know it's
> fast. So take some time to get used to
> it. And if the answer's "no"—well, at
> least, I'll feel you took me seriously
> enough to think it over.

>   DOROTHY
>   (feebly)
> Will you forgive me . . . I feel faint.

CONTINUED

CONTINUED

> LES
> Well, if you're not the god-darndest,
> most feminine little thing I've met in
> my whole life. Come on, I'll take you
> home.

> DOROTHY
> (rising)
> Would you mind terribly . . . I just
> need to be alone. I'd like to start
> thinking it over as soon as possible.

And she rushes away from the table.

> FADE OUT[2]

Jot down your notes on protagonist, antagonist, problem, and structure. How do they compare with ours?

Protagonist? Michael in his disguise as Dorothy.

Antagonist? Les, Dorothy's suitor.

Problem? Michael-Dorothy knows Les wants to propose and wants to let him down gently.

BEGINNING.   This opening part takes us up to the point that Les announces he has something he wants to say. Michael-Dorothy tries to cut him off, but Les rushes on. The problem emerges in the immediate form of Les's relentless drive toward the proposal.

MIDDLE.   Les makes his boots, feet, and photograph marriage proposal speech as Michael-Dorothy, trying to be kind, finds he has put himself in the position of listening to the proposal he'd wanted to cut off at the pass. Crisis.

END.   Michael-Dorothy is confronted with saying yes or no after all, and if not immediately then soon. He flees the situation. Climax.

Consider the scene now from the point of view of emotional realism.

A man fumbles, proposes; a woman is flustered and runs away. Nothing could be more familiar or clichéd. But knowing Dorothy is really Michael lends the scene another dimension, and we are in the amusing and revealing position of seeing that all of Dorothy's reactions are not

2. Larry Gelbart, *Tootsie* (unpublished manuscript, March 1982), pp. 116–119.

only appropriate to her as a woman, but also appropriate to her as a man disguised as a woman trying to be kind. Michael's kindness is his downfall, just as it would be if he had actually been Dorothy. The dividing line between the sexes is amusingly blurred—we see it is not as sharp as we had thought. This is certainly one of the central aims of *Tootsie*.

We said this scene was also full of familiar comedic conventions. One of the oldest of these, going back to the New Drama of Greece in the third century B.C., is the use of mistaken identity. What greater mistake about identity could Les make? Another of these is the love triangle, equally old in lineage. Here Michael loves Julie (who loves a man called Ron from whom Michael-as-Dorothy helps Julie break away); Julie loves her father, of course; and her father loves Michael-as-Dorothy. This is inherently the stuff of comedy.

What makes it work here in a contemporary update? The *premise*, a term you should start getting used to. It has two meanings, actually. The first refers to a brief typed statement you would leave with a studio or network executive responsible for buying likely ideas for shows or films. Without giving the plot, you would try to present in it the essential idea of a story you'd like to be hired to write. The second meaning refers to the essential idea of a story or individual scene, pure and simple, as you would try to give it to someone conversationally, in a few sentences at the most. Terminology varies, and *idea* and *premise* are often interchangeable.

What makes these comedic conventions amusing in the present scene is basically the idea, or premise, behind the story: an out-of-work actor successfully impersonates a woman, attains great success as an actress, and simultaneously becomes plunged into relationships with others as a woman. In any scene you write, you should be able to state the underlying premise as easily and in as few words. After every scene assignment in this text, you must be able to state the premise just so briefly.

Now, do you entirely accept Michael-as-Dorothy? Do you believe that a man could fall in love with Michael-as-Dorothy? Do you think Les could have Michael-as-Dorothy in his arms, dancing, and suspect nothing? It makes for wonderful comedy, but do you entirely believe it? The fact is you do believe because of the emotional realism of the scene and because of your willingness to identify with the scene for the sake of the fun, but the premise has built-in problems. There is an ultimate nagging doubt.

Let's look at the last sample scene.

A Brief Word on Premise

The emotional realism of a scene is crucial to the audience's acceptance. But the underlying premise, the idea on which the story is based, as well as the significance, meaning, or message of the story, also contributes an element of realism that affects the response to your characters. We could call this element *dramatic realism* as well as *emotional realism*. By this we don't mean reality, but the believability of your premise. That can put an element of distance between the audience and your characters or bring the audience unexpectedly close to them. It is almost easier to believe in the people of *Star Wars* behaving as they do long ago and far away than it is to believe that Les, holding Michael-Dorothy in his arms as they danced, couldn't sense something was funny.

Both the briefly summarized scene from *Rocky* and, to a lesser extent, that from *Tootsie* were flawed or depended on our accepting a premise of a not wholly convincing nature. We can believe that Adrian might be attracted to Rocky, but not that he would so easily overcome her inhibitions or find her so conveniently pretty. To the extent there was a problem with Michael-Dorothy and Les, it was in the underlying idea.

So add this consideration about premise, as it affects believability, to your notes on emotional realism after you read the next scene. Compare those with ours on the premise, too.

A Crucial Scene from Kramer vs. Kramer

This is what you need to know as background for the next scene. Ted and Joanna are married and have a young child, Billy. Some time ago, Joanna abandoned Ted and Billy and disappeared. They have not heard from her in a long time. Ted had been a poor father, entirely career oriented, until the time Joanna left. In the time since her departure, however, he has been transformed into a devoted father and as much of a mother as he can be, and he has dropped his obsession with his career. Billy, and family, now come first with him. Just as it seems he and Billy have completed this transformation together, Joanna reappears on the scene and calls Ted. What follows is their first meeting since she disappeared:

FADE IN:

INT.   RESTAURANT, MELONS   (EST) DAY

[CAMERA IS] ON THE DOOR as TED enters and looks around. The OWNER approaches. From his attitude, it is clear that Ted and Joanna were regular customers.

CONTINUED

CONTINUED

> OWNER
> Hello, Mr. Kramer. Haven't seen you
> for a long time. Mrs. Kramer's waiting
> in the back.

> TED
> Thank you, Jack.

[FOLLOW TED] as he walks toward the back room of the restaurant. As he reaches the door to the back room

INT.   BACK ROOM, MELONS   DAY

[showing the tables and customers.]

TED'S POV

JOANNA, sitting against the wall, a glass of white wine in front of her. She is still stunningly beautiful. HOLD ON HER FOR A BEAT as she looks up, smiles.

ON TED

[as] he stands watching her, his knees weak. It is impossible not to fall in love with her all over again.

TWO SHOT: TED & JOANNA

as he crosses to her table and sits down.

> JOANNA
> Hello Ted. You look well.

> TED
> So do you.

The WAITRESS appears, carrying a scotch and soda. She sets it down on the table in front of Ted.

> WAITRESS
> The usual, Mr. Kramer.

> TED
> (not taking his eyes off
> Joanna)
> Thanks.

The waitress promptly disappears.

CONTINUED

CONTINUED

> JOANNA
> How's the job?

> TED
> Fine.

There is a self-conscious pause.

> TED
> Look at us, Joanna. Just like any old
> married couple having dinner. Who
> would believe it.

> JOANNA
> Yes . . . How's Billy?

ON TED

The question he has been dreading.

> TED
> He's great . . . except . . .
> (not looking at her)
> Except he had . . . He fell and he cut
> his face. He . . . he has a scar, Joanna,
> from about here to here . . .
> (indicating where and how
> big)

There is a beat of silence. A moment of shared feeling.

> TED (CONT'D)
> (he has to say it to
> someone)
> I can't help but feel somehow . . . it's
> my fault. I keep thinking I could've
> done something—stopped it . . .

> JOANNA
> You can't tell it from a distance, Ted.

For the first time he looks up at her.

> TED
> What?

CROSSCUT BETWEEN THEM

> JOANNA
> I've seen him.

> TED
> You have?

> JOANNA
> A few times. Sometimes I sit in that
> coffee shop across the street and
> watch when you take him to school.

ON TED

speechless.

[BACK TO SHOT]

> JOANNA (CONT'D)
> He looks like a terrific kid.

> TED
> He is.
> (he still can't get over it)
> You sat in that coffee shop across
> from school—

> JOANNA
> (completing the sentence)
> Watching my son . . . Ted, I've been
> living in New York for the past two
> months.

> TED
> (amazed)
> You've been living here, in the city?

> JOANNA
> (a deep breath)
> Ted . . . The reason I wanted to see
> you . . . I want Billy back.

> TED
> You want *what?!*

CONTINUED

CONTINUED

> JOANNA
> (firm)
> I want my son. I'm through sitting in
> coffee shops looking at him from
> across the street. I want my son.

> TED
> Are you out of your mind?! You're the
> one that walked out on him,
> remember?

> JOANNA
> (trying to explain)
> Ted, listen to me . . . You and I, we
> had a really crappy marriage—
> (hastily)
> Look, don't get defensive, okay? It
> was probably as much my fault as it
> was yours . . . Anyway when I left I
> was really screwed up—

> TED
> Joanna, I don't give a—

> JOANNA
> (she *will* be heard)
> Ted, all my life I'd either been some-
> body's daughter or somebody's wife,
> or somebody else's mother. Then, all
> of a sudden, I was a thirty-
> three–year–old, highly neurotic
> woman who had just walked out on
> her husband and child. I went to Cali-
> fornia because that was about as far
> away as I could get. Only . . . I guess
> it wasn't far enough. So I started going
> to a shrink.
> (leaning forward, very
> sincere)
> Ted, I've had time to think. I've been
> through some changes. I've learned a
> lot about myself.

CONTINUED

CONTINUED

> TED
> (like a shot)
> Such as?

Silence [as he waits].

> TED (CONT'D)
> (boring in)
> Come on Joanna, what did you learn?
> I'd really like to know.

Silence [as he waits].

> TED (CONT'D)
> (relentless)
> One thing, okay? Just tell me one god-
> damn thing you've learned.

There is another beat of silence, then:

> JOANNA
> (quiet, determined)
> I've learned that I want my son.

ON TED

He reacts as if he has been slapped.

> TED
> Joanna, go be a mother. Get married;
> have kids. Don't get married; have
> kids. Do whatever you want. I don't
> give a damn. Just leave me out of it—
> *and leave my baby out of it.*

> JOANNA
> Ted, if you can't discuss this ra-
> tionally—

> TED
> (getting to his feet)
> Joanna, go fuck yourself!

CONTINUED

CONTINUED

And with that he turns on his heels and stalks out of the restaurant.

FADE OUT[3]

Now, let's compare notes again.
Protagonist? Ted.
Antagonist? Joanna.
Problem? Joanna's desire to take Billy from Ted.

BEGINNING.   The beginning lasts up to the point when Joanna says, "I want Billy back." Problem. Until then they have asked the inevitable surface questions and avoided real issues.

MIDDLE.   In this heated section, Joanna tries to explain herself under Ted's relentless prodding to tell him one way in which she has changed—his way of trying to make it obvious that what exists between him and Billy now should not be changed. At the end of this, Joanna reconfirms her desire for Billy. Ted has failed. Crisis.

END.   Ted fiercely denounces Joanna and refuses to give in to her desire. Climax. He storms out.

This scene grips us. How human they both are. How awkward with each other, amazed they're together. Joanna makes it clear in the scene how bad she felt about herself when they were still together, how desperate she was then, and how she now feels she has straightened herself out. She adds the touching detail that for some two months she has been quietly watching Billy. It is easy to feel her ache, to realize that she is not unfeeling: it has taken her all that time to decide to see Ted. She is not a villain.

Neither, obviously, is Ted. He has every reason to feel and behave as he does. This one scene is self-explanatory for his motivation in itself. It is made clear at the beginning he is still attracted to her, that seeing her is hard for him. The nature of the change he has gone through as a parent is also made clear in his outraged words to Joanna, "Leave my baby out of it." He is not a villain either.

Note how sharply etched is this collision of wills. Joanna wants something. Ted wants just the opposite. She tries to explain herself. Ted refuses to accept her explanation. She reaffirms her desire. He, in effect, declares war. It all matters terribly. How two adults and a child are to live depends on the outcome of the conflict. It will not be easily resolved.

3. Robert Benton, *Kramer vs. Kramer* (unpublished manuscript, September 1978), pp. 72–77.

What about the underlying premise for this scene? It's entirely credible that at some point Joanna would return. There's hardly any surprise that she would want her child back. If she had turned out to be a fool, or heartless, or a flake (California and a shrink have come to be stock laughs in storytelling) a good deal of the weight, of the believability of this scene would have evaporated. But she is evidently none of those things.

Nor is Ted's inevitable reaction anything but believable.

What about the underlying premise of the film, that a wife could abandon her husband and son and find herself elsewhere while they, left behind, were able to find themselves as a warm, loving family in her absence. Could we believe that this bond would be so strong that the husband would be willing to fight to maintain this father-son unit against the wife and mother when she finally returns? It's possible. It's no longer unheard of. It doesn't strain credibility.

You are dealing with a piece of strong writing here. The scene has great dramatic strength because each character seems so reasonable to the audience, yet totally unreasonable to the other. But are people really always so sensible, with so much justification on each side? It's unlikely. We can agree on one point in *Kramer vs. Kramer's* defense: a story certainly could work this way.

Review

You must write a dramatic action.

That action is the collision of your protagonist with some problem he must resolve but has great difficulty in resolving.

The protagonist's problem is caused by an antagonist in the form of another person or persons, a physical or natural obstacle, or by conflict within himself.

A scene is both the setting in which dramatic action takes place and a structure of that dramatic action into a BEGINNING, in which the characters are introduced and the problem for the protagonist emerges; a MIDDLE, in which the efforts of the protagonist to solve that problem reach a point of failure (the crisis); and an END, in which the protagonist makes the final effort to resolve his problem one way or another (the climax).

The emotional realism with which characters behave is crucial for credibility; their motivation must be entirely believable.

Your basic idea, or premise, to be effective, must motivate your characters with a need to overcome an immediate obstacle.

The freshness with which you create character and situation matters far more than the conventional elements you may make use of, as with, for example, the comedic traditions taken advantage of in the scene from *Tootsie*.

4. Camera Language and Format

Don't tell it—show it.

Our aim from the beginning has been practical, which means helping you write a salable script. The look and feel of professionalism suggested by the format and use of the camera seriously influences the reading by any buyer of a script written by an unknown screenwriter. You can be sure that if you show ineptitude in covering the significant action in terms of format and camera language you will have small chance of making a sale, regardless of how good a story may be buried in your script.

So take a look at camera language and format before you go on to your first assignment. After you read what follows, go back and look at the three scenes in the last section. We have deliberately treated their camera language and format as if they were the first scenes of their given stories so that you would have a number of examples. We have also treated them as if they were the entire story. That is why FADE OUT appears after each. Last, they represent reasonable examples of the use of shots for writers, neither too many to interfere with their reading, nor too few to make them impossible to visualize. If you flip through this text, you will find many other scenes to look at for their form.

We are talking about making movies, and the language of the camera is the jargon of the trade. But that doesn't mean the language is difficult. A script is written in a way to guide the separate activities of a large number of people diversely engaged in the process of producing it. Properly written, the script focuses the attention of the various collaborative areas and serves two primary purposes. First, it tells a story as you see it: the camera is your eye. Second, it contains a set of instructions for those who are going to film it. The best instructions are brief, clear, cogent, and, above all, do not clutter the story.

Photographing the Story

The chief distinction between film and stage is the mobility and flexibility given the screenwriter by the camera—it gives a dimension of intimacy that the proscenium arch cannot give. This provides the screen-writer with an unrestricted range of visual opportunities, enabling him to probe character more deeply by means of expressions of a subtle nature and adding to his opportunities to present his story more imaginatively, lustrously, and in greater depth. How well the screenwriter exploits these additional dimensions in ways that are original, artistic, and stimulating is a measure of his talent and skill.

But disagreement exists about the extent of a screenwriter's responsibility in relation to photographing the story: a writer is not expected or advised to trespass on the director or cameraman's ground. It is difficult to draw the line between how much or how little photographic detail may be considered proper for the screenwriter to give, and ideas about it vary even among university film teachers. Let us dispose of the philosophy in cinema arts, too often expressed in film study courses, that film is a director's medium. Nothing could be more misleading.

Simply put, a writer is entitled to the full range of his pictorial imagination when he believes that the sight of something will inspire an atmosphere, mood, or reaction that he considers to be important in the telling of his story. Admittedly, one cannot underassess the director's most creative contribution to the artistic sense of a film in theatrical release films, though that contribution is less in television. But it is almost ludicrous to disenfranchise the writer in the process of giving the director due credit! The bulk of films would never see the light of day were it not for the individual who draws from the fountainhead of his imagination that which makes all the subsequent contributions a reality. Nonetheless, the current trend favors the most economical use of camera instructions in a script, almost to the point of including only the essentials that set and describe the scene or sequence, and the characters involved.

This position is difficult to challenge in television, where time is money and costs are astronomical. Complicated camera instructions are not highly negotiable commodities in a marketplace where the chief concern is the clock. Moreover, there is an assembly-line numbness in most series to any departure from fixed production ideas.

Yet the more we search for some specificity on this viewpoint, the more we sense an equivocation caused by instructors' concern for the infatuation most beginning writers have for *irrelevant* angles and shots that muddy the story and rob the script of readability. A writer should realize that if he put in all the shots of a typical movie, there would be over six hundred in his script, which would make it unreadable.

Historically, it was expected that writers would provide scripts with each shot carefully numbered and conceived for shooting. Slowly this function was taken over by the director, in part influenced by the impact of the European auteur theory and in part reflecting the lessening of the initial literary influence that appeared in films with the development of sound. There is no doubt that an extreme application of either approach is wrong. A writer should no longer pepper his script with hundreds of numbered shots, yet the final script of a teleplay or screenplay should be a writer's complete, personally edited version of the action as he would want it seen and experienced by the audience. To this end, he should indicate how the camera might best be used to evoke the dramatic emphasis of whatever he considers genuinely significant to convey his meaning. In the final analysis, the aim of satisfying the reader who might purchase the script is what it's all about.

On the whole, then, it's reasonable to say that the camera should not be called into play beyond the obvious setting of scene and action unless it serves to make a significant dramatic point. At such a moment a writer should never hesitate to call the camera into play to make that point. There *may* be times when a writer will want to use an OVER THE SHOULDER angle, a CLOSE-UP, or some character's POV (point of view) to dramatize appropriately the emotional impact or significance of a scene, and in such cases when it is not already perfectly apparent he should. But this also seems a good place to emphasize the extreme necessity of the writer's keeping the dramatic action of the story foremost in his mind and writing it so that the impact and sense of that story can survive any number of debates between writer, director, and cameraman about whether a particular moment should be shot one way or another. Remember the playwright writes an action, not just words or shots.

Writing to Cover the Action

A screenplay's substance could be set out in what are called "master scenes." In such a procedure a writer would establish the scene and thereafter concern himself chiefly with the characters in the scene and their dialogue, without placing the camera or describing the moves that may be necessary to illustrate the action. The serious dramatist should avoid this procedure: it is not generally acceptable as a finished product.

This treatment or one only slightly more detailed is common practice among those who write for television situation comedies. These shows invariably confine themselves to one or, at the most, two sets, and generally use the three-camera technique, which largely makes unnecessary setting up the shots that apply when only a single camera is used. Another reason is that a talent for comedy is far more rare than the ability to manage a camera; the emphasis is placed accordingly.

This way of generalizing camera use might also be sufficient when a writer has an on-going relationship with the director or producer. Apart from these exceptions, the dramatist of integrity prefers to describe his screenplay with those shots he thinks necessary to communicate his meaning. We reemphasize that last point. Clearly indicate setting and action, but don't go after camera effects that try to be directorially artistic. USE the camera to underscore the significant dramatic values of your story.

For instance, consider a situation in which the dramatist is more concerned with the reaction of one character than he is with the action of another. In that case he would direct the attention of the camera to an angle that FAVORS the reactor rather than the actor. Imagine a scene in John and Mary Adams's living room.

INT.   ADAMS'S LIVING ROOM   DAY

JOHN enters the room quickly followed by MARY. He crosses to the couch and sits. Mary sits beside him.

Obviously, if our camera is covering the entire scene, we must be distant from John and Mary. To involve us more intimately with what they are going to say or do, we should be closer. We so direct the camera:

TWO SHOT: JOHN & MARY

> MARY
> I asked you: did you see that girl last night?

> JOHN
> (he looks at the floor)
> I said no.

> MARY
> John—look at me—

John continues to stare at the floor.

> MARY (CONT'D)
> John, will you look at me? Please?

ANGLE: FAVORING JOHN

He slowly looks up at Mary, his eyes clouded with guilt.

In other words, we FAVOR him with the camera because we want to see the guilt in his eyes.

There might be a time, as noted above, when you decide to exclude an actor entirely and call for a CLOSE-UP of the reactor. In such a case we would hear the actor's voice, but he would be OFF SCREEN (O.S.).

EXT.   ANDERSON HOME DRIVEWAY   NIGHT

MED. SHOT: MANNIX

reaching his car parked a distance away from front of house in the circular driveway.

> KELLY'S VOICE (O.S.)
> Mr. Mannix—!

He turns. She appears crossing to him from the side of the house.

Or there may be times when POV is more important than the people in the scene and what they are saying.

> IRONSIDE
> Did anyone else know you were mov-
> ing in?

> FRAN
> Karen didn't know she was leaving till
> the last minute.

> IRONSIDE
> Did you know whether she got any
> calls? Like that?

> FRAN
> I phoned her in New York. She says no.

CAMERA FOLLOWS action as Ironside frowns thoughtfully for an instant, then crosses to the big living room window. He opens the drapes and looks out searchingly at the surrounding buildings.

IRONSIDE'S POV: THE OTHER BUILDINGS

SLOW PAN to SHOW the penthouse is higher than any nearby building, and we can SEE it offers no opportunity for observation from outside. MEANWHILE

> IRONSIDE'S VOICE (O.S.)
> Do any of the windows face another
> building?

> FRAN'S VOICE (O.S.)
> Only the one in the dressing room.

If you as a screenwriter fail to visualize each foot of your story in camera terms, you are like a painter without a canvas. Your canvas is the camera frame. If you fail to visualize the dimensions of your canvas—

the view of your camera—you will stand a good chance of losing your perspective of dramatic values.

As a screenwriter, you will tell your story through images. "Don't tell it—show it" is more than a cautionary bromide: it is the meaning of the film. You must both mirror your scene of action and particularize the nuances of what you want the viewer to see.

Susan Sontag describes the importance of this use of the camera in this fashion: "as people quickly discovered that nobody takes the same picture of the same thing, the supposition that cameras give an impersonal, scientific result yielded to the fact that photographs are evidence not only of what is '*there*' but of what an individual *sees:* not just a record, but an evaluation."

That is your obligation as a screenwriter. Use the camera in such a way that the viewer can properly evaluate what you see. It is, as Sontag explains, your "corner of material reality" that the audience might not see at all until you focus their attention on it. To do this you must master three things: how the camera may be placed, how it may be moved, and the nomenclature for such use.

Organizing Scenes and Using Shots

Apart from dialogue, the body of a script is composed of scenes and shots. A scene is a sequence of dramatic action that runs continuously according to the actual time it takes as the story progresses. If the time of day or the location of the action changes, a new scene begins. Such a scene may contain additional SHOTS that highlight or punctuate or dramatize special parts of the scene. Such a SHOT is a visual unit in the film that is also described as an ANGLE, meaning an angle of the camera, that includes only the people or things that are to be emphasized.

These scenes and shots are numbered from beginning to end in a shooting script—one that is ready to start principal photography. Some students are taught to do this. Why, we don't know. It's likely a script will be changed substantially before it is accepted for production, so it is better left for the production manager who sets up the shooting schedule to number the scenes after the producer has approved all the revisions.

Whenever you give a shot or a movement of the camera in your script, you address the director, the cameraman and his assistants, the gaffer (lighting man), and the key grips. For that reason, always write your camera instructions in all capital letters. This means you write SEE when you want the CAMERA to SEE something.

There are times when the actor is instructed to approach or move away from the camera. Whenever someone or something moves but the camera remains stationary, unchanged, neither the word *camera* nor the instructions are capitalized.

Use all capital letters in two other instances—all audio effects that are addressed to the sound effects man, and the first (and only the first) time you introduce a character. You always write a character's name in all capital letters over his dialogue.

FADE IN:

EXT.   HOLBROOK MANSION   (EST) NIGHT

The place is immense; the grounds are immaculate and beautifully landscaped. There is a circular driveway, with plenty of room for several expensive cars parked there. Among them is a FERRARI. There are LIGHTS on in some of the rooms, and it is quiet. Suddenly, VOICES are raised; there is a MUTED CRASH of GLASS or CROCKERY somewhere.

CLOSER ANGLE: TOWARD UPSTAIRS ROOM

Figures are SEEN to move quickly behind drawn blinds, a pair of VOICES is HEARD—a MAN'S, a WOMAN'S, then both together. Then, a SLAP and a SCREAM. Then, the SOUND of RUNNING FOOTSTEPS APPROACHING CAMERA, which now PANS DOWN to HOLD FULL on the massive front door. There is a SINGLE GUNSHOT; seconds later the door opens and a woman emerges. This is NANCY HOLBROOK, about 25, beautiful—and at the moment, very distraught. Her face is wet with tears as she jumps into the first car she finds with keys, which is the Ferrari, STARTS IT, and ROARS OFF in it.

EXT.   STREET   NIGHT

MED. PAN SHOT: FERRARI

TIRES SQUEAL and the big MOTOR SNARLS as Nancy takes the car through the neighborhood as fast as it will go.

EXT.   PETROCELLI TRAILER AREA   NIGHT

It is peaceful, with crickets and moonlight. From the direction of the partly built house

> PETROCELLI'S VOICE (O.S.)
> There are not that many crickets in
> the entire world. There can't be!

It is unlikely that you will want to use all the wide variety of shots that are available to you, but you should recognize them and their abbreviations.

FULL SHOT (FS)—This ANGLE is taken at a considerable distance and is used to ESTABLISH (EST) the entire scene for the purpose of orientation.

LONG SHOT (LS)—This ANGLE differs from a FULL SHOT in that it is taken from the same long distance of the viewer from the subject, but the LS shows only the portion of the scene that the audience is specifically meant to SEE.

MEDIUM SHOT (MS *or* MED. SHOT)—This ANGLE is neither LONG nor CLOSE. It is a middle distance from the subject.

CLOSE SHOT (CS)—This is not to be confused with a CLOSE-UP. It is a CLOSE ANGLE of two or more elements close to the viewer.

CLOSE-UP (CU)—This SHOT focuses clearly on a single object in a scene, either a person or an object.

EXTREME CLOSE-UP (ECU)—This is simply a tighter CLOSE-UP in which a specific object or feature, such as the eyes or mouth of an individual or a ring on someone's finger, is the subject.

Apart from these, you may also call for a TWO SHOT. When you do this, indicate the two people in the shot:

TWO SHOT: JOHN & MARY

You might want a THREE SHOT or a FOUR SHOT. Indicate the names of the characters in these, too. If there are more than four people in the shot, you would call for a GROUP SHOT and *not* list the characters' names after it.

A shot can MOVE WITH the action it is photographing, for example, with an automobile, an airplane, a runner, or people walking. In this case the camera can be mounted on a separate vehicle that moves in concert with your characters. You simply describe it as such:

MOVING SHOT: THE CADILLAC

to SEE it race down the block and turn the corner.

A MOVING SHOT is not the same as a PAN or a DOLLY. These last two are not shots but simply movements of the camera that modify a shot while it is on the screen. A PAN is a swiveling movement of the camera on its mount as it turns right or left on a horizontal plane to sweep the scene or FOLLOW an element that moves across it. It is a direction of an existing shot, not a shot in itself.

ANGLE: THE KITCHEN DOOR

as a waiter comes through the door and crosses the restaurant to the cashier. PAN with him.

A DOLLY is a movement into the scene, decreasing the field of vision or the reverse. If you want to move the camera closer in a given shot, you DOLLY IN; if back, you DOLLY OUT.

Much use today is made of the ZOOMAR lens for a similar effect of decreasing or increasing the field of vision without moving the camera. The terminology here is ZOOM IN or ZOOM OUT. Beginning writers often abuse this perfectly legitimate direction.

Use ZOOM IN or OUT and the following more sophisticated ANGLES with caution. If you have a good reason for using one of these, don't hesitate, but it had better be good!

LOW ANGLE—when the camera shoots up from below.

HIGH ANGLE—when the camera shoots down from above the subject.

FAVORING—selects the character to be favored in the SHOT.

OVER THE SHOULDER—Shooting from behind one person over his shoulder to see the face of another when two characters face one another. Beginners find this especially tempting to overdo.

REVERSE ANGLE—an ANGLE the opposite of the one that precedes it.

OVERHEAD SHOT—looking down at a subject, for instance, at a pool table.

POINT OF VIEW (POV)—a SHOT that gives the viewer a close look at what a person in the scene is looking at. This is usually preceded by a CLOSE SHOT of the individual to make clear the direction of his POV. Beginners are advised to label these shots with the character's name to whom they belong, for example, "IRONSIDE'S POV."

TILT (UP or DOWN)—moving up or down in a vertical plane. This is also described as a PAN UP or PAN DOWN.

When a scene or a shot changes on the screen from one to the next, this is a CUT. This takes place automatically, and there is no need to indicate it at the end of each shot. Writers do occasionally indicate CUT TO or CUT or SMASH CUT simply to communicate the feeling of pressure or abruptness to the reader or editor.

A DISSOLVE is a laboratory procedure that is created when one picture fades out and is combined with the fade in of the next. DISSOLVE is seldom used now. In a LAP DISSOLVE, which is still used when appropriate, the picture fading in overlaps the picture fading out. Finally, you have the FADE IN, which goes from a blank screen to a full picture, and the FADE OUT, which does the reverse. These transitions have the effect of raising or lowering the curtain on the play.

There is always the possibility that you may want to use one of the following special devices that are created in the laboratory:

SUPERIMPOSE (SUPER)—The effect of blending one picture on top of another.

SPLIT SCREEN—The effect of wiping half the picture off the screen and replacing that half with another picture.

Much of this sounds more complicated than you will find it to be once you start putting it to use. Facility comes with application, and in short order you will find it second nature to write with an eye for the camera and the finished product.

The same basic simplicity applies to format. As soon as you realize the reason for structuring a script as it should be, you will doubtless find it the most convenient way to reduce your ideas to dramatic form.

Format

You want to reveal as quickly as possible the who, what, when, where, and how of your dramatic situation. Each of these facets of your screenplay's total information occupies its own special place on your sheet of paper.

Starting with FADE IN, we'll list each function:

FADE IN:

WHERE   WHEN

WHAT HAPPENS

WHO
(HOW he says it)
WHAT he says.

WHERE   WHEN

                                                                           FADE OUT

Or, for example,

FADE IN:

EXT.   SLUM AREA   NIGHT

A section of dreary tenement buildings.

CLOSER ANGLE: ONE OF THE TENEMENTS

Wylie's car is at the curb. He's examining the handwritten tags on the mailboxes in the doorway. Finding the one he wants, he enters the building.

INT.   TENEMENT BUILDING HALLWAY   NIGHT

As Wylie emerges from the stairwell, he looks around at the numbers on the shabby doors, moves to one, presses the doorbell.

CLOSER ANGLE: THE DOOR

There's no response to the bell. Wylie raps with his knuckles. After a moment, the door is opened a crack, still secured by a chain lock. A woman is partially visible.

> WYLIE
>
> Mrs. Landry?

> MRS. LANDRY
>
> Who are you?

> WYLIE
>
> Edward Wylie. I don't know if you remember.

> MRS. LANDRY
> (harshly)
> I remember.

FADE OUT

Notice that you give the time only when a scene is set. It is not used for any of the SHOTS. Those take place within the scene, within the time established when the scene starts.

Notice also that the title of each scene and shot is written in all capitals and that space is left (two line spaces) for any necessary description of what is taking place in that scene or shot. This description is often called "the business." Another two lines separates these descriptions from the dialogue. There is no spacing between the name of the character and what he says or how he says it. Sometimes the directions to the actor in parentheses under a character's name are referred to as "the action," which is very different from what we mean when we speak of dramatic action. The *action* is a direction to an actor for a moment of behavior.

When a conversation takes place between people who are in different locations (scenes) you cover that situation by instructing:

INTERCUT FOLLOWING CONVERSATION (*or, simply*, INTERCUT:)

Another shot you might use is designated PROCESS. This is a production technique wherein a rear projection screen is placed behind actors in a scene shot on a stage. The screen reflects the background of the indigenous scenic action. For example, shooting a scene in a car traveling on a highway is difficult. Usually the background of such a scene is shot separately and then projected on the rear screen while the actors perform in front of it. The auto used in this process is called a MOCK-UP.

A word about the use of CONTINUED or CONT'D at the bottom of certain pages and then at the top of the next: these are used when either a scene or shot is not completed on one page, but runs on to the next. It is also used when one character speaks, a direction is given or a line of description inserted, and the character speaks again. In such a case, the character's name appears again with (CONT) or (CONT'D) next to it.

HARRY (CONT'D)

If you find that you cannot complete a speech at the end of a page (and *don't* keep going until there's no more room), you must use this form:

MARTIN
You can't count on me any longer. I
should have told
(MORE)

CONTINUED

next page:

CONTINUED

MARTIN (CONT'D)
you that sooner.

One last word. Once again we urge you to avoid excessive use of shots. The above is a guide and resource—go back and look at the scenes quoted earlier. You will notice how economical but clear the descriptions and shots are. Model your shots on those: do not clutter your script with REVERSE ANGLES and OVER THE SHOULDER SHOTS or play at being director with HIGH or LOW ANGLES. Use your shots to emphasize a significant dramatic moment: don't give us a series of CLOSE-UPS when a TWO SHOT is perfectly adequate. Think of your dramatic action. What follow are two additional examples of format and shot usage: you will be unlikely to need as many shots in any of your initial scenes:

FADE IN:

EXT.   STREET SCENE   (EST) DAY

Every scene of a screenplay is set in the above fashion. You designate your opening shot ESTABLISHING or (EST). Here you describe briefly the setting for the set designer and prop man. You call their attention to things that must be supplied by putting them in all capital letters.

CONTINUED

CONTINUED

You introduce characters as they appear for the first time by using caps. You give a brief description of the character here, too, so that your reader and casting will know your conception. Also, any sounds for the sound effects man, other than source sounds, are in caps.

> CHARACTER
> (any tonal directions)
> The speeches start here and end
> where you see the word *end*. All
> speeches are single-spaced, and if
> there is a pause in the dialogue, you
> do this . . .
> (beat)
> . . . and continue the speech.

MED. SHOT: CHARACTER & PAL

Now, we introduce PAL (note caps) as he ENTERS. He is a short, bearded prospector.

> PAL
> (timidly)
> His speech is typed in the same limits
> as the speech above.

ANOTHER ANGLE

This is the way you get a different look at the same SHOT. You could have decided to FAVOR THE CHARACTER. Any reference to camera coverage is also in all caps.

> CHARACTER
> Now go on with the dialogue, and
> develop your situation.

CLOSE SHOT: PAL

CLOSE SHOTS are used for dramatic effect, to show important details, or to emphasize the importance of what is being said.

CLOSE-UP: CHARACTER

This differs from CLOSE SHOT in that it is always a head shot, but a close shot can be of a person or a thing. For a particularly CLOSE SHOT on a thing, you might want to use an INSERT, as

INSERT

showing a wrapped box in Pal's hand. Remember to follow a CLOSE-UP or an INSERT with a new shot to bring you out of the very narrow visual field of those shots, or to use

BACK TO SHOT (*or* BACK TO SCENE)

which returns us to the previous shot before the CLOSE-UP or INSERT. Use

FADE OUT

once your story has ended.

The obvious rule here is to orient the audience first to the total scene for the sake of visual clarity and then to cover the details more closely with appropriate SHOTS and more specific, action-related descriptions, where necessary.

Here's the second example:

FADE IN:

EXT.   WASHINGTON, D.C. (STOCK SHOT)   (EST) NIGHT

HIGH AERIAL ESTABLISHING SHOT, emphasizing the nation's Capitol with its light-enhanced dome.

EXT.   A STREET (PENNSYLVANIA AVENUE)   NIGHT

LONG SHOT: CAPITOL DOME IN BG

CLOSER ON TRUCK

as it comes to a halt. We can SEE TWO MEN sitting in the cab.

INT.   CAB OF TRUCK   NIGHT

The TRUCK DRIVER is a pleasant-looking, middle-aged nondescript character whom we'll never see again. Next to him sits GIFFORD JACKSON. Gifford, despite his country bumpkin appearance, is a nice-looking, likable, lanky young lad with a sunny disposition who could be anywhere between 20 and 25 years of age. A cute mongrel dog with soulful eyes sits at his feet with its paws up on Gifford's knees.

> TRUCK DRIVER
> Well, Gifford, this is as close as I can
> take you to your destination. From
> (MORE)

CONTINUED

CONTINUED

> TRUCK DRIVER (CONT'D)
> here on, you and—
> (smiling at dog, and ruf-
> fling its head affectionately)
> Miss Jones here are on your own.
> (he points O.S.)
> There's the seat of our government . . .

Gifford looks O.S.

GIFFORD'S POV: CAPITOL IN THE DISTANCE

> TRUCK DRIVER'S VOICE (O.S.) (CONT'D)
> . . . and you'll find the Senate Build-
> ing somewheres around there.

LONG SHOT: THE TRUCK

We SEE Gifford, carrying a small suitcase, get out of the truck. Miss Jones jumps out after him. Gifford exchanges some pleasantries and good-byes with the truck driver, MOS from this distance, and closes the cab door. As the truck roars off, Gifford waving to the driver, we

> DISSOLVE TO

INT.   U.S. SENATE BUILDING—A CORRIDOR   NIGHT

CAMERA SHOOTS DOWN the fairly long night-lit corridor with closed office doors visible on each side, then ZOOMS IN ON GIFFORD, sprawled out in front of one of the doors, his head resting on his suitcase. He's asleep. Miss Jones is stretched out at his feet, snoring gently. CAMERA MOVES IN ON SIGN ON DOOR which reads: SENATOR LUCIUS WALEBROOM.

BACK TO SCENE [or BACK TO SHOT]

as, from O.S., comes the SOUND of APPROACHING, RATHER UNEVEN, FOOTSTEPS. Gifford stirs, slowly opens his eyes, looks sleepily down the dimly lit corridor as the FOOTSTEPS COME CLOSER.

GIFFORD'S POV

From way down the length of the corridor, a figure drags itself up the silent corridor, not walking straight, but leaning a little to the north, then rotating to the east, next to the west, like the world was spin-

CONTINUED

CONTINUED

ning. This is SENATOR LUCIUS WALEBROOM—called "Uncle Loosh" by Gifford.

UNCLE LOOSH is between 45 and 50 years old, has a fleshy and kindly face, watery blue eyes covered by specs, and a shock of rather unruly red hair. He's of medium height and a little on the heavy side.

Review

Little is said in the above, yet a good feel for character and situation is nonetheless provided. We can tell by Gifford's appearance, as well as his arrival and how he arrives, a good deal about him before any action transpires. We don't have to hear Uncle Loosh say anything to get the sense of someone colorful, eccentric, and endearing. We had only to hear Bonasera speak to know he was in distress. Communicate through action, through what is seen and heard whenever you can, whenever those will do what words could do: save your words for all those other moments you must use them. Format and camera language give a set of directions to a production team, yes, but used right, they are your means of opening the audience's senses—all of them—to your vision. That is why it is essential you master these, starting simply from inexperience and remaining spare once you reach mastery. A detail can speak volumes: but volumes of speech, unless in a moment of rare and felicitously rendered passion, put us to sleep. One precise image can communicate as much as a moment of verbal eloquence: both must be rendered with exactitude. You represent an image of reality in a screenplay, permitted by the camera to have that image virtually seem to be reality itself—or how reality could be. It's a wonderful gift to a writer. Don't abuse it or underestimate it, either.

Your First Assignment

It's your turn to think of a story and write a short scene from a crucial moment in it or write an entirely self-contained story. Make this first one short, perhaps only two typewritten pages. Don't take more than five. Get your feet wet. Give your protagonist a problem. Quickly develop it into a clash of wills arising from two characters who want to solve the problem differently, like Joanna and Ted or Bonasera and Don Corleone. Give the protagonist an urgent need to solve the problem.

"Okay," you say, "but . . . where do story ideas come from? How do I make one up?"

Story Sources

We are awash with cinematic images and dramatic situations.

Your unconscious mind dreams one story after another every moment of your life. Every night you dream more stories. The material may be crude and irrational, but many stories have developed from such fantasy and dream.

Your waking life is full of stories, too.

Newspapers and newscasts are full of stories.

You and your friends are constantly telling each other stories, inventing motivations, devising climaxes and resolutions. We call it gossip. Whenever you tell a lie and maintain it, you are living a story you invent on the go.

It doesn't matter whether your creativity flowers in a dream or in the mature work of an accomplished writer. It's there. All it needs is stimulation and direction to become accessible.

Start keeping a notebook to hold ideas and stories in as they occur to you. You must write them down: they won't stay in memory. Look at people closely. Notice when they reveal their inner selves. Ask yourself what motivated someone to do or say what they did. Sit back and speculate if you don't know. Write it down.

Make it a small notebook so you can carry it with you. Whip it out whenever you come across a good story that you see, hear, or imagine—you never know when a unique character or situation will pop into mind. You may have fantasies of revenge over some actual or imagined insult, or in a moment before the mirror in the morning you may dream of doing some magnificent thing. What if you let a character do either of those? Or a line of clever dialogue may flash into your mind in search of a character.

Look within your life with an aware and creative eye. Your life belongs to you. Don't let a false sense of Oh-I-couldn't-write-about-*that!*-could-I? get in your way.

The "What If . . ." Game

Make a game out of inventing your scene, just like we did with our example about Sally, the injured Olympic skier, earlier. Call it the "What If . . ." game. *What if . . .* an athletic young woman is badly hurt in an accident? *What if . . .* it's so bad, everyone gives up hope on her, even her parents? *What if . . .* she refuses then to give up herself, but nothing seems to be happening? Does she have the strength to go on? *What if . . .* determination is rewarded in her case, and she starts to get better? *What if. . . ?*

Remember that by far the most interesting thing about you as a potential writer is your uniqueness, the way you see and interpret your own experiences, not how anyone else may. Trust your mind. Let your imagination go. Writing is a method of applying your original point of view to all that impinges on you. No one like you has ever existed before or ever will again. Your job here is to begin the difficult but rewarding journey toward discovering, then using professionally, your own unique voice.

Let's review the assignment.

Create a protagonist, and place him or her in a problem-solving situation. Introduce an antagonist, an obstacle or force that opposes any solution. The opposition to the protagonist will generate a conflict, a collision of wills or forces or circumstances. Your protagonist must act to get his way. Action will lead to reaction until your protagonist actually succeeds—or fails.

Now, give it a try!

Note: This chapter was adapted in part from Ben Brady, *The Keys to Writing for Television and Film* (Dubuque, Iowa: Kendall/Hunt, 1982), pp. 137–180.

Part Two: Developing Character and Conflict

5. Introduction

We're going to break scenes down to their constituent elements in this section. First, we'll look closely at establishing character and conflict and then at the demands of developing character through conflict to a point of crisis at which some definitive action must be taken. We'll examine the kind of motivation needed to justify a significant, climactic moment and look at the necessity for change in characters through dramatic action. We'll deal with the use of overtly thematic material and conclude by considering dialogue and the pure use of action without dialogue to convey story. Grappling with these issues in a sequence of assignments should help you lay the groundwork for larger projects.

In essence, we will review the main features of plotting within the confines of our short scene assignments and in the sample material in the text. There is nothing mysterious about plotting: it is the story structure of your scenes by which you introduce and develop characters and conflict to a critical and finally a climactic point. Normally we would look for the clear emergence of the dramatic conflict of a story at the end of its first act (BEGINNING), the appearance of the crisis by the end of the second (MIDDLE), and the climax in the third (END). You must swiftly establish a problem and conflict in each of your assigned scenes and bring your characters through a crisis and climax each time, though we will emphasize only part of that overall dramatic structure in each assignment.

As you have already seen in Part One, each individual scene uses the same structure: it is the nature of dramatic conflict to structure itself in this way. Part of the accessibility and popularity of screenplays resides in their continuing to honor the plot structure of problem and conflict-crisis-climax because it lends great drive and clarity to a story. You will find thinking in those terms a considerable help when the time comes to write your own miniscreenplay. We want to emphasize this point of thinking about your story in this way: it is a way of thinking about behavior, of how one action leads to another until critical moments are reached—moments of seeming failure, moments of final effort. You will not find screenplays actually written in "Act 1," "Act 2," "Act 3" segments, anymore than you will find many contemporary stage plays utilizing that same structure on the page. But you will find in every successful screen and stage play that the story can be broken down and analyzed in just such terms as we have been doing. Only in television with its more conventional approaches do you find scripts prepared with act breaks, and those frequently are not honored in actual broadcast because the act endings are determined by required commercials.

Not all the sample material we quote will consist only of one self-contained scene, as in Part One where we wanted to keep things as simple as possible. It is often convenient for the screenwriter to take advantage of the enormous flexibility of the camera to show brief sequences or miniscenes to give dramatic expression to material needed for major scenes. This is a significant difference from writing for the stage, in which the dependence on exposition within major scenes is necessarily greater and subjects a playwright to a constant pressure to justify yet more material emerging at each moment. The camera permits you to give a single shot of a troubled face, as in the start of *Kramer vs. Kramer*, or to offer brief snippets of action, as in the opening of *Tootsie*, to show literally in moments information or states of mind or emotion that would require considerably more effort to establish otherwise. Screenplays have an immediacy and a fluidity we do not wish you to forget as you work on your own scenes. While each assignment requires you to write a major, self-contained scene, you may also find it right to use a few quick images to establish your material.

Remember you must include a brief premise for every scene that you write. For example, we might write the premise of the scene we quoted from *The Godfather* in Part One this way:

PREMISE.   A man is prepared to give up his reliance on conventional paths of justice in order to get revenge for the beating of his daughter by appealing to the Mafia. This scene will also introduce us to how the Mafia, in the person of the Godfather, works.

6. Establishing Character and Conflict

Openings

No doubt you found your first scene something of a struggle. Don't worry: each effort will help you to grow closer to fulfilling your own potential.

Perhaps you were too novelistic in your descriptions in the business? Did you try to tell us rather than reveal things about your character's life we had no way of knowing? Remember, all we know in a screenplay is not what we read, but what we actually see and hear. Or maybe you were too vague when you created a character called, say, the OLD WOMAN? What kind of old woman was she? How was she dressed? Why was she where she was? What about motivation? Was there a reason for what happened? Or is it possible that nothing really happened? Don't be frustrated. Beginning something isn't as hard—or as easy—as you imagined. Let's start over.

How do you begin? How do you establish a character and a conflict so that the audience is drawn in, held, and believes the happening you have created? Look at how the scenes covered in Part One swiftly draw us in. Start by going back to the short opening scene from *The Godfather*. Our analysis there emphasized how quickly Bonasera draws us in with his demand for justice over his daughter's beating and how quickly he runs up against an obstacle, Don Corleone. It's a contest, as every dramatic story has been since drama's beginnings in Greece. No time is lost getting to the contest. We saw how fast Adrian displays discomfort with Rocky and how quickly Les's determined flow prevents Michael-Dorothy from letting him down gently. These are real issues joined with speed.

Let's take a close look at the opening sequence from John Huston's classic *The Treasure of the Sierra Madre*.

FADE IN:

CLOSE-UP: LOTTERY LIST

SHOWING the winning numbers drawn in the MEXICAN NATIONAL
LOTTERY, AUGUST 5, 1924. CAMERA PULLS BACK to INCLUDE
DOBBS.

EXT.   STREET—MEXICO   (EST) DAY

Dobbs is slowly tearing a lottery ticket into bits. CAMERA DOLLIES
AHEAD of him as he turns away from the list. The tribes of bootblacks that people the streets do not pester Dobbs. He is too obviously on his uppers. His clothes are ragged and dirty and his shoes
broken. He hasn't had a haircut in months and there is several days'
growth of beard on his face. He stops a passing AMERICAN.

> DOBBS
> Can you spare a dime, brother?

The American growls, moves on.

CLOSE-UP: THE BURNING CIGARETTE

in the gutter.

CLOSE SHOT: DOBBS

He moves a step towards the gutter, then halts and looks right and
left to make sure no one is watching. This brief delay costs him the
cigarette. One of the swarm of bootblacks swoops down on it. Dobbs
pulls his belt in a couple of notches and continues on up the street.
PULL BACK.

THE STREET

as CAMERA DOLLIES AHEAD. Something Dobbs sees OUT OF SCENE
causes him to increase his pace. He catches up with an AMERICAN
who is dressed in a white suit.

> DOBBS
> Brother, can you spare a dime?

White Suit fishes in his pocket, takes out a tostón and gives it to
Dobbs who is so surprised by this act of generosity that he doesn't
even say thanks. For several moments he stands rooted looking at
the coin in his palm. Then he closes his hand around it, making a
fist. Putting the fist in his pocket, he cuts across the street. CAMERA

CONTINUED

CONTINUED

PANS with him to a tobacco stand where he stops to buy a package of cigarettes, then hurries along. CAMERA PANS him to a sidewalk restaurant.

FADE OUT[1]

We see a ragged, dirty man beg, miss a chance to pick up a cigarette, and beg again. No one needs to tell us that Dobbs is down and out—we see that—and how when he gets some money he instantly spends it. Dobbs will never be able to keep what he gets. He'll get a fortune in gold and lose that, his friends, and his life. If Dobbs wasn't a born loser, would he be where he is here at the start? We experience his life with him. Everything is clearly described, economically enacted, immediate.

Go back and look at the opening shot of the ticket for the lottery that Dobbs didn't win. He is going to be persuaded to take another chance, which will pay off and fund his prospecting expedition to the mountains, the meat of the film. There are no wasted details: what we are given is used. Nothing else!

Turn now to something equally effective but a little more sophisticated, the opening from *Tootsie*.

FADE IN:

MACRO SHOT: LIKE AN ABSTRACT PAINTING

Only one area is in focus. It is an actor's CHARACTER BOX. We SLOWLY PAN to SEE: a MONOCLE, different pairs of EYEGLASSES, rubber APPLIANCES, various MAKEUPS, a collection of DENTAL APPLICATIONS, an assortment of brushes. A HAND COMES INTO THE FRAME and removes a small bottle. WE FOLLOW to see it is SPIRIT GUM. The OTHER HAND ENTERS FRAME and uncaps the bottle. FOLLOW on hand as it applies the spirit gum to a cheek. WE SEE ONLY A PORTION OF THE CHEEK. Now the hands apply spirit gum to a rubber scar. Again we FOLLOW the hands as they place the scar upon the actor's cheek. The ritual continues as we watch a mustache being applied. The hands then search out the dental appliances and pick one. We study the movement as the appliance is inserted into the actor's mouth. Throughout the above we HEAR someone MUMBLING, but we cannot

CONTINUED

1. John Huston, *The Treasure of the Sierra Madre* (unpublished manuscript, January 1947), p. 1.

CONTINUED

make out the words. Suddenly we HEAR:

> A VOICE
> Next!

A BLACK SCREEN: OR SO IT SEEMS

REALLY A DARKENED THEATER. We're looking out toward the
auditorium.

[INT.   THEATRE   DAY]

> VOICE (CONT'D)
> Michael . . . Dorsey, is it?

PULL BACK to HOLD ON MICHAEL in foreground, looking out toward
the darkened auditorium. He is an actor, forty years old. He holds a
script.

> MICHAEL
> That's right.

CAMERA CIRCLES to reveal Michael's face. The scar is present, as is
the moustache. He also has perfect teeth.

> VOICE
> Top of twenty-three . . .

> MICHAEL
> (with feeling)
> "Do you know what it was like wak-
> ing up in Paris that morning? Seeing
> the empty pillow where . . . wait a
> minute, cover your breasts! Kevin is
> downstairs! My God—what *are* you?"

PAN to reveal a BURLY STAGE MANAGER, cigar butt in mouth.

> STAGE MANAGER
> "I'm a *woman*. Not anyone's mother.
> Not Kevin's wife . . ."

> VOICE
> Thank you. That's fine. We're looking
> for someone a little older.

[INT.]   ANOTHER BARE STAGE—MICHAEL WITH ANOTHER STAGE
MANAGER   [DAY]

Michael is dressed in cut-offs, a T-shirt and sneakers. He plays with
a yo-yo.

> MICHAEL
> "Mom! Dad! Uncle Pete! Something's
> wrong with Biscuit! I think he's
> dead!"

> VOICE
> (from the darkness)
> Thank you. Thank you. We're looking
> for someone a little younger.

[INT.]   A THIRD BARE STAGE—MICHAEL WITH ANOTHER STAGE
MANAGER   [DAY]

Michael has dark makeup on, his hair slicked back, wears a zoot
suit, another moustache. He has a "Walkman" stereo hanging from
his neck, and wears earphones.

> STAGE MANAGER
> (eyes on script)
> "No, Julio, no. Get out of the Barrio
> while you can."

> MICHAEL
> "I don' go wi' out Esthella . . ."

He suddenly whips out a knife and flicks it open under the Stage
Manager's chin. The Stage Manager looks up from the script in
terror.

> MICHAEL
> ". . . an I wan' you to look at me
> when I walk, mon. Look at me!"

> VOICE
> Thank you, that was very good, but
> we're looking for someone less ethnic.

MUSIC UP: (A LA "ON BROADWAY")

CLOSE   SCRAPBOOK PAGES   MAIN TITLES BEGIN

The early years.

CONTINUED

CONTINUED

A) A six-year-old Michael in a school play. "My first play," scrawled beneath the picture.

B) A high school newspaper article about Michael Dorsey.

c) In another costume, older now . . . a high school play.

> VOICE OVER
>
> Next!

[INT.]   ANOTHER BARE STAGE—MICHAEL   [DAY]

Deeply moved, in tears, reading from *Henry IV*

> MICHAEL
> "Old men forget
> Yet all shall be forgot,
> But we'll remember with advantages
> What fears we did that day.
> Then shall their names . . ."

He suddenly breaks off as we and he HEAR MUMBLING from out in the dark house.

> MICHAEL
> Is it my acting interfering with your
> talking? . . . because I can keep this
> down. I mean, I wouldn't want to dis-
> turb you. Just tell me if I'm
> interfering.

CLOSE   THE SCRAPBOOK   MUSIC AND TITLES

A) A parchment award. "The John Barrymore Award."

B) A moustache encased in cellophane.

c) A piece of a program from *Cyrano De Bergerac*.

EXT.   A RUN-DOWN STORE FRONT   NIGHT

A run-down storefront converted into a theatre showing *Richard III*. Beneath the title is Michael's name. We [HEAR DIALOGUE] from inside.

INT.   A CONVERTED STORE—THEATRE   NIGHT

Michael as Richard, finishes a speech, moves off stage.

CONTINUED

CONTINUED

The audience, consisting of about TWELVE PEOPLE, applaud. The most enthusiastic response comes from a thirty-four–year–old endearing blonde named SANDY.

BACKSTAGE

such as it is, the DIRECTOR grabs Michael.

> DIRECTOR
> Dammit, Michael, I told you to sit on
> the edge of the stage and talk to the
> audience!

> MICHAEL
> (pulling away)
> I'm supposed to be Richard, the third,
> not Judy Garland!

INT.   THEATRE-IN-THE-ROUND   A REHEARSAL   NIGHT

Michael as an old man, wrinkled skin, bald head, lies on one side of the stage. Several ACTORS hover over him.

> 1ST ACTOR
> Quick! Get a priest!

> MICHAEL
> No! No priest.

> 2ND ACTOR
> But you're dying, Count Tolstoy.

A "PRIEST" runs up to Michael, who strikes out feebly.

> PRIEST
> "In the name of the Father, the Son,
> and the Holy Ghost . . . I commit
> your soul to God."

From the house:

> DIRECTOR
> That was super, Michael luv, but I
> wonder if you could cross to the cen-
> ter stage on the last speech and then
> die. The left side of the house can't
> see you.

CONTINUED

CONTINUED

> MICHAEL
> (slowly)
> You want me to . . . stand up during
> my death speech and *walk*⁇

> DIRECTOR
> I know it's awkward but we'll have
> to do it.

> MICHAEL
> Not with me as Tolstoy.

SCRAPBOOK—MUSIC AND TITLES

A) A telegram wishing Michael "Good luck in New York!"

B) A good review in an "Off-Off" Broadway play.

C) A Mailgram notifying him of an Obie nomination.

D) A wedding photo of Michael and a pretty girl.

E) A clipping in "Variety": "Due to creative differences Michael
Dorsey has been replaced by Terry Bishop in *Petrified Forest* at
the Dy Lys."

[INT.]   ANOTHER BARE STAGE—MICHAEL AND ANOTHER STAGE
MANAGER   DAY

Michael angrily slaps the script against his thigh.

> MICHAEL
> Just a second, now, could I start
> again? I just didn't start it right.

> VOICE
> (from darkness)
> No, no, it was very good. Really, it
> was fine: you're just the wrong
> height.

FADE OUT[2]

Starting with Michael's character box is a colorful, unexpected way of
driving home immediately that he is an actor: Michael will make his

2. Gelbart, *Tootsie*, pp. 1–5.

fortune by a really unexpected piece of impersonation. That and the short takes with Michael in different roles make us wonder, Who is Michael?—a question that will end up involving gender confusion, too. The contrast of the miniscenes with scrapbook shots is an excellent use of the camera to make the past something immediate. Instead of enduring a character's tedious exposition, we see and feel the development of Michael's career and its contrast with his present frustrated situation just as he experiences these. He is too tall or short; too young or old; not ethnic enough; and always too abrasive. He offends the directors he needs to give him a job! He's his own worst enemy.

When later his agent tells him no one wants to hire him because he is impossible, we buy it. We have lived something of the crisis he finds himself in. We're ready for him to strike out in some novel, desperate way. The scenes that have shown his frustration have also shown him to be both determined and nearly too bright for his own good.

Everything is clearly described, economically enacted, immediate.

Everything is visual, contrasting, conflicting, specific.

Everything is emotionally involving, realistic, believable.

Emotional Realism

The importance of emotional realism in a story has already been stressed in Part One. The emotional realism of drama is not a matter of the surface realism of what we, the viewers, witness in any given scene, but the reality of the emotional give-and-take between characters.

Effective writing makes us believe its reality despite all the training to rational disbelief in the imagination that has been inflicted on us. A child or a primitive doesn't analytically separate fact from fancy. They have to be restrained from getting involved in a movie's action or reassured that nothing is happening: faith is our natural franchise. But even as *we* see the first images flow across the screen, we find ourselves ready to believe in the story's world, suspending our matured disbelief.

How is our belief confirmed? We will believe in your story to the extent you make us feel for your characters. You must arouse our emotions through your characters' necessary attempts to resolve their conflict by overcoming their obstacles. Then we will feel empathy and sympathy or, it may be, antipathy toward them as they react to their dilemma in a credible way, that is, as their emotions fit their situation. Their situation on the surface may be fantastic, perhaps a long time ago in another galaxy, but your *characters make their dramatic situation real to us by the credibility and force of their response.* That is emotional realism in drama. Once we feel for and with the characters, feel sympathy and empathy or even antipathy for them, we believe this is real.

Look at Bonasera. We hear that he is under stress: his voice is strained. We know something is wrong before we know what happened to his daughter. It's impossible not to feel immediate sympathy for him. Wouldn't we be tempted to go for such help if our daughter or wife or girlfriend had been beaten and we knew where to go? Vengeance tastes sweet when you hunger for it. So our empathy—our ability to feel for and live through another—is aroused. Bonasera, though frustrated and vengeful, makes sense. His willingness to pay the Godfather's price is the essential token of his desperation. In fact, it is the Godfather who behaves more conventionally, who tempers the vengeance to fit the crime. He rouses our interest and empathy in turn: the reasonable man, willing to do a favor for a friend, but not for money. He is not a hired gun. His is a world that makes sense, one into which Bonasera has not fallen, but moved. It all hangs together, far from our own situation as it seems at the beginning, because of the emotional realism these characters show in response to their problems.

Turn to Dobbs. He is a beggar. He is unshaven, unwashed, ragged. His eyes follow the flight of a cigarette. He's desperate. He hesitates too long to pick up the butt and loses it. He moves on, begging.

Who would want to be in that situation? Poor guy! We don't have to like him to feel for him. Every detail hangs together: his appearance, his behavior, even the lottery ticket he throws away at the beginning. He is a born loser.

Dramatic reality is emotional reality. It is not the setting an action takes place in, but the action itself. Even the most realistic of settings is not real: it is a set or a picture of something. Character in action makes for reality, just as people in action make their own lives real to themselves. Drama—fiction—imitates actions. When we can follow the characters through their actions, any setting becomes real, as long as it stays consistent with itself. This is why we emphasize the view of plot structure (Act 1, BEGINNING: establishment of problem and conflict; Act 2, MIDDLE: effort to solve the problem failing—crisis; Act 3, END: final effort to solve problem—climax) as a way of thinking about action, behavior, instead of an arbitrary structure to be imposed on your story. It is the skeleton of its essence.

The opening miniscenes and images from *Tootsie* underscore this difference between surface realism and dramatic realism. Experiences don't flash by like the miniscenes or alternate with shots of a scrapbook. We accept all of this as a stylistic convention. Some conventions look very much like what we call reality. Some don't. But there's no difference formally between the opening scenes of *Tootsie* and those of *Star Wars* that culminate in Luke's decision to become a Jedi warrior after his adoptive family is slaughtered. What counts is that a character, who is caught in a particular situation and must act because of what has happened to him, arouses our emotions through our empathy and the accessibility of those feelings. What would not be real would have been Dobbs's pulling a hundred dollar bill out of his pocket, or Luke's laughing over his adoptive parents' skeletons, or Don Corleone's beginning a war against the established system for Bonasera's sake. If Dobbs, Michael, or Bonasera were real we might never want to invite them to dinner, but as far as they make us feel for their situation they make us live with them intimately for the brief duration of their lives in a darkened auditorium.

Now, perhaps, you can understand better why the specificity of detail and description in a given scene is praiseworthy, as is the writer's economy in choosing and giving these. You aren't asked to write this way for some abstract reason or because some rule says, "You must be specific and economic in detail and description." You show instead of tell because seeing *just* this person doing *just* this thing in *just* this place and at *just* this time is essential to our being able to empathize with that character.

Dramatic reality is emotional reality.

Character

Determining Sources

Characters can come from anywhere.

What are characters? They are people you invent—even if they're robots like those in *Star Wars* who show more fear, uncertainty, indomitability, and resourcefulness than the human characters around them.

The source for a character can simply be someone you read about in the newspapers or someone you see on television. Maybe the character is based on an actor who fascinates you. Perhaps she is like a friend or someone you heard about. He may arise from the "What if . . ." technique or may be created from separate observations you jot down in your notebook. She can be a family member or someone you have loved or hated for a long time. Your characters will only arouse emotion, hold interest, and generate the progress of your story as they are driven to action by their problem and the opposition they encounter trying to solve it, revealing themselves as they stretch to their limits—the limits of your, the writer's, imagination.

Some characters may wake you up from a dream or daydream, demanding that you learn more about them. Remember that there is more to your mind than you know and you need that "more" as a writer. Put those unexpected characters down on paper. Sort out who is the protagonist and who, the antagonist. Find out what they will do with the problem they very likely drag in their wake. You won't know everything about a character until you take him through an action, no matter how systematic and thorough you become (and you need to become systematic) in planning your story.

Characters can so obsess a writer that they spill out from one drama to another and flow into everyday life. Sophocles needed three plays to get rid of Oedipus and wrote the last play, *Oedipus at Colonus*, at age 94, confounding his children who were trying to have him judged senile. Jolly, fat, cowardly Falstaff was a nuisance in Shakespeare's imagination once invented: he wrote a special play for him, and when Falstaff threatened to take over yet another play, *Henry V*, Shakespeare had to kill him off. George Lucas needed three screenplays for Luke, Han Solo, and Darth Vader and originally had nine in mind! Spock of the Starship Enterprise became so popular his death and resurrection took up two of the first three Star Trek films. Superman has been reincarnated in four films after an absence from television for some years and isn't done yet, nor is his rival as the contemporary Heracles, Tarzan.

When a character is fully alive in your imagination, all of your mind's levels will have been called into play and through your character, ours. You may sometimes have the sensation your character is leading you, instead of the reverse. That is one of the problems and delights of a writer's experience. Be happy when your characters refuse to stay in the leaden mold you thought to fix them in: take a risk, and see where they want to lead you. You own the blue pencil.

Certain characters and dramatic situations seem less invented than perennial inhabitants of our hearts. The loss of the beloved and attempts to revive her stretch from the days of Orpheus to the present. The rebellious son, the abandoned woman or child, the fallen father (hero, athlete, politician) given a second chance, the too-faithful daughter, the young lover, the ingenue, the villain not beyond hope, the proud man cast down, the lowly man who rises to heroism and justice are only a few that are renewed generation by generation. They have this staying power because they touch central portions of our experience. Their wrestling with their problems renews our experience. A character trying to comprehend his experience, to the extent he has maintained our belief in his emotional realism, represents us in our own attempt to comprehend our experience. This is the true meaning of *empathy*. Never hesitate to use such a given character (or situation), but look always for your particular version. They're raw material to be worked with freshly, not finished givens.

Defining Your Character

Let us say your character has put in his appearance. Now is the time to get methodical. Start making a very specific list.

Is the character a man? A woman?

What does your character look like?

How old is your character?

What does he or she wear?

What is his race? If not human, then what?

Does he have any special physical characteristics?

Is he a hunchback with a withered hand, and does he walk onto the stage saying, "Now is the winter of our discontent," as Richard III does? Or do we discover him as he feeds a collection of pigeons and see from his face that he has been in a few fights. Will we be able to guess he is going to get thoroughly beaten up again at the climax, as Terry does in *On the Waterfront*?

How does your character talk? In dialect? Which one? Or does he talk as you do?

What is the social class of your character?

Is she poor? Is he nouveau riche? Is theirs inherited wealth? Is he just middle-class, but she an Alsatian princess?

Is she well educated? Did he never finish grade school? Is he an illiterate from a slum working his way up? As what?

Is she a professional? Or does she clean homes for a living?

For each character there is a well-defined answer to each question. And these are just basics. Consider these:

Is your character moody or gay? Sharp or dull witted?

Dream up a list of opposites: which terms fit your character?

Has life dealt him a good hand? How? If not, how? What has he done with that hand? Despaired? Or has she never given up despite everything? Despite—what?

Just where is this character now? In an office? What kind of office? Is she in a park? Is he making dinner? What does the kitchen look like? Maybe he's working out on a gymnast's vault? Or is he flying a jet? Is she pasting up a layout? Modeling? Committing a crime? Which one?

Does he drink? Is he lying unconscious on a dock? How is it he came to be that way on the dock? Was he beaten up? Is it from drink? What will his wife say when she hears? To whom is he married? Is he just living with someone instead?

Does she take drugs? Is it the first time? Has she shot up so often there's hardly a place left for the needle?

If these aren't enough to start you thinking, add some of the following:

What's wrong with your character? Does he want something that he can't have? What? What is she going to do about that? Who else is involved? Husband? Family? Friends? Professional colleagues? Gang members? Who is opposed to what your character wants?

Above all:

What's your character's problem? How much does it matter to him emotionally?

What's your character's obstacle? A person or circumstance? Or himself?

What's at stake for your character? What dramatic issue are you raising? What does it matter how his struggle comes out?

Clearly, as character occurs to you, you must:

1. Begin to visualize that character clearly.

2. Consider what kind of character you've got on your hands; meaning, what are his traits?

3. Think·about the nexus of relationships that character is in, the life situation in which the character finds himself.

4. Start defining what the character's problem is, and why the character can't solve it easily; that is, start imagining the root of the conflict.

Take out a sheet of paper. Take the first character that pops into mind and subject him or her to some of the questions just asked. See what kind of character that first, sketchy person becomes. What's the problem that character has? If she hasn't brought one with her, imagine one to yourself: "What if. . . ." For it is by stress aroused through conflict, by the feeling aroused in your character and the feeling that he consequently arouses in us, by which your character becomes real to us and is able to show what he or she is. There's no other way to break through the surfaces, to reveal and surprise and discover. The kind of mirror you will hold up to human behavior will reflect a process of struggle that defines a person's reality.

Conflict

Sources of Conflict

The sources of conflict can be as various as those for character.

We are assaulted with stories of conflict in the papers, on television, in our daily lives. There is such a wealth of material it can feel almost impossible to make a choice. In a perfect world, there might not be conflict: in ours, it seems the nature of reality. What seems important to you? Or funny? What obsesses you? What must you write about? You must pick what moves you, what jars your interest, rouses your excitement or indignation. Why else would you want to write about something?

Be specific. Are you going to write of a wife about to leave her husband? A young man about to go out on the street into a gang fight despite his girlfriend's pleas? A man about to pit himself against a better fighter, an established politician, a crime figure? A district attorney confronted with admitting an error in the middle of a political campaign? A young couple divided over abortion? A madman on a murderous spree? A killer trying to kill another in cold blood? A family trying to cope with a child's injury when circumstances seem against them? A man confronted with the need to take revenge and too divided in himself to act? Another man trying to survive in the wilds with too little experience? The list can go on and on.

You may dream of a story as well as a character. Your character probably will bring his conflict in tow with him when he occurs to you and you define him.

Define your conflict just as you define your character. It will fall into one of the three categories mentioned above:

Man versus a physical obstacle or a circumstance

Man versus man

Man versus himself

If it is man versus an obstacle, is it Jeremiah Johnson trying to light a fire beneath a snow-laden tree, a tinhorn almost too inexperienced to learn to survive as a mountain man in the nineteenth-century American West? Is it the biologist in *Never Cry Wolf* who was set down in the contemporary Canadian arctic to study wolves and was as raw and ignorant as Jeremiah Johnson? Or is your character Oedipus in Sophocles' play who, after being told he would kill his father and marry his mother, flees his home to defy such a fate, only to bring it about?

If it is man versus man, is it Michael-Dorothy trying to fend off Les's advances? Or Bonasera trying to get vengeance through the Godfather? Is it Ted denying Joanna her son? Or something as simple as Dobbs's begging the American for money?

If it is man versus himself, is it Hamlet wondering whether to commit suicide or Clint Eastwood's character in *Tightrope* who starts to behave like the sex-killer he's trying to find?

It is always some *particular* character, not any character, dealing with some *particular* problem. That is why you must imagine your character clearly and imagine your problem clearly. It is close to being a chicken-and-the-egg dilemma. No character in conflict—no action; no character in action—no play.

When you define your problem, make it simple for yourself: my character *must* take revenge, *must* get an abortion, *must* win an election or beg for money or refuse a marriage proposal. The more specific and clear your conflict, the more you free your imagination to fill out your character and action.

The Issue of Conflict

So far we have talked about conflict very simply, as a collision of wills involving the character in some immediate problem in which he believes he has to overcome some immediate obstacle in order to survive. That kind of conflict must be present in every scene if you are going to generate action. But in a full screenplay you will have many scenes full of such conflict without any one of them being the same as the overall conflict of the screenplay. You need to differentiate between the immediate, necessary conflict of any given scene and the bearing of that scene on the central conflict of your play—the issue of conflict.

For example, Bonasera's immediate problem is to enlist the Godfather's help. But his asking for such help raises an issue that goes to the heart of the play, namely, the role of the Mafia in our conventional society that Bonasera feels has let him down. His action also prompts the closely allied question of whether someone involved with the Mafia can remain free of it.

Or take *Star Wars*. Over and over Luke has to confront and try to solve immediate problems—whether to seek help from some mysterious figure in the desert, whether to become a Jedi knight, whether to join Obi when his family is killed. Each scene has its own local conflict: cumulatively the scenes flesh out forcefully the issue of conflict of the play—whether Luke and the forces of good can prevail over evil.

Or consider *Tootsie*. However well the opening miniscenes define Michael, they are only preparation for the fateful moment when he chooses to impersonate a woman, which he must do in order to survive as an actor. That is a much larger issue of conflict than his much simpler, immediate problem of auditioning for a job.

In other words, when you write your play you do so with a structure of dramatic scenes that have their own immediate conflicts, but which together explore the larger issue of conflict that is central to the entire story. We end by experiencing that conflict as a totality by living it dramatic moment by dramatic moment, aspect by aspect, as does your character. That is, in fact, how any experience is lived, so that later we say, Ah, that's what it was all about!

Two questions will help you to keep clear the relation between a scene's immediate conflict and the larger issue of conflict.

First, What is immediately at stake in your scene? If nothing is, your character has no problem: he has no need to act, and there is no drama.

Second, What is ultimately at stake in your scene? What larger issues are raised by the consequences of the immediate action? And how does that relate to the entire story you are trying to tell, to your play's objective?

You will be writing the dramatic essence of the immediate conflict when you write the premise for your assigned scenes. You will link both the immediate with the overriding issue of conflict when you write the premise for your miniscreenplay later. For present purposes, they will tend to coincide in your self-contained scenes.

Example: Opening of Kramer vs. Kramer

Let's take a look at a scene, with some preparatory miniscenes, that successfully establishes character and conflict in a more substantial way than we have seen so far.

Let's try and recreate the writer's process of imagination that culminated in the opening of *Kramer vs. Kramer*. We'll use the "What if . . ." game to help.

Imagine that you want to write something about families, about the changing roles of men and women as parents. It seems a relevant issue to you. *What if* . . . it is the wife who feels a deep need to find herself, while the husband is completely preoccupied with his career?

What's stopping the wife from finding herself? *What if* . . . she is not only married, but a mother? *What if* . . . the child is young, and she loves him (we don't want things to be easy for her)? *What if* . . . we put the wife in crisis and have her walk out on her husband and child who will then be at the center of the story, an abandoned man and child instead of an abandoned woman and child?

Is she attractive? In this case, beautiful. How long has she been suffering? *What if* . . . for years, since being a teenager?

Who is her husband? He's . . . modestly successful in his field (What field? He's an artist. Long hair? No, he's a commercial artist.) and so busy he just doesn't see her. He's insensitive to her needs and his son's.

We have certainly given her a problem! Is she going to act, act *now?* Yes. We'll have her pack her bags to go without her husband's even being aware of her state of mind as he comes home. What's more, we'll make this day a very successful one for him up to the moment he comes home in order to dramatize as strongly as possible the revolution in their lives that results from her action.

Finally, *what if* . . . her husband fights to have her stay?

After you read the scene, jot down your ideas for its structure, immediate premise, and what is immediately and ultimately at stake.

FADE IN:

CLOSE-UP: JOANNA KRAMER

She is staring into CAMERA. Her face is a mask, completely impassive. There is no sound. HOLD FOR A BEAT, then

INTERCUT A SERIES OF SHOTS OF TED KRAMER

during his hectic day at the office, wheeling and dealing, laughing and joking at a business lunch, etc. All motion, noise, color. . . . [The SHOTS OF JOANNA KRAMER SHOW her continuing to stare] straight ahead, always silent, her expression never changes.

INT.   O'CONNOR'S OFFICE, AD AGENCY   (EST) [DAY]

O'CONNOR stands behind his desk, a number of rough layouts spread out in front of him. TED stands in front of the desk, watching nervously. Scattered around the office are six or seven 'regulars' including PHYLLIS BERNARD.

There is a BEAT of silence as O'Connor studies the layouts.

                    O'CONNOR
          I like it . . .
               (then)
          I love it . . .
               (then)
                    (MORE)

CONTINUED

CONTINUED

> O'CONNOR (CONT'D)
> It's fabulous . . .
> (to Ted)
> Okay, Ted, you got it . . .
> (to the rest)
> All right. Hold it down . . . Hold it
> down. I think everybody here ought
> to know I'm putting Ted Kramer on
> the Northern Airlines account.

There are general cheers and good-natured jokes. A couple of people start to yell "SPEECH."

> TED
> (embarrassed, but he can't
> stop grinning)
> All I can say . . . All I can say is this is
> maybe one of the five best days in my
> whole life.

INT.   CHILD'S ROOM, KRAMER APT.   NIGHT

The room is dark, the only light coming from a small night light.

We SEE a beautiful five-year-old boy, BILLY KRAMER. He lies in bed, half asleep. HOLD FOR A BEAT as a beautiful woman, JOANNA KRAMER, leans over, kisses the child and hugs him tightly to her.

> JOANNA
> (intense)
> I love you, Billy . . .

> BILLY
> (drowsy)
> I love you too, Mommy . . .
> Goodnight . . .

ON JOANNA

as she gets up from the bed and starts toward the door of Billy's room.

> JOANNA
> Sleep tight . . .

CONTINUED

CONTINUED

> BILLY
> Don't let the bedbugs bite . . .

Joanna stops in the doorway, silhouetted against the light. She turns, takes a last look at her son, then steps outside.

INT.   HALLWAY   [NIGHT]

Now that the light is brighter, we can SEE Joanna more clearly. In her mid-thirties, she is beautiful, dressed in a style that can best be described as Bloomingdale's. HOLD FOR A BEAT as she leans against the door. It is clear from her expression that she is terribly upset. Then, making up her mind, she crosses to a closet and takes out a suitcase. . . . [FOLLOW HER] as she carries it into the bedroom, lays it out on the bed and opens it.

[IN THE BEDROOM]

She crosses to a closet, grabs an armload of clothes and dumps them helter-skelter into the suitcase.

INT.   O'CONNOR'S OFFICE   NIGHT

It is some time later and the only people left are Ted and O'Connor.

> TED
> (in the midst of a story)
> So I'm over at the airlines, right? And
> the place is full of suits, right? And
> I'm up there and I'm making my pitch
> and it's going great. I mean, I've got
> 'em right where I want 'em. And all of
> a sudden this old guy starts to cough.
> So I keep on pitching and he keeps on
> coughing and I keep on pitching and
> he keeps on—

> VOICE, O.S.
> G'night, fellas.

[TED'S] POV

The door to O'Connor's office. A fellow worker, NORMAN FISHER.

CROSSCUTTING BETWEEN THEM

> TED
>
> Where you goin' Norm, it's early—

> NORM
>
> Got to get home.

And he disappears.

[ON TED]

> TED
> (glancing at his watch)
> Oh, Christ, I'm late . . . I gotta get out
> of here.
>> (nevertheless, he settles
>> back and resumes his
>> story)
> So, anyway, I look over and the old
> guy is starting to turn blue. Jim, I
> swear to God the only thing I can
> think about is that this poor
> sonofabitch is gonna die on me and
> screw up the pitch.

INT.   KRAMER APT.—BATHROOM   [NIGHT]

Joanna stands at the medicine cabinet, going through it, packing things in a travel kit: rollers, deodorant, makeup, birth control pills. She starts to take a small bottle of perfume that has only an eighth of an inch of fluid left inside, hesitates, then puts it back.

EXT.   OFFICE BUILDING, MIDTOWN   NIGHT

. . . as the doors to the outer lobby open and Ted and O'Connor appear. Ted starts to hail a taxi. O'Connor stops him.

> O'CONNOR
> C'mon, what's the rush? Walk me a
> couple of blocks.

> TED
> Jim, I've got to go. I'm already late—

CONTINUED

CONTINUED

> O'CONNOR
> Listen, Ted . . . I just wanted to tell
> you that if this campaign does what I
> expect it to, I've got a pretty good idea
> they'll make me a partner and when
> they do . . .

He starts off down the street.

> O'CONNOR (CONT'D)
> . . . I just want you to know you'll be
> the next creative director.

ON TED a moment as he hesitates, then turns and follows O'Connor.

INSERT

A long and meticulous list that Joanna is making of the phone numbers and addresses of the various doctors and hospitals, of what each of Billy's medicines is for, and of the foods that Billy is and isn't permitted to eat. . . . [DRAW BACK TO SHOW]

INT.   KRAMER APT.—[DINING ROOM]   NIGHT

where Joanna] sits at the dining room table working on the list with total concentration.

EXT.   STREET: [TRACK WITH TED AND O'CONNOR]   NIGHT

as they walk along in no particular rush.

> O'CONNOR
> Look, Ted, these guys are dumping six
> million into a national account, right?
> And they're looking to change their
> corporate image, right? Ted, I'm tell-
> ing you it's a wet dream. You can start
> writing your acceptance speech for
> your Cleo now.

> TED
> C'mon, Jim, don't say that. Don't talk
> like that. It gets me very fatootzed
> when people talk like that. We go in,
> we give them our best shot. That's all
> we can do.

INT. KRAMER APT.—FOYER NIGHT

ON JOANNA'S SUITCASE, now packed and by the door.

IN THE KITCHEN

CLOSE ON THE LIST OF INSTRUCTIONS that Joanna wrote out. It is neatly laid on the kitchen counter with a box of whole grain cereal and a small bottle of vitamins beside it.

INT. KRAMER APT.—LIVING ROOM NIGHT

[Joanna sitting] at a desk. There is an envelope with a list that she has made for herself. As she crosses off one of the items, and starts to go through her wallet, the front door opens and Ted steps in.

JOANNA'S POV

Ted with a big grin on his face. He is so full of himself that he fails to notice anything is wrong. He kisses her lightly and starts for the phone.

>   JOANNA
>   Ted—

But it is too late. He has gone to the phone, started dialing.

>   TED
>   Just a minute. I forgot to call the—
>   (into the phone)
>   Listen, this is Ted Kramer. I'm gonna
>   need that stuff outa the retoucher,
>   Tuesday latest. Okay?

As he hangs up the phone, he turns to Joanna.

>   JOANNA
>   (like ice)
>   Ted, I'm leaving you.

>   TED
>   What?

Joanna opens her purse, takes out her keys and wallet.

>   JOANNA
>   Here are my keys. I won't be needing
>   them any more.

[Ted doesn't believe this. It must be] one of her moods—

>   CONTINUED

CONTINUED

> TED
> (sardonic)
> I'm sorry I'm late, all right? I'm sorry
> I didn't call—I was busy making a
> living.

. . . Joanna doesn't bother looking at him. She opens her purse, takes
out her wallet and begins removing credit cards.

> JOANNA
> My American Express . . . My Bloom-
> ingdale's Credit Card . . . My check-
> book—

> TED
> (the martyr)
> Okay, okay . . . What is it this time?
> What did I do now?

> JOANNA
> (ignoring this)
> I took two thousand out of the savings
> account. That was what I had in the
> bank when we got married.

> TED
> Joanna, whatever it is, believe me, I'm
> sorry.

> JOANNA
> Here are the slips for the laundry and
> the cleaning. They'll be ready on
> Saturday.

> TED
> (hard lining it)
> Now listen, before you do something
> you'll really regret you'd better stop
> and think—

> JOANNA
> (not bothering to look up)
> I've paid the rent, the Con-Ed and the
> (MORE)

CONTINUED

CONTINUED

> JOANNA (CONT'D)
>
> phone bill, so you don't have to worry
> about them.

She checks off the last item on her list as her husband watches,
dumbfounded.

> JOANNA (CONT'D)
> There, that's everything.

Joanna gets to her feet and starts towards the front door. In an instant Ted is after her.

> TED
> (panic starting)
> For God's sake, Joanna, would you at
> least tell me what I did that's so
> terrible!

. . . . At the door.

> JOANNA
> Look, it's not your fault, okay? It's me.
> It's my fault—you just married the
> wrong person.

Joanna opens the door and steps out into the hallway.

INT.   HALLWAY OUTSIDE KRAMER APT.   NIGHT

> JOANNA
> (tears starting)
> Ted, I can't . . . I tried . . . I really tried
> but . . . I just can't hack it
> anymore . . .

> TED
> (stiffening)
> What about Billy?

> JOANNA
> I'm not taking him with me.

> TED
> What?

CONTINUED

CONTINUED

> JOANNA
> (from her gut)
> Ted, I'm a terrible mother! I'm an
> awful mother. I yell at Billy all the
> time. I have no patience. No . . . No.
> He's better off without me.
> (unable to look at Ted)
> Ted, I've got to go . . . I've got to go.

> TED
> Okay, I understand and I promise I
> won't try and stop you, but you can't
> just go . . . Look, come inside and talk
> . . . Just for a few minutes.

> JOANNA
> (pleading)
> No! Please . . . *Please* don't make me
> stay . . . I swear . . . If you do, sooner
> or later, maybe tomorrow, maybe next
> week—maybe a year from now—
> (looking directly at him)
> I'll go right out the window.

[We HEAR THE] ELEVATOR COMING. . . . There is nothing more that can be done; this is the last moment of intimacy.

> TED
> Joanna, please . . .

> JOANNA
> Ted, I don't love you anymore.

> TED
> (quietly)
> Where are you going?

The elevator door opens, Joanna stepping inside.

> JOANNA
> I don't know . . .

The elevator door closes behind her and it starts to descend.

CONTINUED

CONTINUED

. . . . [Ted] stands for a moment, stunned, unable to move.

FADE OUT[3]

These opening miniscenes are not as flamboyant as those from *Tootsie*, but they more succinctly and pointedly draw us immediately into the problem. First we see Joanna's impassive face. We don't know what's wrong, but know something is. Then we cut to Ted happy in the office. Ted has just scored a coup. We cut back to the apartment as Joanna says an intense goodnight to Billy, "I love you Billy." Her child matters to her a lot, but then Joanna gets a suitcase and starts packing.

How swiftly our emotions are worked on by this simple compare-and-contrast sequence of miniscenes. No one tells us about her unhappiness or his insensitivity: we see an unhappy woman, guess an insensitive man through his obliviousness to what is going on at home. We're prepared for a major collision as Ted dawdles and Joanna packs, makes lists, and waits.

This is clear, straightforward, intense dramatic writing with the information we need for understanding communicated to us in a series of actions. Ted walks in without noticing list or wife waiting with her suitcase and instantly makes a call. If we hadn't gotten the point about his insensitivity, that little piece of action shows it! She immediately precipitates a conflict: "Ted, I'm leaving you." She does not make a speech about her motivation, causes, reflections, and final decision, only methodically gives him the list, keys, and her credit cards. Her actions show that her leaving has been planned for a time and down to the last detail. Ted can't believe it—as Joanna goes on about the laundry, rent, and Con-Ed bill. When she heads for the door, Ted starts to believe her.

Ted demands to know how he is guilty. Joanna turns it around: this is not going to be a simple-minded thing. She is the problem: she "can't hack it anymore." He married the wrong person, innocently. We begin to see Ted's insensitivity differently in this light: he has his faults, clearly, but he is not the villain. Who is? No one. How should they have been different? The question isn't asked, but we begin to feel it. That is essential preparation for the issue of conflict.

What about Billy? She's leaving him behind with Ted. Second bombshell for Ted. We wonder, What kind of mother is she? "I'm a terrible mother!" she says. We think, This is a troubled, honest woman. We're

3. Benton, *Kramer vs. Kramer,* pp. 1–9.

wholly into the scene's conflict, our empathy aroused by such an intense confrontation between the characters.

Now, when Joanna does try to explain herself, it is because Ted tries to keep her and she must get away. What she says is aimed at making him do something immediate—let her go. Force opposes force. Things are so bad she might try suicide if she has to stay. She delivers the clincher: "Ted, I don't love you any more." "Where are you going?" "I don't know." She disappears into the elevator.

Compare your notes with ours.

What is immediately at stake? Joanna's leaving.

Ultimately at stake? How will Ted and Billy manage on their own? Can Ted be father and mother enough for his child?

Issue of conflict? Can a man hold a family together today, or is he unable to break out of his traditional role?

Protagonist? Joanna in this scene, but Ted for the story that ensues.

Problem? Joanna's need to leave.

Antagonist? Here, Ted.

BEGINNING.   Ted comes home and starts telephoning, ignoring Joanna. She hits him with her decision. Immediate problem and conflict.

MIDDLE.   She tries to leave, and Ted stops her, forcing her to explain herself. He even promises not to stop her, but begs her to come in and talk "just for a few minutes." Not even her warning about suicide works. Crisis. Imminent failure stares her in the eyes.

END.   She tells him she doesn't love him anymore, overcoming his resistance, getting her way. Climax. The elevator doors close.

A Word on Back Story, Exposition, and Preparation

This is a good place to define *back story, exposition,* and *preparation,* terms that frequently recur in any discussion of dramatic material. *Back story* is all the information you gather about your characters and story that explains what took place before the action began. If Joanna was your character, you might have imagined her education, her parents, the nature of her home life, or the circumstances of her marriage. But you use only what you need to make the immediate situation clear. Much that you gather in back story will never appear in your play, but it will deepen your understanding of your character and condition your handling of character and situation.

Exposition is information you convey during the action that we need to know in order to understand the present situation and behavior of the characters. Joanna explains herself to Ted under direct, dramatic necessity—this is why I am doing what I am doing. Good-bye! Bonasera tells his story to get Don Corleone's help. The opening of *Tootsie* lets us experience the exposition directly in the scrapbook shots and in the mini-scenes of Michael's botched auditions.

You know you have gone astray in your handling of exposition if a character tells us something without there being an immediate, dramatic need to say it to someone in order to do something. Exposition is also one of the oldest devices for giving information in the present that is necessary for us to be able to understand some later action in a proper way. But a good writer tries to make even this kind of exposition seem motivated by a character's present need—even if that character seems to take advantage of the moment to tell us more than we think we need to know just then.

Preparation is a detail or action carried out in the immediate moment of the scene we are experiencing that prepares us for later action. Seeing Joanna pack her bags prepares us for the confrontation with Ted. Observing Dobbs's behavior prepares us to understand he can't keep what he has. Witnessing Michael's argumentativeness prepares us for his need to do something unexpected to break down the barrier he has raised against himself.

Your Second Assignment

Write a scene in which you establish character and conflict in five type-written pages, no more or less. Introduce your characters and initiate an action by establishing a conflict in reaction to a problem in which the wills of your characters clash. Take it to some conclusive action. Give swift, accurate descriptions of shots and characters in the business. Don't be novelistic. Don't tell us what a character is thinking: show that thought by appropriate behavior and speech. That's the only way we experience anything in drama.

Don't hesitate to use the camera's freedom to give yourself a mini-scene or two to establish character or situation for your major scene.

Be specific. Who are your characters? What is your conflict? Define them as we've shown you.

What is immediately at stake? What is ultimately at stake? Are these two different? That is, does your issue of conflict transcend this particular scene?

A simple word to the wise in terms of working procedure. Don't judge what you write before or while you write it—judge it afterward. Too many students never let themselves get off the ground because they don't know when to write freely and when to sit back and judge. Don't cramp yourself in the beginning. Only after you have text should you begin to judge your effort.

A tremendous amount of the art of writing is in revision. Do a first draft, and then concentrate on the revision. When you write that first draft, be free with it: do anything and everything that occurs to you as you write it, above and beyond whatever you may have planned. When you revise your draft, you can develop the best ideas that appear in the scene.

Have a good time with this one!

7. Developing Character and Conflict to Crisis

The Nature of the Dramatic Obstacle

We suspect you wrote your character and conflict with a great deal more specificity in your last assignment. You probably got to the problem, and to more of a problem, more swiftly and with better definition: if you didn't, you were likely a good deal more aware of that. Good writing doesn't waste time bringing the story into troubled waters.

But several problems are likely to have occurred. You may have had a good idea for your scene, but somehow failed to see the extent of the opportunity your idea offered for drama or comedy, so you came away feeling you had missed the boat. Or you may have hurried your development to the point of crisis too quickly with the result that your characters and conflict seemed sketchy.

You may have asked yourself once your protagonist had his problem: Where do I go from here? How do I maintain that development, create suspense, reveal motivation, and bring a character to the crisis where he makes a final, self-defining effort to triumph, regardless of whether he triumphs or fails?

We said to define your conflict, just as you must define your character, yet how do you keep that conflict in clear view when the form the protagonist's immediate problem or obstacle takes seems to change moment by moment as he encounters opposition? Even as simple a scene as that from *Rocky* turns out to be deceptive when looked at more closely. We said the immediate problem was overcoming Adrian's resistance, yet nowhere do you encounter resistance in general. What you do encounter is a series of related changes. First, she wants to talk to her brother. Then, she doesn't think she should stay. Next, she gets to the door. She doesn't want to take her glasses off or her hat. She starts to weep. When kissed, she doesn't immediately respond. These are the actual obstacles.

It's also too easy to say that the fun as well as your insight and inventiveness is in how your characters try to solve their problems, when you now realize, reviewing the scenes quoted so far in the text, that there are layers of problems confronting characters. There is the basic dilemma for the protagonist set out in the premise. There is a *series* of forms that the immediate problem or obstacle takes in a given scene. There is a relationship between what is immediately at stake and what is ultimately at stake with regard to the main issue of conflict. Then there are obvious complications that befall characters, like Rocky's falling in love, Les's proposing to Michael-Dorothy, or Joanna's coming back for Billy, some of which may seem directly related to the main thrust of your story, some less so.

In fact, two problems have emerged: one is how to master the actual technique for developing character and conflict moment to moment; the other is how to relate that development to the various turns the story structure of your material takes, to the turns in the plot. There are two concepts you need to understand in order to solve these problems.

First, your protagonist is subjected, moment by moment, to a series of minor *reverses* because each effort your protagonist makes to overcome his obstacle fails, partially, as we have pointed out, because of the opposition he or she encounters from the antagonist, be that a person or force or division within the protagonist himself. Each reverse leads to a new effort on the part of the protagonist to get his way and a new effort on the part of the antagonist to block him. The obstacle takes on new shades and shapes necessarily as a consequence. When we speak of an action-reaction pattern in drama, this is exactly what we mean, this constant metamorphosis of the conflict as it is generated by the first attempt and relative failure of the protagonist to solve his problem. *The development of a scene is made up of several reverses leading to the crisis that, climactically, your protagonist must resolve.*

The second key to developing character and conflict is how you invent and use *complications* in the action. Rocky's falling in love is a complication; Joanna's returning for Billy is a complication. Complications are crucial turns in the story, in the plot: reverses make up the texture of action within individual scenes. If speaking of reverses helps us understand the growth of the action within a scene, speaking of complications gives us an additional way to think about the larger problems from which specific scenes flow. The two can overlap, especially when a complication is introduced, as in the scene from *Kramer vs. Kramer* when Joanna demands Billy: normally they are quite different.

Let's look at reverse and complication more closely.

Reverse

Some screenwriters and directors talk about plot structure in a jargon you should avoid. For instance, you hear terms like *plot point* bandied around, a term that can be used to justify any moment in a story a writer is in love with. *Reverse* is an older and more acute term and gives a real handle on the endlessly changeable nature of the obstacle your protagonist encounters. Its roots go back to the Greeks. They called a reverse a *peripeteia*, and by it meant the crucial, climactic moment in which the tragic hero recognized his irreversible failure to solve his problem as he would have wanted. The most famous peripeteia in dramatic literature is in Sophocles' *Oedipus Rex* when Oedipus, who thought he had avoided the fate pronounced for him—that he would kill his father and marry his mother—discovers he has inadvertently done both. At the moment he discovers this, he cries out:

> OEDIPUS
> O, O, O, they will all come,
> all come out clearly! Light of the sun, let me
> look upon you no more after today!
> I who first saw the light bred of a match
> accursed, and accursed in my living
> with them I lived, cursed in my killing.[1]

In a moment he falls from a king to a man all others but his daughter Antigone, who is also his sister, despise. He rushes off to find that his wife-mother, Jocasta, has hung herself. He blinds himself and is led off by Antigone, no more than a beggar.

At the end of *The Treasure of the Sierra Madre* Dobbs, with a line of burros carrying a fortune in gold dust, runs into three bandits. He tries to pretend he is unconcerned, but they, making sure he is alone, become threatening. Dobbs pulls a gun and tries to shoot, but it refuses to work. The bandits crush his skull with a stone and knife him with a machete. They don't recognize the value of Dobbs's bags of gold dust and slice them, letting the gold pour out and blow away in the wind. Dobbs had slaved for this gold and thought he had killed his best friend to have all of it. Meeting with bandits is a complication: what happens to him as a consequence is a reverse.

These are examples of major reverses—literally, complete reversals of fortune. Ted encounters one in *Kramer vs. Kramer* when he comes home after a superlative day, only to have Joanna abandon him. Every scene can't have a major reverse in it: they appear only at strategic turning points in the story. But every scene is made up of the texture of the minor reverses a character encounters trying to get his or her way.

---

1. Sophocles, *Oedipus the King*, trans. David Grene, in vol. 3 of *The Complete Greek Tragedies* (New York: Modern Library), p. 76.

Michael undertakes one tryout after another in hope—why else would he be at one?—only to find they turn out badly for one unexpected reason after another. He undergoes, swiftly, multiple reverses. Or he meets with Les, and moment to moment is stopped from letting Les down gently until the proposal he came to prevent is made: he meets another series of reverses. Even something as simple as Dobbs's hesitating to pick up the cigarette and having it stolen from him is a reverse.

Think of the simple reverses in the first scene we quoted in this text, when Bonasera is methodically rebuked by Don Corleone in *The Godfather* for not coming for help before, for demanding too severe a punishment for his daughter's attackers, and for offering to buy help. These are all reverses. *Each reverse is a moment of dramatic action containing an action and a reaction* within the flow of the scene. Each of these moments also marks a particular shading or change in the immediate obstacle the character is trying to overcome. That obstacle will appear in a slightly new form because of each reverse. A new effort, a new ploy, a new inspiration, a new offer—a new response is called for, reverse by reverse, from the protagonist because he fails to get his way and from the antagonist's efforts to keep things that way!

Complication

A complication is a development in the process of events that affects the overall objective of the protagonist. It is an event that has an ongoing impact, providing the basis for a scene or a number of scenes or an entire screenplay. A reverse is a given moment of action-reaction within a scene that works out contrary to what the protagonist wants. A reverse is never good, while a complication in itself can be neutral: it is how your protagonist handles a complication that is important. There is nothing bad about Rocky's falling in love or Dobbs's winning the lottery that lets him go prospecting. Everything depends on how these characters handle the consequences of each complication. Rocky builds a relationship; Dobbs goes mad with greed from the gold he finds. Similarly, Michael's decision to imitate a woman and become Tootsie represents a real complication in his life, but it becomes impossible only because of the complications that follow from that action on his part: he falls in love with a woman who believes he is a woman, and her father falls in love with him.

Clint Eastwood in *Pale Rider* plays a providential drifter who helps a group of poor miners against a single wealthy, greedy miner trying to corner all claims. He persuades the man to buy out the poorer miners at a reasonable price instead of calling in hired guns, but the miners decide to stick it out from motives of dignity. They desire gold only as a means to build a decent community. This is a complication that now makes their resistance look not foolhardy but heroic, and the antagonist's seemingly generous offer becomes merely an example of mindless greed.

A complication can also be bad. Luke in *Star Wars* becomes involved with Darth Vader and his minions as he tries to help Princess Leia, the first consequence of which being that he sees his adoptive family destroyed. There is nothing positive immediately for Ted in Joanna's leaving. Your premise will contain both your primary idea for your story and the primary complication, with the shading the action gives that for better or worse.

A story can have a few complications or many. There is a delicate line to walk here. Too many complications and we begin to chuckle and wonder, What next? One of the techniques of comedy depends on this multiplication of complications. Used right, even apparently serious material can be given a comedic nature not at odds with a writer's intentions. Complications abound in *Prizzi's Honor*, starring Jack Nicholson as Charlie Partani, a Mafia man Friday who investigates, kills, and organizes with equal dexterity. First complication—he falls in love with a non-Mafia woman. Second complication—she turns out to have stolen "family" money. Third complication—she is an expert hit man in her own right. Fourth complication—instead of killing her, he marries her. Fifth complication—the daughter of one of the sons of the ruling Prizzi godfather tells her father Charlie raped her and sets him off in a quest for vengeance. Sixth complication—the father hires Charlie's wife to hit Charlie.

When Charlie overcomes all problems and the Prizzi godfather asks him to run the family's business, a moment of great triumph for Charlie, he is ordered to kill his wife. Why? Charlie's wife had shot a woman, a witness to a kidnap (another complication), to prevent her from identifying the Mafia members involved. That woman turned out to be a policeman's wife. The police are consequently on a rampage against the Mafia (a complication caused by a complication), even though their salaries are cut in half by the withdrawal of Mafia bribes. Now Charlie must run the family, and straightening out this mess is his first assignment. He is horrified and refuses, but is driven to a moment of insight. If he doesn't kill his wife, he must leave the family, and he realizes he can't imagine a life outside the family. He encounters a major reverse because of this complication. He kills his wife.

Now let's turn to three scenes from three very successful screenplays widely separated in time and place to illustrate and develop these points: *The Graduate, On the Waterfront,* and *Fanny and Alexander*.

A Seduction Scene from The Graduate

The Graduate is a film that caught the disillusionment of the 1960s when it first appeared with its mingled portrayal of innocence and hope corrupted by the beaten in spirit. Ben returns home from college only to discover nothing of great meaning or value awaits him. He is adrift and enticed, teased, and seduced by a woman old enough to be his mother, Mrs. Robinson, a close friend of his parents. Her husband is his father's partner. Her daughter, Elaine, is Benjamin's age. Later Ben and Elaine will fall in love and end up together despite her mother's affair with Ben.

What follows is the scene in which Mrs. Robinson seduces Ben. He has just been maneuvered by her into taking a hotel room, where he is waiting for her as the action begins. Jot down what you think are the BEGINNING, MIDDLE, and END. List the complication that has brought Ben here, which we have indicated for you, and then list what you think the reverses are in this scene.

FADE IN:

INT.   HOTEL ROOM   (EST) NIGHT

Ben steps in, moves to the window. We SEE the pool area through the window. Ben closes the blinds.

There is a KNOCK on the door. Ben crosses to the door and opens it.

> MRS. ROBINSON
> Hello, Benjamin.

> BEN
> Hello, Mrs. Robinson.

Mrs. Robinson moves to the bureau and puts her purse and gloves on it. She looks at herself in the mirror for a moment, then turns slowly, looking at the room, finally ending on Ben's face. She steps towards him.

[TWO SHOT: BEN & MRS. ROBINSON]

> MRS. ROBINSON
> Well?

He clears his throat and kisses her.

> BEN
> Well.

> MRS. ROBINSON
> Benjamin.

CONTINUED

CONTINUED

> BEN
>
> Yes?

> MRS. ROBINSON
>
> I'll get undressed now. Is that all
> right?

> BEN
>
> Sure. Shall I—I mean shall I just stand
> here? I mean—I don't know what you
> want me to do.

> MRS. ROBINSON
>
> Why don't you watch?

> BEN
>
> Oh—sure. Thank you.

She takes off her jacket.

> MRS. ROBINSON
>
> Will you bring me a hanger?

> BEN
>
> What?

> MRS. ROBINSON
>
> A hanger.

Ben opens the closet door.

> BEN
>
> Oh—yes. Wood?

> MRS. ROBINSON
>
> What?

> BEN
>
> Wood or wire? They have both.

> MRS. ROBINSON
>
> Either one will be fine.

> BEN
>
> Okay.

He brings her a hanger. She puts her jacket on it.

CONTINUED

CONTINUED

> MRS. ROBINSON
> Will you help me with this, please?

She turns her back.

> BEN
> Certainly.

He undoes the zipper at her neck.

> MRS. ROBINSON
> Thank you.

> BEN
> You're welcome.

She turns and looks at him. He backs away.

> MRS. ROBINSON
> Would this be easier for you in the dark?

> BEN
> Mrs. Robinson—I can't do this.

> MRS. ROBINSON
> You what?

> BEN
> This is all terribly wrong.

> MRS. ROBINSON
> Benjamin—do you find me undesirable?

> BEN
> Oh no, Mrs. Robinson. I think—I think you're the most attractive of all my parents' friends. I mean that. I find you desirable. But I—for God's sake, can you imagine my parents? Can you imagine what they would say if they just saw us here in this room right now?

> MRS. ROBINSON
> What would they say?

CONTINUED

CONTINUED

> BEN
>
> I have no idea, Mrs. Robinson. But
> for God's sake. They brought me up.
> They've made a good life for me. And
> I think they deserve better than this. I
> think they deserve a little better than
> jumping into bed with the partner's
> wife.

> MRS. ROBINSON
>
> Are you afraid of me?

> BEN
>
> No—but look—maybe we could do
> something else together. Mrs. Robin-
> son—would you like to go to a
> movie?

> MRS. ROBINSON
>
> Can I ask you a personal question?

> BEN
>
> Ask me anything you want.

> MRS. ROBINSON
>
> Is this your first time?

> BEN
>
> Is this—what?

> MRS. ROBINSON
>
> It is, isn't it? It is your first time.

> BEN
>
> That's a laugh, Mrs. Robinson. That's
> really a laugh. Ha ha.

> MRS. ROBINSON
>
> You can admit that, can't you?

> BEN
>
> Are you kidding?

> MRS. ROBINSON
>
> It's nothing to be ashamed of—

CONTINUED

CONTINUED

> BEN
> Wait a minute!

> MRS. ROBINSON
> On your first time—

> BEN
> Who said it was my first time.

> MRS. ROBINSON
> That you're afraid—

> BEN
> Wait a minute.

> MRS. ROBINSON
> —of being—inadequate—I mean just
> because you happen to be inadequate
> in one way—

> BEN
> INADEQUATE!

LONG pause.

> MRS. ROBINSON
> (starting to dress)
> Well—I guess I'd better—

> BEN
> Don't move.

He slams the bathroom door shut. The light in the room disappears.

> FADE OUT [2]

This is at once amusing and sad, full of effective, simple detail, like Ben's asking Mrs. Robinson whether she prefers a metal or wooden hanger and the exaggerated politeness of his using "Mrs. Robinson" to address her. It is similar to the earlier scene from *Rocky*, except now it is the man who is inhibited. How do your notes on structure compare with ours?

---

2. Buck Henry, *The Graduate* (unpublished manuscript, March 1967), pp. 51–54; adapted from the novel *The Graduate* by Charles Webb.

BEGINNING. This first section lasts up to the point the problem takes specific form for Ben, when he says he "can't do this." The obstacle takes the form of guilt.

MIDDLE. From the moment Ben refuses, he searches to find something else to do. Mrs. Robinson derails his attempt by challenging his masculinity. Crisis—his effort to leave seems to have failed.

END. The brief, climactic conclusion builds to Ben's furious "INADEQUATE," which leads to the resolution of his effort to go—by staying.

Immediately at stake: whether Ben can escape the seduction.

Ultimately at stake: whether Ben will slide into a depressing affair after having hoped for better from life.

Complication: as indicated, Ben's seduction by an older woman able to manipulate him at will. His taking the hotel room is a natural outgrowth of Mrs. Robinson's power over him and shows the inevitable connection between a complication and the action it causes.

Reverses:

1. Ben says he can't stay and speaks of his parents' reactions. But in response to Mrs. Robinson he can't imagine what these would be, and when she directly challenges him by asking if he's afraid of her, his first effort to break off the seduction fails.

2. Ben's denial of fear combined with an attempt to substitute a movie fails when Mrs. Robinson again challenges him, this time by implying he is afraid because he is a virgin.

3. Ben denies he is a virgin as Mrs. Robinson simultaneously shifts ground again by speaking of his being afraid of being inadequate. His hot denial forces him to demand that Mrs. Robinson stay.

This is a very simple scene with its easy play on virility. Ben turns out to be as hapless as Adrian, if more artfully maneuvered by Mrs. Robinson than Adrian is by Rocky. She is repellently direct and efficient: his reactions betray exactly how naive and inexperienced he is.

The reverses' minisequences of dramatic action that successively define what is immediately at stake for Ben are nearly identical with the scene's structure. His immediate problem—trying to stop the seduction—undergoes a *series* of transformations. These transformations are caused by the antagonist's successful attempts to deny letting Ben resolve the problem. Specifically, his guilt is changed first to a denial of fear and then to a denial of inadequacy. The artfulness of this simple scene is that by succeeding in overcoming the final form the obstacle in the scene takes—the challenge to his adequacy at the climax—Ben fails to get what he wanted initially. He is drawn into the affair he wanted to avoid.

Looking at a scene's reverses, then, gives us a good hold on the actual development of character and conflict. We can pinpoint the specifics of the changes the protagonist's immediate problem undergoes. We can see that *a character develops only to the extent he encounters reverses.* Thus Ben is checked enough to show his essential naïveté in this scene, but little more is developed beyond the obvious. Three reverses do not give you much room for development. The artfulness of Buck Henry and Mike Nichols' writing is what gives the scene its interest.

Let's look at a more sophisticated scene from Ingmar Bergman's family fantasia *Fanny and Alexander.*

The Punishment Scene from Fanny and Alexander

Good dramatic writing is an international art. Few cinemas have been as popular as the American, with its heavy accent on action, or as respected as the Swedish, led for so long by Ingmar Bergman. Many of his earlier films were somber, brooding stories filled with a dark magic and a deeply pessimistic view of human nature, but his later films often have shown a moving humanity combined with a beautiful sense of scene and detail, evoked in part by Bergman's frequent chief cameraman, Sven Nykvist. The scene we are going to look at is drawn from *Fanny and Alexander*, Bergman's farewell to movie-making.

It evokes many of his earlier themes in his later context of warmth and humanity, powerfully contrasting the life of the warm, material, loving Ekdahl family with the life four of its members lead for a time with Bishop Edvard Vergérus. A figure like Edvard once would have been the protagonist through which Bergman would have wrestled with the modern dilemma of the failure of faith: in *Fanny and Alexander* he is reduced to the antagonist whose torments are juxtaposed to the Ekdahls' worldly-wise comfort.

Alexander, 10, and his sisters Fanny, 8, and Amanda, 12, had lived an idyllic existence at their grandmother's mansion with their parents, Emilie and Oscar. But Oscar dies (first complication) and Emilie falls in love with and marries Bishop Vergérus (second complication). They move to his austere mansion, populated by his unpleasant servants, sisters, and mother, where the children are very unhappy, especially Alexander.

As the scene begins, Alexander has been summoned to Edvard's study to answer charges brought by the children's virtual imprisoner, the housemaid Justine. A short time before Alexander had tried to frighten her in front of his sisters by indulging his streak of fantasy. He told Justine that he had seen the ghost of Bishop Vergérus's former wife, who had drowned with her two children. The wife's ghost, Alexander said, told him that the bishop had imprisoned, starved, and driven his former family into jumping out the window into the river beside the house, where they had drowned trying to reach freedom. Impressed and shocked, Justine immediately left and told Alexander's story to Edvard. Alexander's mother is absent at the time the bishop interrogates Alexander.

Alexander has thus caused a fresh complication for himself with this story. Whether the story is true or not doesn't matter from this perspective: it was at least symbolically true and an entirely ill-advised thing to tell someone devoted to the bishop. The scene that follows is its immediate consequence.

After you read the scene, jot down your notes on its structure, and list the reverses in the scene. Then compare your notes to ours.

FADE IN:

INT.   EDVARD VERGÉRUS' STUDY   GROUP SHOT   (EST) DAY

[showing the austere study with Blenda, Edvard's mother, Henrietta, his sister, Justine, the thin housewife in black, and Edvard as Fanny, Alexander, and Amanda hesitate just inside the door. Edvard gets up from a long table.] Justine gives a brief, uncertain smile.

Alexander is told to step forward. He stands in the middle of the vast room, which is filled with books from floor to ceiling. A great dread, like a sick crab, squirms in his bowels.

> EDVARD
> (gently)
> Alexander, my boy. In the presence
> of your sisters and Justine you have
> accused me of having murdered my
> wife and children.

> ALEXANDER
> It's not true.

> EDVARD
> Justine, please repeat what you
> told me.

> JUSTINE
> Alexander said he had seen the late
> Mrs. Vergérus and her children. She
> (MORE)

CONTINUED

CONTINUED

> JUSTINE (CONT'D)
> had spoken to him. She had said that
> in a fit of wrath His Grace the bishop
> had locked her and the children into
> the bedroom without food or water.
> On the fifth day they tried to escape
> through the window but were
> drowned.

> EDVARD
> Do you recognize the story,
> Alexander?

> ALEXANDER
> No, sir.

> EDVARD
> So you allege that Justine has given
> false testimony?

> ALEXANDER
> She was probably dreaming.

> EDVARD
> Justine, are you prepared to confirm
> your statement on oath?

> JUSTINE
> (bobbing)
> Yes, Your Grace.

> EDVARD
> That is good, Justine. Did Fanny and
> Amanda hear Alexander's story?

> AMANDA
> No.

> FANNY
> (whispers to Amanda)
> Stop pinching.
> (aloud, to Bishop Vergérus)
> No.

CONTINUED

CONTINUED

> EDVARD
> So you deny having heard anything?

> AMANDA
> I only remember that Justine told us
> that the mother and children were
> found under the cathedral bridge and
> that they had to be sawn apart to get
> them into the coffins.

> EDVARD
> Did you say that, Justine?

> JUSTINE
> (whispers)
> Yes, sir.

There is a long silence. Bishop Vergérus's face swells until it is huge, terrible, inhuman. His voice is nevertheless unchanged—quiet and friendly. To Alexander:

> EDVARD
> You maintain that Justine was lying or
> dreaming?

> ALEXANDER
> Yes sir.

> EDVARD
> Are you prepared to take an oath
> on it?

> ALEXANDER
> Of course.

> EDVARD
> It is a mortal sin to swear falsely,
> Alexander. It is called perjury and
> is severely punished.

FAVOR ALEXANDER

> ALEXANDER
> Oh, is it?

Alexander shifts his weight on to the other leg, puts his hand at his

CONTINUED

CONTINUED

side, and licks his dry lips. Nothing matters now. Life is over. God's punishment is going to strike him. Bloody damn vindictive God.

TWO SHOT: BISHOP VERGÉRUS & ALEXANDER

> EDVARD
> Kindly come here to the table. Lay
> your left hand on the Bible and say
> after me: "I, Alexander Ekdahl, swear
> by Holy Writ and by the living
> God . . ."

> ALEXANDER
> (in a firm voice)
> I, Alexander Ekdahl, swear by Holy
> Writ and by the living God . . .

> EDVARD
> ". . . that everything I have said, am
> saying, and will say is the Truth and
> nothing but the Truth."

> ALEXANDER
> . . . that everything I have said, am
> saying, and will say is the Truth and
> nothing but the Truth. May I go now?

> EDVARD
> Do you want to go already,
> Alexander?

> ALEXANDER
> There's nothing more to say. How can
> Justine prove she wasn't dreaming?

> EDVARD
> Tell me something. Are you happy
> with us here in the bishop's palace?

> ALEXANDER
> As happy as a snake in an anthill.
> Though worse.

> EDVARD
> You dislike your stepfather, don't you?

CONTINUED

CONTINUED

> ALEXANDER
> Must I answer?

> EDVARD
> Do you remember the two of us had
> rather an important little talk about a
> year ago. It concerned certain moral
> questions.

[Note: about lying and cheating]

> ALEXANDER
> You can't call it a talk.

> EDVARD
> What do you mean?

> ALEXANDER
> The bishop did the talking and Alex-
> ander said nothing.

> EDVARD
> Said nothing and felt ashamed, per-
> haps. Of his lies.

> ALEXANDER
> I've grown wiser since then.

> EDVARD
> You mean you lie better.

> ALEXANDER
> That's one way of putting it.

> EDVARD
> I don't know what you imagine, Alex-
> ander. Do you think this is a joke? Do
> you think you can smirch another
> person's honor with impunity? Do you
> think you can lie and play the hypo-
> crite and commit perjury and get away
> with it? Do you think we are having a
> game, Alexander? Or do you think
> perhaps that this is a kind of play in
> which we say whatever lines come
> into our heads?

CONTINUED

CONTINUED

> ALEXANDER
> I think the bishop hates Alexander.
> That's what I think.

> EDVARD
> Oh, so that is what you think.
>   (pause)
> Well, I'll tell you something, my boy.
> Something that will perhaps surprise
> you. I don't hate you. I love you. But
> the love I feel for your mother and sis-
> ters is not blind and is not sloppy. It is
> strong and harsh, Alexander. If I must
> punish you, I suffer more than you
> know. But my love compels me to be
> truthful. It compels me to chasten and
> form you even if it hurts me. Do you
> hear what I say, Alexander?

> ALEXANDER
> No.

> EDVARD
> You are hardening your heart. More-
> over, you are misjudging the situation.
> I am much stronger than you are.

> ALEXANDER
> I don't doubt that!

> EDVARD
> Spiritually stronger, my boy. It's be-
> cause I have truth and justice on my
> side. I know that you will confess in a
> little while. Your confession and your
> punishment will be a relief to you,
> and when your mother returns this
> evening it will all be over and done
> with and life will go on as usual. You
> are a wise little man, Alexander. You
> realize that the game is up, but you
> are proud and stubborn, and of course
> you are ashamed.

CONTINUED

CONTINUED

> ALEXANDER
> One of us should be ashamed. That
> is true.

> EDVARD
> You must understand your insolence
> does not help your cause. It merely
> confirms my suspicions.

> ALEXANDER
> I've forgotten what I am to confess.

> EDVARD
> Oh. *Have* you now.

GROUP SHOT

[to show the tense expression on everyone's face as the drama heads
toward its climax.]

After a long pause

> ALEXANDER
> What does the bishop want Alexander
> to confess?

> EDVARD
> You know that I have means at my
> disposal.

> ALEXANDER
> I didn't know, but I do now.

> EDVARD
> Effective means.

> ALEXANDER
> That doesn't sound pleasant.

ON EDVARD

> EDVARD
> In my childhood parents were not so
> soft-hearted. Naughty boys were pun-
> ished in an exemplary but loving
> manner. With the cane. The motto
> (MORE)

CONTINUED

CONTINUED

EDVARD (CONT'D)

was: "Spare the rod spoil the child."
I have a cane too. It is there on the
table. Then we had another means
that was really efficacious, and that
was castor oil. There you see the
bottle, Alexander, and a glass. When
you've swallowed a few mouthfuls of
that you will be a little more docile.
And if castor oil didn't help there was
a dark and chilly bogey hole where
one had to sit for a few hours, until
the mice started sniffing at one's face.
You see, over there under the stairs,
Alexander, a nice big hole is waiting
for you. Then of course there were
other, more barbarous methods, but I
disapprove of them. They were humil-
iating and dangerous and are not applied, nowadays.

TWO SHOT: ALEXANDER & BISHOP VERGÉRUS

ALEXANDER

What punishment will I get if I
confess?

EDVARD

You may decide that for yourself,
Alexander.

ALEXANDER

Why must I be punished?

EDVARD

That is perfectly obvious, my boy. You
have a weakness in your character—
you cannot distinguish lies from the
truth. As yet you are a child and your
lies are a child's lies, however dreadful
they may be. But soon you will be a
grown-up man and life punishes liars
(MORE)

CONTINUED

CONTINUED

> EDVARD (CONT'D)
> ruthlessly and indiscriminately. The
> punishment is to teach you a love of
> the truth.

> ALEXANDER
> I confess I made up that about the
> bishop locking his wife and chil-
> dren in.

> EDVARD
> Do you also confess that you have
> committed perjury?

> ALEXANDER
> Yes, I suppose so.

> EDVARD
> Now you have won a great victory, my
> boy. A victory over yourself. Which
> punishment do you choose?

> ALEXANDER
> How many strokes of the cane do
> I get?

> EDVARD
> Not less than ten.

> ALEXANDER
> Then I choose the cane.

> EDVARD
> Take your pants down. Bend over by
> the sofa. Put one of the cushions
> under your stomach.

GROUP SHOT

Ten not too hard strokes on the cane follow. Alexander makes no sound. He bites his hand, tears fill his eyes, his nose runs, he is dark red in the face, and blood oozes from the weals in his skin.

> EDVARD
> Stand up, Alexander.

CONTINUED

CONTINUED

Alexander stands up.

> EDVARD
> You have something to say to me.

> ALEXANDER
> No.

> EDVARD
> You must ask my forgiveness.

> ALEXANDER
> Never.

> EDVARD
> Then I must whip you until you think
> better of it. Can you not spare us both
> that unpleasant experience?

> ALEXANDER
> I'll never ask your forgiveness.

> EDVARD
> You won't ask my forgiveness?

> ALEXANDER
> No.

> EDVARD
> Take your pants down. Bend over
> the sofa. Put a cushion under your
> stomach.

Raises his arm to strike.

> ALEXANDER
> No more, please!

> EDVARD
> Then you beg my forgiveness?

> ALEXANDER
> Yes.

> EDVARD
> Button up your pants. Blow your nose.
> Lend him a handkerchief, Justine.
> What are you to say, Alexander?

CONTINUED

CONTINUED

ALEXANDER
Alexander begs the bishop's
forgiveness.

EDVARD
For the lies and perjury.

ALEXANDER
For the lies and perjury.

EDVARD
You understand that I punished you
out of love.

ALEXANDER
Yes.

EDVARD
Kiss my hand, Alexander!

ALEXANDER
(kissing Bishop Vergérus's
hand)
May I go to bed now?

EDVARD
Yes, my boy, you may. But so that you
will have an opportunity of thinking
over the day's events in peace and
quiet, you are to sleep in the attic.
Justine will provide a mattress and a
blanket. At six o'clock tomorrow
morning Henrietta will unlock the
door and you are free. Is this understood, Alexander?

ALEXANDER
Yes, Your Grace.

FADE OUT[3]

3. Ingmar Bergman, *Fanny and Alexander*, trans. Alan Blair (New York: Pantheon Books, 1982), pp. 132–139. English translation copyright © 1982 by Alan
Blair. Reprinted by permission of Pantheon Books, a Division of Random House,
Inc. Please note that the screenplay was not accessible to the authors; camera
directions, screenplay format, and all bracketed material have been added by
the authors.

Before we analyze this scene, compare your notes on structure with ours:

BEGINNING.   The problem appears instantly: did you tell such a story? No, Alexander replies. No time is wasted getting to what is immediately at stake: whether Alexander can avoid punishment for his story.

MIDDLE.   The scene proceeds through the point at which the bishop tells Alexander about the type of punishments available to him and used in the past, and Alexander caves in and confesses. Failure: crisis.

END.   There is an extended climax in which the punishment turns out to be inadequate, and the bishop forces Alexander to beg his forgiveness.

Immediately at stake: Alexander's telling the truth—and then asking forgiveness.

Ultimately at stake: whether the spiritual force is on Alexander's side or the bishop's or, phrased in terms of the issue of conflict, whether the life of this world is better than some other's—religious, or implicitly, any "-ism's."

This is a powerful scene, full of moral terrorism as a much older man breaks a child of ten to his will. But it is also based on several exceptionally simple emotional strands from which Bergman works the seeming complexity of the interaction between the bishop and Alexander. First, Alexander immediately gives himself a bigger problem than having told the story to Justine—he lies to the bishop instead of throwing himself on his mercy. Second, by doing so, he invites a contest that he can only lose and that Edvard *must* win. Third, Alexander hates the bishop: that emotion betrays him into the challenge, just as, fourth, his age and the difficulty he has put himself into leads him simultaneously to attempt to deny everything. These elements work together easily, and it is this blend of the characters' clear motivations and reactions to their situation that give the scene its great emotional reality.

Now compare your list of reverses with ours:

1. Alexander's attempt to lie meets an initial check when Justine is prepared to confirm her statement on oath. Alexander shifts from saying it isn't true to saying that "she was probably dreaming."

2. Alexander is forced to take an oath. We *see* his reaction, in this case, as he shifts uncomfortably and licks his lips.

3. His desire to go is thwarted by the bishop, even though he took the oath.

4. The bishop drives Alexander into admitting he thinks "the bishop hates Alexander."

5. The bishop instead claims he loves Alexander and drives home his having greater strength—which he assures Alexander is spiritual.

6. Alexander's attempt to pretend he has forgotten what he is to confess crumbles before the bishop's list of punishments.

7. Alexander confesses and receives punishment but refuses to ask the bishop's forgiveness.

8. "Never," says Alexander to the bishop's demand to ask for forgiveness, but he is forced to at the threat of further caning.

9. He is done and thinks he can go to bed, but is sent instead to the attic.

The ancient Greek playwright Sophocles would have felt as comfortable with this scene as we do, speaking technically. Alexander and Edvard are locked in a steady cause-and-effect contest. Each time Alexander resists, the bishop must make fresh efforts to get what he wants. In this course of action he reveals his need to triumph over Alexander and shows us, by being content with such a hollow triumph, how far he has fallen away from any true understanding of love or God. We *see* the failure of faith and its replacement by this cruel hypocrisy in action: we can almost feel it as he beats the boy.

Alexander, in turn, by his repeated efforts to defy the bishop, rising to the "never" that the bishop overcomes, dramatizes just how powerful his hate and contempt is for the man, while the behavior he provokes from the bishop only confirms and justifies his feelings despite the hopelessness of his resistance.

Compare this to the scene from *The Graduate*. The number of reverses alone indicates we are dealing with a much more substantial scene. Ben's failure and Mrs. Robinson's success simply confirm what we were able to guess about their characters from the beginning. They are well handled and their scene is interesting as a consequence, but they are not given the opportunity to grow beyond their initial characterizations, something necessary for any major character and something deferred to other scenes for Ben.

Bergman develops much more substantial characters and thematic weight because Edvard and Alexander have so much more to deal with in each other. Alexander's challenge to the bishop provokes real anger in his surprise at its constant renewal ("Do you think this is a joke?"). That repeated resistance draws an ever-stronger effort on Edvard's part to break the child's will to his "moral" authority, finally by resorting to violence. What is more, when Edvard makes his speech about the types of punishment once used but now no longer used, it is hard not to believe he is talking about his own childhood experience. In other words, Alexander drives Edvard into revealing more about himself than the bishop intended at the start, in respect to both the past and present. This is crucial to the sense of the scene's weight and to the larger issue of conflict in the film. Here Bergman is at pains to show that the normally despised experience of the comfortable, worldly middle class is, in fact, infinitely more humane and preferable than lives sacrificed to principles. Very quietly, in other words, he touches on one of the central issues of our times.

Similarly, our feelings about Alexander undergo a steady development as he makes a renewed effort after each reverse to salvage something of his pride. It is one thing to resist once and give in, as is nearly the case with Ben: it is another to resist repeatedly and to give in only to overwhelmingly superior force, as Alexander does. He is a little boy with real grit. Edvard's cruelty dispels our own sense of Alexander's guilt for the story he invented.

Notice, too, that just as Alexander drives Edvard into revealing more than he realized or intended, so too does Edvard drive Alexander into similar revelations. Alexander didn't walk into Edvard's study intending to tell the bishop he hated him, nor did he realize he would have to reveal as much courage as he does show, rising to his hopeless "never." He did not know he would demonstrate how much humiliation he could bear without ceasing to be himself. We are in a different place with regard to these characters than we were at the start, too, and they have certainly grown in unexpected ways through the action in this scene.

This is, in fact, how you, as a writer, develop character and conflict. The protagonist's problem, the obstacle, does not appear in a scene once, but repeatedly, each time somewhat changed or redefined. Look again at the list of reverses. With each reverse, the nature of the obstacle metamorphoses for Alexander from the lie to the oath, to leaving, to being driven to an admission of hatred, to punishment, to forgiveness, and again to leaving (but being sent to the attic). *Action leads to reaction.* Each time what is immediately at stake evolves and so do the characters. One action-reaction does not resolve a scene, but attempts to succeed are repeated until the crisis arrives that provokes the climax that, in turn, resolves the conflict.

A Further Word on Complication

We have stressed the difference between a complication and a reverse, but we don't want you to lose sight of the fact that a complication is also a problem for your characters. We said a complication might, on its first introduction, appear as the actual problem in a scene, as when Joanna reappears and demands Billy from Ted in *Kramer vs. Kramer*. We want to emphasize here how in good writing the complications or problems a character must deal with tend to be integrally related to the thrust of the play. For example, Alexander complicates his life by telling Justine a foolish story. That has a major consequence, as complications do, provoking the next scene with the bishop and several others we aren't going to look at. But notice how Alexander takes the first consequence of that complication and gives it a new twist by trying to lie, with all the results we have examined. The one is directly connected with the other, just as Alexander's being in this dilemma in the first place is directly tied to his mother's having married Edvard. We can push the link of cause-and-effect relations back to his father's death if we like.

Contrast these complications to those in a film like *Raiders of the Lost Ark*. Many of the problems encountered by Indiana Jones are almost unrelated to each other. At one moment he needs to escape from a snake-filled chamber; at another, to get back on a truck he has fallen off. He must ride a submarine externally as it leaves for some unknown destination. These make for good adventures and are all related to his effort to find or regain the ark, but in a casual, episodic way. The same is true of the James Bond films and of action-adventure films in general. It is the inherent tie-in between complications and character development that lends a story the greatest potential emotional weight, the development of conflict and character out of a given situation that you begin by complicating in some fundamental way, as with the death of Alexander's father or, for that matter, of Hamlet's. This is why scripts like *Fanny and Alexander*, *Tootsie*, or *Kramer vs. Kramer* give us a much stronger sense of one event leading *inevitably* to the next. That is the best sort of dramatic writing.

Two Simple Faults in the Business and Dialogue

When Alexander is said to feel a sick crab in his bowels, or the bishop's face is said to swell terribly, or you are told Alexander thinks that "nothing matters now. Life is over. God's punishment is going to strike him. Bloody damn vindictive God," you see the business misused. A film exists in your sight and hearing immediately: you must *show* how a character feels or thinks in and through the action, not tell us. Calling for such an effect on the part of the bishop's face must lead either to a special effect that would destroy the believability of the scene, or call for a piece of acting beyond an actor.

Note, too, the length of the bishop's speeches. We have also seen Bonasera make a long speech in the opening from *The Godfather* and Les make another proposing to Michael-Dorothy in *Tootsie*. These go against normal practice. You should avoid speeches of such length as a beginner, especially. If you take the advice of writing a first draft of each assignment, then at that stage let your speeches run to whatever length seems right at the moment. But in revision break them up. For example, suppose Edvard's speech on types of punishment was yours. You could have revised it into something like this:

> EDVARD
> In my childhood parents were not so
> soft-hearted. Naughty boys were pun-
> ished in an exemplary but loving
> manner.

> ALEXANDER
> How was that?

> EDVARD
> With the cane. The motto was: "Spare
> the rod and spoil the child." I have a
> cane, too.

INSERT

cane on the table.

BACK TO SHOT

as Alexander stares from it to the Bishop.

> EDVARD (CONT'D)
> Then we had another means that was
> really efficacious, and that was cas-
> tor oil. There you see the bottle,
> Alexander, and a glass. When you've
> swallowed a few mouthfuls of that
> you will become a little more docile.

> ALEXANDER
> Would I?

And so on.

That being said, any effective scene is able, through the dramatic tension it generates, to do what the "rules" say you can't do. All the long speeches we have shown are effective, including the steady outpouring of words from Edvard against Alexander's laconic stubbornness. The rules almost exist to be broken. A film like *My Dinner with Andre* is an illustration of how dinner conversation can be extended successfully through an entire film. But don't break the rules of prevailing practice in your scenes unless your material drives you to do so. Then be prepared to defend your choices!

Now let's draw our considerations together by looking at a short sequence of major scenes from the classic *On the Waterfront*, written by Budd Schulberg.

A Sequence from On the Waterfront

On the Waterfront is one of America's memorable films. It has a true-to-life feel about its exposure of dockside corruption and a clarity in cinematography and writing that refuses to be dated. Reruns in theatres and on TV and release for the home video market give it a wide, continuing exposure.

Johnny Friendly runs the corrupt longshoreman's union in the story. Charley is his lawyer. A sympathetic character, he is not one of Johnny's thugs. Charley's younger brother, Terry, is the protagonist. Terry was once a boxer, but his career didn't go anywhere: he's punch-drunk. Now he works, or more accurately drifts, through the days on the docks, given easy jobs because of Charley's connection. Terry is a decent guy, but he is on the fringe of the Friendly organization. The Friendly crowd takes advantage of his naïveté to use him without his knowing to set up a murder at the beginning of the film.

Terry is obviously drifting into worse until he falls in love with Edie (whose brother is the man he set up at the beginning). Through her and the local priest, Father Barry, he finds his long-simmering resentments and conscience start to come to life. A crime commission investigation has been launched against Johnny Friendly, and Edie and Father Barry try to persuade Terry to testify. Terry knows enough to send Friendly to prison, but Terry can't make up his mind. He's under terrible pressure from all directions. The sequence that follows begins with a meeting Friendly has called to deal with Terry. He has gotten wind that Terry is about to break ranks.

FADE IN:

INT.   FRIENDLY BAR—BACKROOM   (EST) NIGHT

It is set up as an informal kangaroo court. Jocko is pointing at

CONTINUED

CONTINUED

Charles Malloy, who is on the hot seat. Johnny Friendly is the judge, flanked by Big Mac, Truck, Sonny, Barney, Specs, J. P. Morgan, and others.

> J. P.
> I didn't hear them, boss, but I sure
> seen them, walking along and smiling
> like a pair of lovers.

Charley looks uncomfortable. He hasn't finished his drink.

> JOHNNY
> (watching him carefully)
> Drink up Charley, we're ahead of you.

> CHARLEY
> (disturbed)
> I'm not thirsty.

> JOHNNY
> (drinking)
> After what we been hearing about
> your brother, I thought your throat'd
> be kind of dry.

> CHARLEY
> So they're walking along and smiling.
> That doesn't mean he's going to talk.
> There's no evidence until he gives
> public testimony.

> JOHNNY
> Thanks for the legal advice, Charley.
> That's what we always kept you
> around for.
> (smiles wisely)
> Now how do we keep him from giv-
> ing this testimony? Isn't that the—
> er—as you'd put it—main order of
> business?

> CHARLEY
> (nervously)
> He was always a good kid. You know
> that.

CONTINUED

CONTINUED

> BIG MAC
> He's a bum. After all the days I give
> him in the loft—he's got no gratitude.

> JOHNNY
> (offended)
> Please Mac, I'm conducting this—
> (nodding to Charley)
> investigation.

> CHARLEY
> This girl and the Father got their
> hooks in him so deep he doesn't know
> which end is up anymore.

> JOHNNY
> I ain't interested in his mental condi-
> tion. All I want to know is, is he D 'n
> D or is he a canary?

> CHARLEY
> I wish I knew.

> JOHNNY
> So do I, Charley, for your sake.

> CHARLEY
> What do you want me to do, Johnny?

> JOHNNY
> Very simple. Just bring him to . . .
> that place we been using. Mac, you
> take care of the details. Call Gerry G.
> in if you think you need him.

> CHARLEY
> Gerry G!! You don't want to do that,
> Johnny! Sure the boy's outa line, but
> he's just a confused kid.

> JOHNNY
> Confused kid? First *he* crosses me in
> public and gets away with it and then
> the next joker, and pretty soon I'm
> just another fellow down here.

CONTINUED

CONTINUED

> CHARLEY
> (horrified)
> Johnny, I can't do that. I can't do that,
> Johnny.

> JOHNNY
> (coldly)
> Then don't.

> CHARLEY
> But my own kid bro—

> JOHNNY
> (cutting in)
> This is for you to figure out. You can
> have it your way or you can have it
> his way.
> (gestures with his palms
> up and his palms down)
> But you can't have it both ways.
> (turns to Sonny)
> Am I right, Sonny?

> SONNY
> Definitely!

> JOHNNY
> (thumbing Charley to his
> feet)
> Okay, on your horse, you deep
> thinker.

Charley rises reluctantly, his confident, springy manner now gone.

DISSOLVE

INT.   TAXICAB (N.Y. B.G.)   [NIGHT]

Charley and Terry have just entered the cab.

> TERRY
> Gee, Charley, I'm sure glad you
> stopped by for me. I needed to talk to
> you. What's it they say about blood,
> it's—
> (falters)

CONTINUED

CONTINUED

> CHARLEY
> (looking away coldly)
> Thicker than water.

> DRIVER
> (gravel voice, without turn-
> ing around)
> Where to?

> CHARLEY
> Four thirty-seven River Street.

> TERRY
> River Street? I thought we was going
> to the Garden.

> CHARLEY
> I've got to cover a bet there on the
> way over. Anyway, it gives us a chance
> to talk.

> TERRY
> (good naturedly)
> Nothing ever stops you from talking,
> Charley.

> CHARLEY
> The grapevine says you picked up a
> subpoena.

> TERRY
> (noncommittal. Sullen)
> That's right . . .

> CHARLEY
> (watching his reaction)
> Of course the boys know you too well
> to mark you down for a cheese-eater.

> TERRY
> Mm hmm.

> CHARLEY
> You know, the boys are getting rather
> interested in your future.

CONTINUED

CONTINUED

> TERRY
> Mm hmmm.

> CHARLEY
> They feel you've been sort of left out
> of things, Terry. They think it's time
> you had a few things going on for you
> on the docks.

> TERRY
> A steady job and a few bucks extra,
> that's all I wanted.

> CHARLEY
> Sure, that's all right when you're a
> kid, but you'll be pushing thirty soon,
> slugger. It's time you got some
> ambition.

> TERRY
> I always figured I'd live longer with-
> out it.

> CHARLEY
> Maybe.

Terry looks at Charley.

> CHARLEY (CONT'D)
> There's a slot for a boss loader on the
> new pier we're opening up.

> TERRY
> (interested)
> Boss loader!

> CHARLEY
> Ten cents a hundred pounds on every-
> thing that moves in and out. And you
> don't have to lift a finger. It'd be
> three-four hundred a week just for
> openers.

CONTINUED

CONTINUED

> TERRY
> And for all that dough I don't do
> nothin'?

> CHARLEY
> Absolutely nothing. You do nothing
> and you say nothing. You understand,
> don't you, kid?

Struggling with an unfamiliar problem of conscience and loyalties:

> TERRY
> Yeah—yeah—I guess I do—but there's
> a lot more to this whole thing than I
> thought, Charley.

> CHARLEY
> You don't mean you're thinking of tes-
> tifying against—
> > (turns a thumb towards
> > himself)

> TERRY
> I don't know—I don't know! I tell you
> I ain't made up my mind yet. That's
> what I wanted to talk to you about.

> CHARLEY
> > (patiently, as to a stubborn
> > child)
> Listen, Terry, these piers we handle
> through the local—you know what
> they're worth to us?

> TERRY
> I know, I know.

> CHARLEY
> Well, then, you know Cousin Johnny
> isn't going to jeopardize a setup like
> that for one rubber-lipped—

> TERRY
> > (simultaneous)
> Don't say that!

CONTINUED

CONTINUED

> CHARLEY
> (continuing)
> —ex-tanker who's walking on his
> heels—?

> TERRY
> Don't say that!

> CHARLEY
> What the hell!!!

> TERRY
> I could have been better!

> CHARLEY
> The point is—there isn't much
> time, kid.

There is a painful pause, as they appraise each other.

> TERRY
> (desperately)
> I tell you, Charley, I haven't made up
> my mind!

> CHARLEY
> Make up your mind, kid, I beg you,
> before we get to four thirty-seven
> River . . .

> TERRY
> (stunned)
> Four thirty-seven—that isn't where
> Gerry G. . . ?

Charley nods solemnly. Terry grows more agitated.

> TERRY
> Charley . . . You wouldn't take me to
> Gerry G. . . ?

Charley continues looking at him. He does not deny it. They stare at each other for a moment. Then suddenly Terry starts out the cab. Charley pulls a pistol. Terry is motionless, now, looking at Charley.

> CHARLEY
> Take the boss loading, kid. For God's
> sake. I don't want to hurt you.

CONTINUED

CONTINUED

Hushed, gently guiding the gun down towards Charley's lap.

> TERRY
> Charley . . . Charley . . . Wow . . .

> CHARLEY
> (genuinely)
> I wish I didn't have to do this, Terry.

Terry eyes him, beaten. Charley leans back and looks at Terry
strangely. Terry raises his hands above his head, somewhat in the
manner of a prizefighter mitting the crowd. The image nicks
Charley's memory.

> TERRY
> (an accusing sigh)
> Wow . . .

> CHARLEY
> (gently)
> What do you weigh these days,
> slugger?

> TERRY
> (shrugs)
> —eighty-seven, eighty-eight. What's it
> to you?

> CHARLEY
> (nostalgically)
> Gee, when you tipped one seventy-
> five you were beautiful. You should've
> been another Billy Conn. That skunk
> I got to manage you brought you along
> too fast.

> TERRY
> It wasn't him!
> (years of abuse crying out
> in him)
> It was you, Charley. You and Johnny.
> Like the night the two of youse come
> into the dressing room and says, "Kid,
> this ain't your night—we're going for
> the price on Wilson." *It ain't my*
> (MORE)

CONTINUED

CONTINUED

>   TERRY (CONT'D)
> *night.* I'd of taken Wilson apart that
> night! I was ready—remember them
> early rounds throwing them combina-
> tions. So what happens—This bum
> Wilson he gets the title shot—out-
> doors in the ball park!—and what do I
> get—a couple of bucks and a one-way
> ticket to Palookaville . . .

More and more aroused as he remembers it:

>   TERRY (CONT'D)
> It was you, Charley. You was my
> brother. You should of looked out for
> me. Instead of making me take them
> dives for the short-end money.

>   CHARLEY
>   (defensively)
> I always had a bet down for you. You
> saw some money.

>   TERRY
>   (agonized)
> See! You don't understand!

>   CHARLEY
> I tried to keep you in good with
> Johnny.

>   TERRY
> You don't understand! I could have
> been a contender. I could've had class
> and been somebody. Real class. In-
> stead of a bum, let's face it, which is
> what I am. It was you, Charley.

Charley takes a long, fond look at Terry. Then he glances quickly out the window.

[EXT.]   MEDIUM SHOT   WATERFRONT   NIGHT

from Charley's angle. A gloomy light reflects off the street numbers: 433— 435—

INT.   CLOSE   CAB   ON TERRY AND CHARLEY   NIGHT

> TERRY
> It was you, Charley . . .

> CHARLEY
> (turning back to Terry, his
> tone suddenly changed)
> Okay—I'll tell him I couldn't bring
> you in. Ten to one they won't believe
> it, but—go ahead, blow. Jump out,
> quick, and keep going . . . and God
> help you from here on in.

[EXT.]   LONGER ANGLE—CAB   NIGHT

as Terry jumps out. A bus is just starting up a little further along the street.

EXT.   MEDIUM LONG SHOT—RIVER STREET   NIGHT

Running, Terry leaps onto the back of the moving bus.

INT.   CAB—RIVER STREET   NIGHT

> CHARLEY
> (to driver as he watches
> Terry go)
> Now take me to the Garden.

Charley sinks back in his seat, his hand covering his face. The driver turns around, gives him a withering look, steps on the gas, and guns the car into—

EXT.   MEDIUM LONG SHOT—RIVER STREET   NIGHT

the garage they have reached, and which the car now zooms into through the entrance. We catch a glimpse of Truck, Sonny and Big Mac.

> FADE OUT[4]

The first scene from *On the Waterfront* is simple, direct: its pattern of reverses and complications are nearly synonymous with its BEGIN-NING, MIDDLE, and END, as in the scene between Ben and Mrs. Robin-

---

4. Budd Schulberg, *On the Waterfront* (Carbondale and Edwardsville: Southern Illinois University Press, 1980), pp. 96–105. Copyright © 1980 by Budd Schulberg; used by permission.

son. It works because of its threatening nature and Charley's horror at his situation, and because it immediately propels us forward. But note how changed Charley is in this scene—far more than Ben was or Adrian in *Rocky*. Charley starts just worried: he leaves with a life-and-death situation on his hands. Much more is at stake for him, and because more is at stake, it was possible for Schulberg to write with more emotion and meaning.

All their motivations make sense and give the scene a strong emotional reality. How swiftly Charley is established: he is the one they keep for advice, but not for the real dirty business. For that you need the unseen but menacing Gerry G. We know Charley is upset: he can't drink. We know he cares about Terry: he puts up a spirited defense right away. But a real complication has entered Charley's life, a menacing problem in this scene, and the cause of the next scene: Friendly puts the life and death of his brother in his hands or those of Gerry G. The efforts Charley makes to placate Johnny Friendly suffer a serious reverse at that point, which coincides with the crisis. Charley is in danger, too. There is no middle ground for him with Johnny Friendly, with whom he is hopelessly implicated in any wrongdoing. If Charley doesn't carry through, then everyone is in trouble. Climax: Charley will try to solve the problem.

Note the elements of preparation. First, Big Mac calls Terry a bum, someone who bites the hand that secured him the cushy job in the loft unloading ships. Then set up are Gerry G. and that there will be consequences if Charley fails with Terry. All three of these bear fruit immediately.

Jot down your own sense of the second scene's structure. What complication has set it off? What complication does it introduce? What are its reversals?

BEGINNING.   Charley introduces the problem quickly for Terry: he doesn't want him to testify and is prepared to bribe him with better money at the docks.

Reverses:

1. Terry is easily deceived about the purpose of going to River Street.

2. His resistance to having a better job is not overthrown but compromised by Charley's bribe to keep him silent.

MIDDLE.   The bulk of the scene, steadily rising to the point at which Charley pulls out his gun and threatens Terry, preventing him from leaving, makes up the second part. Crisis: Terry's efforts to talk fail. A series of reverses move the scene forward:

3. Terry demands not to be called "a rubber-lipped ex-tanker who's walking on his heels": he could have been better. Charley tells him he doesn't have the time.

4. Terry can't believe Charley would take him to Gerry G. When he does, he tries to flee.

5. Charley stops his flight with a gun. Terry pushes the gun aside. Crisis.

Complication: Terry discovers what not having time means: he must make an immediate choice one way or the other. His effort to temporize, which he persuades Charley to go along with, results in Charley's being driven to see Gerry G.

END. The appeal to Charley, the passionate outburst of how Charley had failed him, of how Terry could have been someone, finishes the scene. Climax: Charley lets him go.

6. The climax and the sixth reverse are the same: the appeal succeeds.

Reverses aren't necessarily events that happen opposite of the way your protagonist wants but only in some way he doesn't expect: he may even get his way—after a struggle—as Terry does when he persuades Charley to let him go. Reverses are minisequences of action—the action-reaction pattern we emphasized in *Fanny and Alexander:* Terry has to defend himself against being called rubber lipped or a used-up boxer; Terry discovers to his great surprise he's being taken to Gerry G. and then fails to escape.

The relation between reverse and insight is also particularly clear here. Terry is incredulous at Charley's taking him to River Street: what kind of man is this who calls himself his brother? Neither Terry nor Charley is a villain, any more than Joanna or Ted Kramer. That is a crucial element in the emotional realism of the scene. So when the gun is pulled, the most important fact is that Charley can't use it. Instead, stung to passion, Terry forces a moment of reckoning between the brothers neither knew was coming that night. Both are changed by that: Terry by having it out in the open at last, Charley by hearing it and realizing it is so.

The cause-and-effect relation between the reverses is also particularly clear here. Terry comes to talk: he's talked to. He insists on his right to talk and not be called names: he's told he doesn't have time. He can't believe where he's going—he tries to get out. Charley's stopping him prompts his outburst. Moreover, step by step through the reversals, Charley is upholding Johnny Friendly and again letting Terry down, just as he did in the past. The accusation Terry finally levels against his brother has been exemplified in the immediate action for us. It doesn't depend on Terry's accidentally assuming a boxer's position and setting off a casual train of memory in Charley: past and present failure are intimately related. Every reverse is leading these characters to the perception of that linkage between past and present.

The Appearance of the Past

This brings us to a crucial understanding about good writing and the function of complication and reverse. No matter how light the subject, you are not creating some sort of machine for killing time when you write. At the very least you are creating the illusion of people suddenly having to make sense out of their lives that have been profoundly disturbed by some fundamental complication. But most of our lives exist either in the past, almost all of which we forget, or in the future, all of which is unknown. Our present experience, gone in the moment we think about it, is a meager point of light between these two oceans of our unknowing. We can fantasize about the future, but being in ignorance of it, our fantasies will tend to project our inner conflicts on the future's blank screen. Or we can try to understand how we have become what we are at the same time we struggle to realize who we are.

That is why we have stressed the appearance of the past in Bergman's and Schulberg's scenes. The pressure they subject their "people" to, the accumulation of complication and reverse, forces their characters to search for that understanding as they struggle to justify some immediate, dramatic decision. "You can't do this, because . . . ," Terry says and reaches into his heart to find that "because." "You must give in to me, because . . . ," Edvard says to Alexander and searches for one reason after another until we sense he has bared some of the punishments that warped him as a child. "You must let me go, because . . . ," Joanna says to Ted, and his resistance forces her to say more than she wanted, to reach both into the past and to admit the thing in the present (her lack of love) that she had never been under enough pressure to bring out to Ted before.

This pressure toward the past as something immediately bearing on present action typifies all of the most enduring writing. We could instance *Oedipus Rex* again, in which present action propels Oedipus systematically to recreate his past as he tries to dispel a plague for his city. During these efforts he discovers that how he had seen his past was wrong: that, in fact, he had done everything he thought he had avoided. In *Hamlet*, the protagonist spends the greater part of the play trying to establish in his mind whether or not Claudius really is guilty of his father's murder, an event that happens before the action of *Hamlet* begins.

Tennessee Williams's *A Streetcar Named Desire,* one of our most enduring contemporary plays, also recounts a search of the past. Successfully produced as a movie with Marlon Brando and Vivien Leigh and recently adapted for television with Treat Williams and Ann-Margret, the play centers its action around the relentless attempt of its hero, Stanley Kowalski, to penetrate the truth about the past of his wife's sister. Any drama—for stage, screen, or television—that takes place wholly in the present, must, of necessity, be impoverished because so little of our lives can be found there.

Whatever it is a character reaches in a moment when the present action forces something of his or her past into the present may have lain on the heart a long time, without the character knowing that or ever having found the way to say it. At a critical moment it emerges. Neither Ben nor Mrs. Robinson has recourse to the past, nor Rocky or Adrian. In consequence, whatever else may be said of their scenes, they are simply not as meaningful to us. But in those scenes in which the past is brought in as a necessity to explain and propel the present action forward, then we are given, as an audience, through our identification with the protagonist, a sense of some of the mystery of human life being illuminated. This is equally true in comedy, even in a scene as light as that between Les and Michael-Dorothy. The moment of critical dramatic action that plumbs the past and uses it, as Terry does in his outburst to Charley, brings a sense of meaning into human struggle. In that moment we share the characters' sense of illumination, the sudden ending of their blindness or self-deception. Through them we have the experience of seeing the past truly and how, as a result of that perception, present action must be changed. As we have seen, Charley is changed because of that moment: he lets Terry go, even though Friendly has threatened him with consequences if Terry testifies. This creation of the meaning of lives through conflict, however upsetting it may also be for your characters, is utterly central to dramatic writing and profoundly satisfying to us as the audience.

Another practical point is important here. Authors write, too, to be remembered. It is unlikely that we would still be looking at Schulberg's drama if he had avoided the past and let the scene turn into a shallower debate between Terry and Charley about being a canary or sticking with the boys. The more you give your characters to deal with, the more you can achieve dramatically. The more emotion and tension you build up in them through their struggles, the more you build in yourself. Then when you reach the critical point with your characters, you will be able to supply out of your imagination the answer to the question: how can I justify the action my character wants to take now? Reverses challenge you to insight, just as they lead your characters to the same things. You show your vision through your characters' actions and reactions. "Vision" is deliberately used here in place of "motivation" to emphasize the real source and nature of motivation. A piece without vision is worthless.

The connection between complication and reverse is also particularly clear in *On the Waterfront* and bears on this point. The real complication in Terry's life began years ago, before the story begins, namely, that moment when he took a dive and started his slide into being a bum. The story slowly brings that out and gives him a chance to redeem himself. He innocently sets someone up, who is killed. Then he falls in love. Double complication. That involves him with Edie and Father Barry and opens him to the crime investigation, which he wouldn't have responded to otherwise. He turns to his brother for help, and his brother is killed. Because of that, he testifies. Because he testifies, he becomes persona non grata on the docks. Because of that, he directly challenges Johnny Friendly and, despite being beaten up, leads the dockworkers to work in place of Johnny Friendly. There is a constant, implicit link between complication and reverse. In the end, the bum Terry has become a hero.

We said at the start archetypal patterns underlie much of what is written. The making of a hero is one such pattern, and typically the hero starts off as a fool or a compromised innocent of some kind, just as does Terry. The oldest example that springs to mind is Beowulf from the epic of the same name, a heroic slayer of monsters and leader of his people, who, we are carefully told, as a young man seemed less able and less bright than others. Schulberg didn't set out to do something of this kind: that overtook him as he wrote, *because* he wrote well, *because* he was not content to write a dock exposé. Demanding more, he asked himself, Who are these people? and that question inevitably propelled him into the past.

Change

We began this chapter perplexed by the way in which the immediate obstacle for the protagonist seemed to change constantly within a scene, even though what was ultimately at stake within the play remained consistent. Now it is time for you as a writer to realize that in good writing, change is constant. *Your characters constantly change.* Certainly your protagonist is never the same at the end of the scene as at the beginning, if you have done your job as a writer.

Go back to the beginning of this book. Remind yourself how Bonasera changes from a man asking for justice to a man who receives it at the price of compromising his integrity. Or look at Michael in *Tootsie* in his persona of Dorothy. He sets out to let Les down gently, fails, and leaves the restaurant in confusion—as confused as a "woman." He too has undergone a change from how he began in that scene.

Look at the protagonists in this chapter. Ben tries to avoid being seduced and fails. Alexander tries to defy the bishop and is broken by the cane and spiritual hypocrisy of the man. Charley is forced to do Friendly's bidding, only to have Terry change him. Terry begins by wanting advice but ends in a passionate lament of a disappointment long suffered in silence. He leaves emotionally transformed, even more firmly holding onto his nascent conscience.

Not just protagonists but antagonists undergo the same process of change: Charley with Terry; the bishop, forced to reveal indirectly ever more about himself, with Alexander; even Mrs. Robinson, who arrives sure of a conquest but then has to reconquer all over, with Ben. If you are generating conflict, if your characters are acting and reacting on each other, they inevitably, necessarily change each other. Change in drama is constant, constantly building toward climactic revelations, insights, and efforts that pull all the changes together in some final, defining climactic moment of meaning and capacity for the protagonist.

So remember: *dramatic action changes characters.* It is to see those changes, to feel them, to comprehend them, that we are fascinated with drama, for every character is an act of the human imagination working on our humanity itself: they are possibilities of existence.

Your Third Assignment

Write a scene in which you concentrate on the development of your characters as we have discussed it. Get to your problem as fast as possible so that you can devote your time to your protagonist and antagonist's struggle. Look at your first draft for its reverses. What material are you giving yourself to work with?

Are there any complications within the scene? What complication sets the scene in motion? Be succinct and clear in the brief premise you write for this scene.

What is immediately at stake? What, ultimately?

We have sometimes assigned a love scene to our students at this point, requiring that the characters either break up or come together in a significant way. We don't indicate what has caused this necessity: you must invent the problem that precipitates the crisis. The past must have a bearing in such a situation: how to use it meaningfully as part of the present action is the critical question in this assignment. You may have other ideas you prefer, but put your characters at some immediate pitch of decision.

Think about how they have changed by the end, once you have done a draft. If they have not changed, you have a problem. If you write a love scene, it might challenge you to have your characters start with the opposite intention from the result you intend—intending to stay together in the scene in which they end by breaking up or the reverse in which coming together is the result.

The outcome of your scene must matter to your characters desperately. And it must be hard—and getting harder moment by moment—for your characters to do what they attempt.

And that is enough for now!

8. Achieving Crisis and Climax

USING CHARACTERIZATION TO ACHIEVE CRISIS AND CLIMAX

No part of a scene or screenplay poses more of a challenge to your characters or through them to you than the crisis and climax. All the efforts of your protagonist lead to the crisis and climax: in these the challenge to your craft and insight reaches its peak. It is your handling of the crisis and climax that gives you a chance to achieve something memorable as a dramatist, and by *memorable* we mean something very practical and simple: a story worth remembering.

Discovery, Revelation, Clarity

The protagonist always has an objective—the cessation of conflict with his triumph over the problem that has generated the action of the story. Yet the problem he faces refuses to be solved and forces him constantly to renew his efforts to overcome it, because any effective dramatic story plunges its characters into a state of continuous crisis. Thus the protagonist is always reacting to the immediate conflict as it is shaped by reverses and complications and never knows all he needs to know to get his way or, consequently, what getting his way really means.

Terry in *On the Waterfront* does not know that he is involved in an action that involves his transformation from a bum to a hero. He is driven to that ultimate change moment by moment. Michael in *Tootsie* only knows he is desperate to find work. He has no idea that he will have to face being both a man and a woman or that he will discover that success, which he thought all-important, is less important to him than the love of a woman. Alexander in *Fanny and Alexander* is nearly overwhelmed by his moment-to-moment need to survive the complications of his father's death and his mother's remarriage to Bishop Vergérus. He doesn't think of himself as caught in a growing-up process; he doesn't know that he will have the opportunity, magically, to participate in the bishop's death. Michael in *The Godfather* thinks he will be able to pursue a non-Mafia career, but events lead him to assume increasing power in the family until he takes the actions that make him the new godfather.

Hamlet has no idea when he comes home that the ghost of his father will ask him for revenge against his murderer—his mother's new husband, Hamlet's uncle. Nor does Hamlet know when he begins to try and prove his uncle's guilt to his own satisfaction that he will be plunged into a confrontation with himself that will paralyze him. At the crisis, when he realizes the depth of his previous failure, he finally reveals himself capable of action and avenges his father. But his climactic outburst continues his bungling: the play ends with the stage strewn with bodies, including his own.

A character, then, begins in the dark. He thinks his problem and objective are one thing but discovers they are something else as he is tested and changed by the conflict. He finds his way. His moments of discovery are all-important, especially when he discovers his efforts seem about to fail at the crisis. Three things happen at that point:

1. The final nature of the problem the protagonist must face or overcome is revealed.

2. The protagonist's response (the climax) reveals the ultimate extent of his physical, intellectual, moral, and creative resources.

3. The protagonist's final effort lays bare the deepest wellspring of his motivation.

Flip back to the scene between Terry and Charley from *On the Waterfront*. At the crisis as Charley pulls the gun Terry discovers, first, what problem really faces him: be quiet or be killed. In response, second, he evokes the past and makes Charley see it was he, Charley, who was betraying him then, just as he is now. Third, Terry's lament peaks when he says, "I could've had class and been somebody." The revelation of that lament is that Terry once again wants to be someone: this time Charley doesn't stop him.

Even 007 in the James Bond series is constantly challenged until he finally finds a way to pull victory out of the jaws of defeat. In winning he reveals the capacities that make him the best agent. In *Private Benjamin*, successful as a movie with Goldie Hawn and then as a situation comedy on television, Julie reveals the ability at the crisis to shake off her dependence on others, associated with a comfortable, high society life-style, in favor of independence and perhaps a renewed career in the despised Army. Whether in comedy or drama *a dramatic action, then, rises to a culminating moment of revelation.*

That revelation can be of an ultimate capacity in a protagonist (he "has what it takes"), an uncovering of something in the past that still determines motivation, the true nature of a character or situation, or a piece of all-important knowledge. These are usually found together with varying emphases.

We want to emphasize the active nature of revelation, too, that it emerges from the final struggle your protagonist makes to overcome the crisis. Moreover, that final struggle to overcome the apparently final defeat offered by the crisis also forces the obstacle that has confronted and thwarted the protagonist to take its final shape. Everything becomes clear—the nature of the antagonist, what your hero or heroine must do, and what he or she can do. *The culminating moment of action in the climax brings a final clarity to your story.*

We said characters constantly change in effective dramatic writing: your protagonist changes decisively. That change is dramatized most sharply through the protagonist's response to the crisis (the climax).

Motivation

Motivation is a vast subject: just the volumes written to explore Hamlet's motivation would fill a small library. Why a character behaves as he does, how the reasons for his behavior are affected and transformed by the conflict, and how the dramatic action generated by conflict brings a character to a final testing at the crisis and climax go to the heart of any drama. As an audience we are constantly judging a character's motivation, asking ourselves whether or not it makes sense and is justified by the premise or subsequent complications or moment-to-moment reverses. Your insight as a writer is being judged constantly in this way, for the wellspring of motivation shown by a character is only what you can envision for him or her.

Yet two things need to be said: First, central as considerations of motivation are in judging the success or failure of a story, they cannot be talked about in the abstract. We must always talk about some particular character in some particular conflict. Second, however much prior thought you may give to a character's motivation and the structure of the story that will reveal and explore it, the entire depth or variety of a character's motivation must emerge immediately and gradually through the actual structure of conflict reverse by reverse, complication by complication.

There are multiple aspects to motivation. When we spoke of emotional reality, we emphasized that your characters' behavior must always seem appropriate to their circumstances. Whether we believe how they feel and, by extension, how they make us feel as the audience depends on their responses to the immediate challenge they face being neither excessive nor inadequate. Believable motivation in this sense is simply contingent on the ability of a writer to make his characters respond to any immediate challenge in a way that makes good emotional sense to those of us in the audience. Then we will feel with them, and that fellow-feeling will create a sense of a shared reality.

This lets us emphasize a second aspect. If the dramatic obstacle to your protagonist always appeared in one way or if his first act was decisive, there would never be a need to talk about motivation except in its first appearance. But your protagonist finds himself in an on-going struggle, so his initial motivation is constantly challenged and redefined. That conflict tests a protagonist's motivation, makes him find more options as any one act fails to resolve the conflict, and puts him in different situations in which existing motivation appears in a new light.

This brings us to two more aspects. Look again at the simple scene from *The Godfather* in which Bonasera seeks vengeance for his daughter's beating. The Godfather reminds Bonasera how he has tried to fit into conventional society and creates the crisis by telling Bonasera, in effect, to sleep in the bed he has made. At that point Bonasera reveals what no one had known up to that point, namely, that he wants help so badly, his motivation for help is so strong, he will agree to anything the Godfather asks. He will even permanently compromise himself, although he certainly had no intention of doing so at the start of the scene! Because of what happened in the past he is so upset that he *changes* his life. First, motivation leads your protagonist to change in order to get his way, and, second, at that immediate moment of change, the past is revealed as crucial.

Revelation, motivation, and the past always culminate together.

This might have seemed complex at the beginning of this book: here, perhaps, you realize with something of a creator's thrill how the immediate pattern of reverses naturally leads a writer to such moments of crisis and climax within a scene or scene by scene within a screenplay, with its attendant complications, as a natural outgrowth of the characters' urge to end conflict by overcoming their obstacles. But at the actual moment of crisis, no matter how well prepared for, the writer is left alone with a challenge for climactic insight and action. This is as it should be and what all the careful establishment of character and conflict and their development is meant to lead to.

Now a brief word on sustaining motivation. This is an old topic: inevitably, you sustained motivation in your last assignment as you paid attention to developing character and conflict from your initial premise for your scene through your pattern of reverses and whatever additional complications you introduced. Your protagonist, like Bonasera or like Alexander in *Fanny and Alexander*, faces multiple reverses. His motivation may go through as many changes as Alexander's, from a desire to lie to cover his tracks to an intention to never ask forgiveness. Like Ben in *The Graduate,* your protagonist may be maneuvered into demanding the opposite of what he began the scene wanting if the antagonist can manipulate his motivation artfully enough. That, too, reveals a great deal about your character. Your protagonist begins to *discover* what kind of a person he is and what he can or can't do as each change or modification of his motivation in response to the developing conflict reveals something more. In other words, the multiple action-reaction structure of a scene provides the basis for sustaining and developing motivation that is inseparable from establishing and developing character and conflict.

From now on ask yourself simple, direct questions about motivation as you work on your scenes.

1. What does your protagonist want to do immediately? Why does he want to do that?

2. As you develop that desire, what does it show about your protagonist?

3. Is he reacting with emotional appropriateness to the situation?

4. What does he discover about himself?

5. How powerfully does the past appear as a motivating force?

6. How do these elements of immediate motivation, past motivation, discovery, and revelation combine and culminate at the moment of crisis, and what is your character's response to that, the climax?

A Council of War from The Godfather

As the following scene starts, the sons of Don Corleone wrestle with the problem of vengeance while Don Corleone lies in the hospital, critically wounded by an assassination attempt. Sonny, the Godfather's heir apparent, has already begun to strike back at the other Mafia families. Michael has joined the war council, though he sits in silence, not expected to make a contribution. His face is bandaged because of a blow he had taken from Captain McCluskey, a corrupt policeman, when Michael single-handedly saved the stricken Don's life at the hospital after all his guards mysteriously disappeared. Moved by his father's condition at the hospital, Michael has promised to stay with him now. Sollozzo and the Turk are the same man; he is the Mafia head whom the Corleones believe is responsible for the assassination attempt. Hagen is Sonny's and Michael's brother, adopted as a child by Don Corleone, and now a coun-

cilor and a counselor for the family. Some Corleone henchmen are also
at the table, including Tessio and Clemenza.

FADE IN:

INT.   DON CORLEONE'S OFFICE   (WINTER 1945)   (EST) DAY

[A war council is in progress, including Sonny, Hagen, henchmen
Clemenza and Tessio, and other close retainers.] Sonny is excited and
exuberant.

> SONNY
> I've got a hundred button men on the
> streets twenty four hours a day. If Sol-
> lozzo shows one hair on his ass
> he's dead.

He SEES Michael, and holds his bandaged face in his hand, kiddingly.

> SONNY (CONT'D)
> Mikey, you look beautiful.

> MICHAEL
> Cut it out.

> SONNY
> The Turk wants to talk! The nerve of
> that son-of-a-bitch! After he craps out
> last night he wants to meet.

> HAGEN
> Was there a definite proposal?

> SONNY
> Sure, he wants us to send *Mike* to
> meet him to hear his proposition. The
> promise is the deal will be so good we
> can't refuse.

> HAGEN
> What about the Tattaglias? What will
> they do about Bruno?

> SONNY
> Part of the deal: Bruno cancels out
> what they did to my father.

> HAGEN
> We should hear what they have to say.

CONTINUED

CONTINUED

> SONNY
>
> No, no Consiglere. Not this time. No
> more meetings, no more discussions,
> no more Sollozzo tricks. Give them
> one message: I WANT SOLLOZZO. If
> not, it's all out war. We go to the mat-
> tresses and we put all the button men
> out on the street.

> HAGEN
>
> The other families won't sit still for
> all out war.

> SONNY
>
> Then THEY hand me Sollozzo.

> HAGEN
>
> Come ON Sonny, your father wouldn't
> want to hear this. This is not a per-
> sonal thing, this is Business.

> SONNY
>
> And when they shoot my father . . .

> HAGEN
>
> Yes, even the shooting of your father
> was business, not personal . . .

> SONNY
>
> No, no, no more advice how to patch
> it up, Tom. You just help me win,
> understand?

Hagen bows his head: he is deeply concerned.

> HAGEN
>
> I found out about this Captain Mc-
> Cluskey who broke Mike's jaw. He's
> definitely on Sollozzo's payroll, and
> for big money. McCluskey's agreed to
> be the Turk's bodyguard. What you
> have to understand is that while Sol-
> lozzo is guarded like this, he's invul-
> nerable. Nobody has ever gunned
> (MORE)

CONTINUED

CONTINUED

> HAGEN (CONT'D)
> down a New York Police Captain.
> Never. It would be disastrous. All the
> five families would come after you
> Sonny; the Corleone family would be
> outcasts; even the old man's political
> protection would run for cover. So
> just . . . take that into consideration.

> SONNY
> (still fuming)
> McCluskey can't stay with the Turk
> forever. We'll wait.

> MICHAEL
> We can't wait. No matter what Sol-
> lozzo says about a deal, he's figuring
> out how to kill Pop. You have to get
> Sollozzo now.

> SONNY
> The kid's right.

> HAGEN
> What about McCluskey?

> MICHAEL
> Let's say now that we have to kill Mc-
> Cluskey. We'll clear that up through
> our newspaper contacts later.

> SONNY
> Go on Mike.

> MICHAEL
> They want me to go to the conference
> with Sollozzo. Set up the meeting for
> two days from now. Sonny, get our in-
> formers to find out where the meeting
> will be held. Insist that it has to be a
> public place: a bar or a restaurant at
> the height of the dinner hour. So I'll
> feel safe. They'll check me when I
> (MORE)

CONTINUED

CONTINUED

> MICHAEL (CONT'D)
> meet them so I won't be able to carry
> a weapon; but Clemenza, figure out a
> way to have one planted there for me.
> (Pause)
> Then I'll kill them both.

Everyone in the room is astonished; they all look at Michael. Silence. Sonny suddenly breaks out in laughter. He points a finger at Michael, trying to speak.

> SONNY
> You? You, the high-class college kid.
> You never wanted to get mixed up in
> the family business. Now you wanta
> gun down a police Captain and the
> Turk just because you got slapped in
> the face. You're taking it personal, it's
> just business and he's taking it
> personal.

Now Clemenza and Tessio are also smiling; only Hagen keeps his face serious.

> MICHAEL
> (angrily, but cold)
> Sonny, it's all personal, and I learned
> it from him, the old man, the God-
> father. He took my joining the Ma-
> rines personal. I take Sollozzo trying
> to kill my father personal, and you
> know I'll kill them, Sonny.

Michael radiates danger. Sonny stops laughing.

FADE OUT[1]

The Corleones's situation is made clear immediately as Sonny relates the number of "button men" on the street and then finds himself in conflict with Hagen over how to get the Turk. Michael does not need to say anything because his desire for revenge is theirs, too; nor do they see any reason to ask anything of him. They know that Michael has just

---

1. Puzo and Coppola, *The Godfather*, pp. 69–72.

saved his father at the hospital, but not that he told his father, "I'm with you now." Your protagonist must have an immediate need to act in order to begin the process of revealing and developing his motivation. Hagen provides Michael with that need by wearing down Sonny's ardor and resolution.

Michael's intervention is at once smart and brutally direct. He doesn't directly challenge Hagen's statement that everything is business: he simply makes it clear that they must act because Sollozzo is still trying to kill their father. Then, without directly challenging Sonny's capacity, Michael offers a cogent plan to do what hasn't been done (kill the police captain) in one artfully planned meeting—alone.

Sonny's laughing rejoinder asserts (a) that Michael's motivation is trivial and (b) that Michael's motivation is purely current. The crisis has appeared: Michael's effort to intervene is almost laughed away largely because of the view the others hold of his past. He is the brother who stood aside. What can he know or do?

His climactic response underscores the weight of his reversal of their position by putting himself in a more direct line than themselves with the Godfather: "It's all personal, and I learned it from him, the old man." Michael knows the lessons of the past better than they do, and they are different from what his brothers thought they were. His motivation to act now is linked to the past resoundingly. Simultaneously he reminds them he was a Marine. They know he was decorated for bravery. He can do what he says. He is a dangerous man. The revelation of this new Michael silences them.

The elements associated with crisis and climax operate succinctly.

CRISIS.   Michael is nearly laughed away: failure seems imminent. Because of that imminent failure, a new and definitive effort must be made to succeed.

CLIMAX.   Michael makes a new effort. He *reveals* he has a better handle on the past and so a better understanding of the present, and he also demonstrates greater immediate capacity than they do.

Note that in part the conflict over the past centers as much around what it means, as well as what it is. Moreover, the truth and meaning of the past that are raised in a scene are never Truth or Meaning but some particular truth and some particular meaning for those characters directly involved.

We emphasized earlier the importance of change in good writing. Michael's role in the family and how we view him are transformed by this scene. He puts himself at the center of the family. So strong are his grief and anger as motivating forces that he abandons his past goals. *Mo-*

tivation leads to action: action leads to change. Drama makes both of these overt, and brings them into sharp focus through crisis and climax.

Not every response to a crisis succeeds, however. Earlier we saw how artfully Ben in *The Graduate* is made by Mrs. Robinson to want his failure. Ted does not succeed in holding onto Joanna in *Kramer vs. Kramer*. Alexander cannot successfully resist Bishop Vergérus in *Fanny and Alexander*. Let's look at another scene from *Kramer vs. Kramer* in which Ted, unlike Michael Corleone, deliberately chooses failure.

A Choice of Failure in Kramer vs. Kramer

Earlier we looked at the scene in which Joanna returns and demands to have Billy back. Ted refuses her, and, as we saw, storms out of the restaurant. A bruising courtroom struggle ensues for custody of Billy in which both Ted and Joanna are mercilessly cross-examined. Billy is not asked to testify, however, and so is spared that experience. As we pick up the action, the courtroom confrontation has just ended. Ted has been waiting to hear what the decision of the judge is. He goes to meet his lawyer Shaunessy in a fashionable bar and there is told the judge's decision.

FADE IN:

INT.   MEN'S BAR, MIDTOWN   (EST) DAY

A crowded, rather posh watering spot. Shaunessy sits alone at a table for two, a drink in front of him.

REVERSE ON THE DOOR

as Ted enters, spots Shaunessy and starts in his direction.

CLOSER ON SHAUNESSY'S TABLE

as Ted sits down.

> TED
>
> Well?

ON SHAUNESSY

as he looks up at Ted, says nothing.

ON TED

He realizes that they have lost.

> TED
>
> *Oh, Christ!*

CROSSCUT BETWEEN THEM

> SHAUNESSY
> That judge went for motherhood
> straight down the line.

> TED
> I lost him? I lost him?

> SHAUNESSY
> I can't tell you how sorry I am.

> TED
> Oh, no . . .

> SHAUNESSY
> (reading from a piece of
> paper)
> Ordered, adjudged and decreed that
> the petitioner be awarded custody of
> the minor child, effective Monday the
> 23rd. of January. That the respondent
> pay for the maintenance and support
> of said child four hundred dollars each
> month. That the father shall have the
> rights of visitation: every other week-
> end, one night each week to be mutu-
> ally agreed upon and one half of the
> child's vacation period.
> (looks up at Ted)
> That's it.

> TED
> (grim)
> What if I fight it?

> SHAUNESSY
> (matter of factly)
> We can appeal, but I can't guarantee
> anything.

> TED
> (determined)
> I'll take my chances.

CONTINUED

CONTINUED

> SHAUNESSY
> It's going to cost.

> TED
> (his mind is made up)
> Don't worry. I'll get the money.

There is a beat of silence, then:

> SHAUNESSY
> I've got to tell you something, Ted.
> This time it'll be Billy that pays. This
> time I'll have to put him on the stand.

CLOSE ON TED

as his last hope goes crashing to the ground.

> TED
> Oh, Christ no . . . I can't do that.
> I just . . . can't . . .
> (he looks up at the lawyer
> in despair)
> Excuse me . . . I'm sorry . . . I just . . .

That is all Ted can manage to say. He gets to his feet and rushes for
the door.

> FADE OUT[2]

Ted is placed in an archetypal situation as old as the biblical confrontation of the contending mothers before Solomon, where love is
proved by the woman who lets the child go rather than sacrifice him in
a tug of war with the other. This is Ted's terrible choice: to hurt Billy in
order to try and keep him or live with the judgment. His grief and anger
are instantly apparent and provide ample motivation for him to pursue
the case, but he chooses not to when he realizes the cost to Billy.

What we want to stress here is the clarity that the crisis and climax
bring to a character and story. Ted's choice makes it clear that he has
indeed been transformed after Joanna's departure into so loving and devoted a father that he is prepared to let his son go rather than keep him if
that means hurting him. It is a rare moment and a noble choice. Simultaneously the nature of Ted's struggle to keep Billy becomes clear; namely,

2. Benton, *Kramer vs. Kramer*, pp. 121–123.

he fought because of love, not as a way to take vengeance and inflict hurt on Joanna. Last, his objective in the story takes its final shape: not to hurt the child he truly loves.

These are crucial facets of crisis and climax. It is already apparent from the scene with Michael (above) that the protagonist is revealed in his true colors through the crisis and climax. But in addition to the way a character's nature and the past become clear, the final objective of a character, as character and conflict have evolved, is shown to have undergone an evolution to which the crisis and climax give a final clarification.

We'll bring our discussion to a head by looking at two substantial scenes from *On the Waterfront* and the successful stage-cinema-television drama *A Streetcar Named Desire*.

The Climax from On the Waterfront

In the last chapter we read the scene from Schulberg's *On the Waterfront* in which Terry wins his release from Charley through his passionate outburst at how Charley, even more than Johnny Friendly, had betrayed him in the past. Guilt-stricken, Charley let Terry go.

Johnny Friendly then has Charley killed. Terry, beside himself with grief and fury, goes to the bar where Johnny Friendly and his confederates do business. He has a gun, and he intends to kill. Father Barry arrives and dissuades Terry from violence. There's something better, more decisive, he tells Terry: go testify against Johnny Friendly. That is the very action Johnny had sent Charley to stop Terry from taking; that is the action around which the struggle for Terry's conscience has become centered; that is the action that represents Terry's rediscovery of his right to act as a free moral agent, something he had surrendered as a bum.

Terry testifies with great impact, but the hearings and trials have a long way to go before they will reach a definite end. Johnny Friendly remains in power on the dock. He threatens Terry's life. Terry discovers that what he has done isn't enough yet to avert the failure of his efforts, the crisis that arrived with Charley's murder. He has to do more.

But Terry is baffled. At home he finds all the pet pigeons he had tended on the roof have been killed by a boy who until then had looked up to him. The consequence of being the "canary," the man who has "ratted," grows on him. His girlfriend Edie finds him on the roof. She's moved by the slaughter of the pigeons, frustrated, afraid Terry will be another pigeon who will be killed. She begs Terry to leave the docks for good, to move somewhere else, and perhaps become a farmer. We pick up the action as Edie follows Terry into his room, demanding that he do what she says.

FADE IN

INT.   TERRY'S ROOM   (EST) [DAY]

as Terry enters. Edie's voice follows him in as she trails behind him. He sits on the bed and looks at the cargo hook hung on a peg on the wall.

> EDIE
> Doesn't that make sense!

[Note: She means leaving the docks and starting anew, maybe starting a farm.] Terry doesn't answer her. He takes the cargo hook from the wall and jabs it viciously into the floor.

> EDIE
> I don't think you're even listening
> to me!

He pulls the cargo hook out and jabs it into the floor again.

> EDIE
> . . . are you?

He looks up at her, frowns and then studies the cargo hook, tapping it into his hand with pent-up feeling. The feeling is a strong and infectious one. Edie senses it and accuses him—

> EDIE
> You're going down there!

He looks at her again for a moment and then works his hand over the handle of the hook.

> EDIE
> (her voice rising)
> Just because Johnny warned you not
> to, you're going down there,
> aren't you?

He doesn't say anything but the determination in him seems to be steadily mounting.

> EDIE
> You think you've got to prove some-
> thing to them, don't you? That you are
> not afraid of them and—you won't be
> (MORE)

CONTINUED

CONTINUED

> EDIE (CONT'D)
> satisfied until you walk right into
> their trap, will you?

His silence maddens her. She seems on the verge of striking him out of frustration and impotent rage. Her voice is hysterical.

> EDIE (CONT'D)
> Then go ahead—go ahead! Go down
> to the shape-up and get yourself
> killed, you stupid, pigheaded, son
> of a—
>   (struggling to control
>   herself)
> What are you trying to prove?

With a decisive gesture Terry takes the hook and sticks it through his belt. Then he goes to the wall and lifts Joey's windbreaker from the nail on which it has been hanging. He puts the windbreaker on in a deliberate way, and grins at her as he does so; then walks to the door with a sense of dignity he has never had before.

> TERRY
>   (quietly)
> You always said I was a bum. Well—
>   (points to himself)
> not anymore. I'm going down to the
> dock. Don't worry, I'm not going to
> shoot anybody. I'm just going to get
> my rights.
>   (rubs sleeve of the jacket)
> Joey's jacket. It's time I started wear-
> ing it.

He goes.

QUICK DISSOLVE

EXT.   PIER—SHAPE-UP   [DAY]

Big Mac facing the semicircle of several hundred men. Into this circle walks Terry. Other longshoremen instinctively move away from him as he approaches.

CLOSE: BIG MAC

> BIG MAC
> I need fifteen gangs today. Everybody
> works!

He picks men out very quickly and they move forward from
the mass.

MEDIUM CLOSE: TERRY   PIER   DAY

He has taken his stand defiantly, with his hands in his pockets, looking Big Mac in the eye. Big Mac picks men all around Terry. He
makes it obvious by reaching over Terry's shoulder to pick men behind him. Finally there are only a handful left around Terry, and then
they are chosen. Terry is left standing there alone.

> TERRY
> (brazenly)
> You're still a man short for that last
> hatch gang, Mac.

> BIG MAC
> (without looking at Terry,
> calls to Sonny)
> Hey, Sonny, go across to the bar and
> pick up the first man that you see.

Now Big Mac looks at Terry for the first time.

> BIG MAC
> Where are them cops of yours,
> stoolie? You're gonna need 'em.

He turns away. Terry stands there seething. He looks around at Pop,
and the others ready to enter the pier. They look away, still fearful of
Big Mac and the power of the mob, and feeling guilty for their
passivity.

INT.   JOHNNY FRIENDLY'S OFFICE ON WHARF   DAY

Johnny looks across at the isolated figure of Terry. Sonny, Truck, and
Specs are with Johnny. On the desk are tabloids with the headlines
reading NAME JOHNNY FRIENDLY AS WATERFRONT MURDER BOSS.
Under the bannerhead is a large picture of Johnny.

> TRUCK
> That ain't a bad picture of you, boss.

CONTINUED

CONTINUED

Johnny glares at him and pushes the paper aside angrily.

> SONNY
> I wish you'd let us go to work on that
> cheese-eater.

> JOHNNY
> (with both hands working)
> After we get off the front page. Then
> he's mine. I want him.

EXT.   CLOSE: PIER ENTRANCE   ON TERRY & BIG MAC   DAY

As the other Sonny returns with "the first man he saw"—MUTT MURPHY. Mutt and Terry glance at each other.

> SONNY
> Here's your man, Mac.

> BIG MAC
> Okay.

Mac nods Mutt onto the pier, the one-armed derelict turning back with an apologetic gesture. Terry's fury grows. Mac growls at him—

> [BIG MAC]
> You want more of the same? Come
> back tomorrow.

Terry looks at him, and then across at Johnny's office on the wharf. His hands begin to tremble.

He turns and starts walking slowly, resolutely, down the gangplank leading to Johnny's headquarters.

INT.   JOHNNY FRIENDLY'S OFFICE   DAY

> SONNY
> (seeing Terry through the
> window)
> He's comin' down!

> JOHNNY
> He's gotta be crazy!

> TRUCK
> (glancing out, growls)
> Yeah, here comes the bum now. I'll top
> 'im off, lovely.

CONTINUED

CONTINUED

Behind Johnny's back the click of a revolver safety latch is heard.
Johnny whirls on him quickly.

> JOHNNY
> Gimme that.

> TRUCK
> (offended)
> How are we gonna protect ourselves?

> JOHNNY
> Ever hear of the Sullivan Law? Carry-
> ing a gun without a permit? They'll
> be on us for anything, now. The
> slightest infraction. Give.
> (turns to the other goons)
> All of you? Give—give—give—

Sonny, Truck and the others reluctantly give up their guns. Johnny
turns to the safe and begins to open it.

> JOHNNY
> We're a law-abidin' union.
> Understand?

As he puts the guns in the safe and slams the safe door.

> JOHNNY (CONT'D)
> A law-abidin' union!

EXT.   UNION LOCAL OFFICE ON WHARF   DAY

Terry walks compulsively down the ramp to the office.

> TERRY
> (shouts)
> Hey, Friendly! Johnny Friendly, come
> out here!

Johnny comes out of his office followed by his goons.

> JOHNNY
> (shouts)
> You want to know the trouble with
> you? You think it makes you a big
> man if you can give the answers.

CONTINUED

CONTINUED

> TERRY
> Listen, Johnny—
>
> JOHNNY
> Go on—beat it. Don't push your luck.
>
> TERRY
> You want to know somethin'—?
>
> JOHNNY
> I said beat it! At the right time I'll
> catch up with you. Be thinkin'
> about it.

As he starts back into his office, Terry advances, steaming himself up.

> TERRY
> (louder)
> You want to know something? Take
> the heater away and you're nothin'—
> take the good goods away, and the
> kickback and the shakedown cabbage
> away and the pistoleros—
> (indicating the others)
> and you're a big hunk of nothing—
> (takes a big breath if
> relieved)
> Your guts is all in your wallet and
> your trigger finger!
>
> JOHNNY
> (with fury)
> Go on talkin'. You're talkin' yourself
> right into the river. Go on, go on . . .
>
> TERRY
> (voice rising defiantly)
> I'm glad what I done today, see? You
> give it to Joey, you give it to Nolan,
> you give it to Charley who was one of
> your own. You thought you was God
> Almighty instead of a cheap—conniv-
> (MORE)

CONTINUED

CONTINUED

> TERRY (CONT'D)
> ing—good-for-nothing bum! So I'm
> glad what I done—you hear me?—
> glad what I done!

> JOHNNY
> (coldly)
> You ratted on us, Terry.

Aware of fellow longshoremen anxiously watching the duel:

> TERRY
> From where you stand, maybe. But
> I'm standing over here now. I was rat-
> tin' on myself all them years and
> didn't know it, helpin' punks like
> you against people like Pop and
> Nolan an'—

Beckoning Terry with his hands, in a passion of hate:

> JOHNNY
> Come on. I want you. You're mine!
> Come on!

FIGHT ON UNION OFFICE DECK   SERIES OF SHOTS

As Johnny takes an aggressive step forward, Terry runs down the ramp and hurls himself at him. They fight furiously on the deck of the houseboat. A fight to the death. A violent brawl with no holds barred. First one, then the other has the advantage. In B.G., long-shoremen we know creep forward and watch in amazement.

LONGSHOREMEN WATCHING

> LUKE
> That kid fights like he useta!

Others nod but show no inclination to join in and face the goons.

BACK TO FIGHT

Which mounts in intensity as CAMERA FOLLOWS it around the nar-row deck bordering the union office. Johnny knees Terry but Terry retaliates with desperate combinations that begin to beat Johnny to the deck. Both of their faces are bloody and hideously swollen.

ANOTHER ANGLE: GOONS

At this point Sonny, Truck and the other goons jump in to save their leader. Terry fights them off like a mad man, under vicious attack from all angles.

> LONGSHOREMEN WATCHING
> They'll kill 'im! It's a massacre! etc.

But they still hang back, intimidated by Johnny Friendly and his muscle.

TERRY FIGHTING

His face a bloody mask, being punched and kicked until he finally goes down. Goons are ready to finish the job when a battered Johnny Friendly mutters:

> JOHNNY
> That's enough. Let 'im lay there.

Terry is crumpled on the deck, senseless, in a pool of blood.

REVERSE: ON EDIE & FATHER BARRY

pushing their way through the crowd of longshoremen.

> FATHER BARRY
> (tight-lipped)
> What happened? What happened?

> EDIE
> (to a young longshoreman)
> Tommy, what happened?

> POP
> Where you goin'?

> EDIE
> (fiercely)
> Let me by.

BACK TO TERRY

Blood seeping from many wounds as Father Barry and Edie run in and kneel at his side, Johnny Friendly near by.

> JOHNNY
> You want 'im?
> (as he goes)
> (MORE)

CONTINUED

CONTINUED

> JOHNNY (CONT'D)
> You can have 'im. The little rat's
> yours.

> FATHER BARRY
> (to longshoremen)
> Get some fresh water.

> EDIE
> Terry . . . ?

> FATHER BARRY
> Terry . . . Terry . . .

ENTRANCE TO PIER   ON BOSS STEVEDORE

In felt hat and business suit, symbols of executive authority.

> BOSS STEVEDORE
> Who's in charge here? We gotta get
> this ship going. It's costing us money.

The longshoremen hang back, glancing off towards the fallen Terry.

> BOSS STEVEDORE
> (waving them towards
> him)
> Come on! Let's get goin'!

The men don't move.

> BOSS STEVEDORE
> I said—c'mon!

> TOMMY
> How about Terry? If he don't work, we
> don't work.

Others around him murmur agreement.

> JOHNNY
> (from background)
> Work! He can't even walk!

JOHNNY ON RAMP

Surrounded by longshoremen ignoring Stevedore's commands tries to
drive them on.

CONTINUED

CONTINUED

> JOHNNY
> Come on! Get in there!
> (grabbing Pop and throwing
> him forward)
> Come on, you!

From force of habit, Pop begins to comply. Then he catches himself and turns on Johnny. Sounding more sad than angry:

> POP
> All my life you pushed me around.

Suddenly he shoves Johnny off the ramp into the water scummy with oil slick and riverbank debris.

JOHNNY IN WATER

Cursing.

POP & LONGSHOREMEN

Cheering Johnny Friendly's humiliation.

> JOHNNY
> (from water)
> Come on, get me outa here!

BACK TO STEVEDORE

> BOSS STEVEDORE
> Let's go! Time is money!

> MOOSE
> You hoid 'im. Terry walk in, we walk
> in with 'im.

Others facing Stevedore mutter agreement.

TERRY, FATHER BARRY, & EDIE

Terry's eyes flutter as they bathe his wounds.

> EDIE
> (to Father Barry)
> They're waiting for him to walk in.

> FATHER BARRY
> You hear that, Terry?
> (as Terry fails to respond)
> (MORE)

CONTINUED

CONTINUED

> FATHER BARRY (CONT'D)
> Terry, did you hear that?
> (trying to penetrate Terry's
> battered mind)
> You lost the battle but you have a
> chance to win the war. All you gotta
> do is walk.

> TERRY
> (slowly coming to)
> . . . Walk?

> FATHER BARRY
> Johnny Friendly is layin' odds that
> you won't get up.

> JOHNNY, OS
> Come on, you guys!

> TERRY
> (dazed)
> Get me on my feet.

They make an effort to pick him up. He can barely stand. He looks around unseeingly.

> TERRY
> Am I on my feet . . . ?

> EDIE
> Terry . . . ?

> FATHER BARRY
> You're on your feet. You can finish
> what you started.

Blood oozing from his wounds, Terry sways, uncomprehendingly.

> FATHER BARRY (CONT'D)
> You can!

> TERRY
> (mutters through bloody
> lips)
> I can? Okay. Okay . . .

CONTINUED

CONTINUED

EDIE
(screams at Father Barry)
What are you trying to do?

ANGLE ON RAMP

As the groggy Terry starts up the ramp, Edie reaches out to him. Father Barry holds her back.

FATHER BARRY
Leave him alone. Take your hands off
him—leave him alone.

Staggering, moving painfully forward, Terry starts up the ramp. Edie's instinct is to help him but Father Barry, knowing the stakes of this symbolic act, holds her back. Terry stumbles, but steadies himself and moves forward as if driven on by Father Barry's will.

TERRY APPROACHING PIER ENTRANCE

As he staggers forward as if blinded, the longshoremen form a line on either side of him, awed by his courage, waiting to see if he'll make it. Terry keeps going.

REVERSE ANGLE: BOSS STEVEDORE   TERRY'S POV

Waiting at the pier entrance as Terry approaches. Shot OUT OF FOCUS as Terry would see him through a bloody haze.

TERRY

As the men who have formed a path for him watch intently, Terry staggers up until he is face to face with the Stevedore. He gathers himself as if to say, "I'm ready. Let's go!"

BOSS STEVEDORE
(calls officially)
All right—let's go to work!

As Terry goes past him into the pier, the men with a sense of inevitability fall in behind him.

JOHNNY FRIENDLY

Hurrying forward in a last desperate effort to stop the men from following Terry in.

CONTINUED

CONTINUED

>   JOHNNY
>   (screams)
>   Where you guys goin'? Wait a minute!
>   (as they stream past him)
>   I'll be back! I'll be back! And I'll re-
>   member every last one of ya!

He points at them accusingly. But they keep following Terry into
the pier.

WIDER ANGLE: PIER ENTRANCE

As Father Barry and Edie look on, Stevedore blows his whistle for
work to begin. Longshoremen by the hundreds march into the pier
behind Terry like a conquering army. In the B.G. a frenzied Johnny
Friendly is still screaming, "I'll be back! I'll be back!"

The threat, real as it is, is lost in the forward progress of Terry and
the ragtail army of dock workers he now leads.

>   FADE OUT[3]

Let's bring together the various analytic tools we have acquired. Take
a piece of paper and jot down the BEGINNING, MIDDLE, and END of this
scene, starting with Terry on the pier. What is Terry's immediate problem, and when is it established? Who or what opposes him? What is the
nature of the conflict? Where does the crisis in the scene fall? Its climax? What are the reverses by which the scene is built? Are there any
complications? What is immediately at stake? What, ultimately?

Then jot down how Terry's objective has grown or changed from seek-
ing revenge against Johnny Friendly for Charley's death. How is the past
involved in the immediate action? How would you judge the emotional
realism of the scene? Does the motivation connect with the past? What
is revealed? What is made clear, finally, in terms of past and present
about Terry and his objective? Compare your breakdown to ours.

Problem? He isn't allowed to work.

Complications? The initial complication is Terry's inability to get
work as the result of his testifying against Johnny Friendly (another
complication), which in turn resulted from the complication of Charley's death.

Antagonist? Big Mac, then Johnny Friendly.

---

3. Schulberg, *On the Waterfront*, pp. 126–140.

Type of conflict? Man versus man.

Immediately at stake? Can Terry win the right to work?

Ultimately at stake? Can Terry survive to live a life of his choice as a fully free and responsible man, not a bum ground down by criminals?

BEGINNING.   The opening section ends at the point Terry moves to take action, joining the type of conflict with his immediate problem by turning from Big Mac and walking to Johnny Friendly's office.

Reverses:

1. Terry appears for work and is not chosen.

2. Terry demands work from Big Mac, and Big Mac sends Sonny to find anyone else.

3. Sonny returns with the apologetic Mutt, and Terry heads toward Friendly's office.

MIDDLE.   Terry confronts Johnny Friendly and they fight. Crisis: Terry loses the fight.

4. Unknown to Terry, Johnny Friendly's goons pull their guns, and Johnny takes them away.

5. Terry's initial challenge to Johnny only draws a rebuke from Johnny, who then heads back into his office.

6. Terry heightens the challenge, and Johnny challenges him to fight.

7. Terry is winning until the goons enter the fight and beat him senseless.

END.   This third section spans the moment of defeat to Terry's final triumph as he leads the longshoremen to work at the climax.

8. As Johnny abandons Terry to Edie and Father Barry, the Boss Stevedore demands that the men go to work. They refuse, waiting on Terry. This includes Pop's pushing Johnny Friendly into the water.

9. Edie and Father Barry try to get Terry up: finally, he stands, but is too dazed to know it.

10. Edie tries to help Terry and is stopped.

11. Terry staggers to the Boss Stevedore who gives the order for them to go to work.

How does the past appear in the scene? Terry's appearance on the docks sets the stage for the struggle over the past by raising the question of his motivation (Why does he go to the docks?) and, inextricably bound up with that, his nature (Is he a bum or not?). The previous scene helps deepen the confrontation scene by showing Terry has considered and rejected alternatives. The action that follows addresses these questions.

Note how the argument over the nature of the past is provoked by *immediate* conflict:

1. Terry's recent behavior creates the problem he faces when he confronts Big Mac. He can't get work because he testified against Johnny Friendly: he "ratted."

2. Thus when Terry confronts Johnny Friendly and raises the issue of historical truth, it is from the perspective of asking who betrayed whom all those years: when did the real act of ratting take place? Who really is a bum, a "hunk of nothing"? What, in short, are the true natures of Terry, Johnny Friendly, and the past?

3. The fight between Terry and Johnny shows Terry can fight "like he useta!" Terry is so deeply motivated he is able to reach into himself and find what he had in the past before he took the first dive in the boxing match for Johnny Friendly.

The emotional realism of the scene is graphic. Each moment rings true because everything Terry or the others do and say is in fitting response to some urgent, immediate need. To succeed, Terry must get work, challenge Johnny Friendly in order to get work, and stagger to his feet in order to overturn Johnny Friendly and win his original objective in the scene. Johnny Friendly's reactions ring true in the same immediate way when Terry goads him into a rage. Edie naturally wants to help Terry. Father Barry restrains her so that Terry can fail or succeed on his own.

How has Terry's objective changed? In the scene between him and Charley, we saw that Terry wanted two things: advice and the right to make up his own mind. The issue of his nature as a person is raised by Terry's outburst about the past, but what that means and how either his nature or the past is related to a challenge to Johnny Friendly have only begun to be clear. Johnny kills Charley and Terry testifies, now motivated by vengeance. That doesn't prove decisive: Terry *discovers* he must either leave, or *he*, not the legal system, must overcome Johnny Friendly. Now we wonder: Is Terry man enough to do that? What is he capable of, really? The questions raised about Terry, the past, and what to do fuse at this point. We have to find out *new* things about Terry through the action to answer these questions. At this point his objective has gone beyond Terry's ability to state it. It is a self-transformation that can only be shown and confirmed by his taking very specific steps that lead to his overcoming "the bad guy." This makes the transformation credible and gives the story a personal weight that makes it more than merely a dockside exposé. That is the source of the story's durability.

The revelation about Terry proceeds reverse by reverse as Terry shows that it is Johnny Friendly, not Terry, who is the ratter and the bum. Terry is obviously acting in a new way, a way no one on the docks, including Johnny Friendly, has seen before. Yet it all finally hinges on a single moment when Terry seems beaten: very simply, all depends on whether he can stand up and walk. The action carries the meaning at the critical moment. And at that moment the past makes a crucial appearance: Father Barry tells Terry that Johnny Friendly is laying odds he won't get up—just as years ago he laid odds knowing Terry would go down. In these scenes as in all drama *the truth of the past and of the protagonist are made clear simultaneously in the climax in a new way as the protagonist discovers he can or cannot carry out the necessary action to gain his objective.*

USING DRAMATIC ELEMENTS TO ACHIEVE CRISIS AND CLIMAX

We need to look at several elements crucial to effective dramatic writing before we bring our examination of crisis and climax to a head with a scene from the Tennessee Williams stage, film, and television classic *A Streetcar Named Desire*. These are the use of silences, moments of action without dialogue, spectacle, symbol, and suspense.

Silences and Moments of Action without Dialogue

Sometimes the use of silence can make us feel the impact of a moment or anticipate an obvious piece of information more effectively than dialogue or action. Look again at the scene between Ted and Shaunessy from *Kramer vs. Kramer*. When Ted asks Shaunessy, "Well?" demanding the outcome of the custody battle, Shaunessy says nothing. Shaunessy's silence is protracted enough for Ted to realize he has lost: "*Oh, Christ!*" Not having Shaunessy speak makes Ted guess, and through him, we guess: we have time to feel more by anticipating the worst. That involves us more deeply.

Look at two other moments of silence from this scene. First, Shaunessy pauses after Ted promises to get the money for an appeal. That moment of silence provokes in us and Ted the feeling that money isn't enough: there must be some other obstacle than the one we would expect. That silence lets us feel and anticipate that obstacle before it takes on concrete terms with Shaunessy's statement that Billy would have to take the stand in an appeal. Second, Ted pauses after that discovery. He needs time to take in what Billy's being put on the stand might mean. We need the time to feel his dilemma and wonder what we would do, what Ted will do. Then, stumblingly, Ted reveals he couldn't do that to Billy.

Turn again to the war council from *The Godfather* as Michael makes his offer to Sonny. The business reads: "Everyone in the room is astonished; they all look at Michael. Silence. Sonny suddenly breaks out in laughter." Inserting that moment of silence after Michael's offer is effective writing. Michael's offer marks the turning point in his role with the family: how better to underscore it than with everyone's speechless amazement? That silence also gives us and Sonny time to question Michael's offer. Could Michael really *do* that? Could *Michael* do that? Could Michael do *that?* Sonny's laughter answers in the negative. That silence and laughter are far more effective than some kind of extended debate. The actual debate that follows is exhausted in one exchange between Michael and his doubter.

Don't use words when silence can carry the emotional impact and indicate the meaning of the action. Words, then, get in the way of your story's forcefulness.

Moments of action without dialogue are often the most effective way to dramatize conflict if a moment's dramatic issues are sharply enough drawn. The entire process of Terry's making up his mind to go down to the docks in *On the Waterfront* happens in silence. All Terry does as Edie rails at him and offers alternatives is look at the cargo hook, take it from the wall, and then jab it into the floor, once, twice. Then he takes Joey's coat. His actions speak louder than words until he goes beyond actions to motivation and tells Edie something new: why he is going down to the docks.

Once Terry is on the dock the gangs are chosen in silence until he stands alone. Once Mutt has been chosen, there is another moment of silence as Terry seethes and wonders what to do. The dockworkers stand in silence too, waiting on Terry's action. The fight with Johnny Friendly is without dialogue, and the moment from Terry's downfall, the longshoremen staring, until Edie and Father Barry appear. Finally, Terry's walk is in silence. Schulberg can rely on physical acts to carry the weight of content because he has developed his story's content so clearly to the climax. That's how it should be done.

Look for the moments in your scenes when the use of silence and physical action without dialogue can show emotion, reveal decisions, and dramatize their impact on critical moments. They are as much a part of the art of dramatic writing as your words. You don't want to find yourself writing a scene that is all talk: whenever you do, you have forgotten that *a dramatist writes action, not words.*

Spectacle

Spectacle is one of the original elements of drama delineated by Aristotle. Its use in drama extends from Aeschylus' spectacular effects to Stephen Spielberg's, from spaceships that occupy more space than can be shown on screen to, in a film like *Never Cry Wolf,* vast natural panoramas. Nature itself can be a character in survival and disaster films, films that usually take names like *Earthquake* or *Hurricane.* There are repeated moments in dramatic history when spectacle seems to become the primary dramatic value, whether in the eighteenth century panoramas that audiences went to the theatre to see exclusively in place of dramas, in the sets that sometimes have overwhelmed Wagnerian productions, or in the current taste for science fiction spectacles. The eye can be enchanted or horrified and in either case spellbound by the spectacular nature of what it sees. The heart can be carried away by large and sweeping effects. Ours has been a century full of torchlight parades and political rallies held in great stadiums, from Mussolini to the present, staged by men aware of the power of mass spectacles to sweep reason and the individual away.

Spectacle isn't an important factor in the scenes quoted in this chapter from *Kramer vs. Kramer* or *The Godfather,* but it is an important element in *On the Waterfront.* Major urban docks are spectacles that are interesting in themselves and representative of one of our crucial economic areas. They fit into Terry's story naturally, just as at the climax having hundreds of men hanging on the outcome of his actions is an appropriate spectacular effect. Action adventures and Westerns depend heavily on spectacle, in the former to fill the story out and in the latter to give the story the dimension of the beautiful, empty land over which the Good and the Bad struggle for control. However, spectacle must be appropriate to the story. It has no place in a film like *Kramer vs. Kramer,* except for the incidental glimpses of the New York skyline; no place in *Ordinary People;* and only limited place in *Places in the Heart* when the protagonist tries to bring in the harvest. A film like *The River* makes a natural use of spectacle (the river and farm versus the plant where Mel Gibson must work to survive). In films like *The Emerald Forest* panoramas of the jungle and of what man has done to it are central to the story.

There is nothing to bar you from writing a screenplay in which nature is, in effect, a character, protagonist or antagonist. You can use moments that depend on mass effects or contemporary spectacle, too. You may conceive of spectacular action, as in the christening scene in *The Godfather* that INTERCUTS between the church ceremony and the slaughter of Michael's opponents. Or spectacle may be incidental, in which case don't let it arbitrarily intrude.

Symbol

Our days and lives are structured around symbols. The cross, the dollar sign, the swastika instantly evoke complex responses. Our dreams fill our nights with symbols; our unconscious minds are a creative ferment of which only symbols give us some idea. Our waking thought is full of symbol and symbolic processes. Symbolic logic is a crucial area of philosophy and science.

Symbols fill screenplays. All good writing makes use of our natural tendency to invent new symbols or use those already familiar to us. How often in Westerns have we seen the hero on a white horse, as in *Pale Rider* and *Silverado*? Such heroes, or a character like Dirty Harry in the Clint Eastwood films, almost always have special guns, shinier or larger than anyone else's. They are as necessary to a hero as his horse and equally symbolic of the potency that enables the hero to triumph and to get the girl. Indiana Jones would be as symbolically castrated without his whip as Samson without his hair. Dracula films use the cross as a symbol of power and as a characterizing element: only someone free of Dracula's power can wield it or bear its touch.

Symbols can move the action swiftly and tellingly because nothing is as condensed and packed with meaning and emotion as an understood symbol. What a reasonable explanation would require a volume to make clear, a symbol can evoke in a moment. What we sometimes struggle to express without success can often be comprehended instantly if we can create a symbol whose meaning is made clear by the dramatic action of our story.

Turn back to the climax from *On the Waterfront*. Terry looks at the cargo hook in the scene with Edie, takes it, and strikes it into the floor. The act shows his anger, but the cargo hook is also the tool of his trade: to give up his right to use it would mean surrendering his potency and signal his defeat. Terry must prove his right to use it. The hook, then, is as much a symbol as the Western hero's gun. The same scene shows a second symbol created out of the action by Schulberg—Joey's jacket. We know from earlier in the screenplay that Joey is the young man Terry naively set up for death at the start of the film. Joey was also Edie's brother. When Terry dons Joey's jacket, he engages in a symbolic act of identification and restitution that he then goes down to the docks to make good.

Schulberg calls our attention to some obvious symbols in *On the Waterfront*, like the suit the Boss Stevedore wears and its meaning. The bandage Michael wears in *The Godfather*'s war council is simultaneously a plain fact—that he was struck defending his father—and a symbol—representing the inner hurt he feels for his father and his changing role in the family. Michael's bandaged jaw is a very mild version of Captain Ahab's damaged leg in Herman Melville's *Moby Dick*. Ahab's wooden leg is also simultaneously a plain fact and a symbol of Ahab's wounded nature. We find it irresistible to give things a symbolic weight.

Symbol has a way of spilling over into the ways stories take on mythical or archetypal patterns. Often the hero in a Western is presented as a non-violent man, a dude, or a man who has given up violence. But the moment comes when violence can no longer be avoided, and the hero has to put on a gun or retrieve one. Eastwood leaves the miners he has been helping as a minister in *Pale Rider* and returns to the town where he had left his gun in a safe deposit box. He gets it out, puts it on, and takes off his minister's collar.

The action for both Terry in *On the Waterfront* and Michael in *The Godfather* is typical of hero-making scenes. Often a hero begins as an innocent, even an incompetent; is challenged and molded by events; and then reveals a climactic capacity to guide others and end conflict. These patterns seem almost to be instinctive in us: stories can't help taking on their coloration, no matter how contemporary and unique they may seem at the start. These patterns, as they are made specific in particular characters in a particular story, give both a greater weight. We feel through characters like Terry or Michael, despite their different achievements, that a human being can overcome seemingly overwhelming odds. We want to believe that even when capacity and hope seem to have been lost, these can be regenerated by an urgent enough effort. Sometimes these things are true.

Examine your own scenes for symbol and symbolic action. Why use them unconsciously when you can martial them to great effect through conscious use? If your scene has no symbolic element, ask yourself if that is appropriate or if its absence is the source of your feeling that something is missing. If you write conflict with force, you will find your material suggests symbols to you. Use them, but remember you must always be sure any symbol, like the use of spectacle or any other detail or dramatic resource, is appropriate to your characters and story.

Suspense

All of the scenes we have looked at so far have generated suspense: scenes can't be effective otherwise. To feel suspense we must be able to sympathize or empathize with the protagonist: then we can care about his fate. We feel suspense about the outcome of the trial for Ted in *Kramer vs. Kramer* and what he will do when the verdict goes against him because we care. If we didn't care about Terry, what would it matter to us when he goes down to the docks or when he lies beaten senseless? Suspense is generated by our concern about some condition or event whose outcome is in doubt but is crucial to the well-being of a protagonist we care about.

The importance of what is at stake greatly affects our feelings of suspense and is another reason that what is at stake must be substantial and cared about deeply by the protagonist. Mrs. Robinson's manipulation of Ben in *The Graduate* amuses us, but we respond more deeply to Bonasera begging the Godfather for help. In *Rocky* we wonder if Rocky will succeed in seducing Adrian, but feel tense over the outcome of *Kramer vs. Kramer*'s confrontations between Ted and Joanna. Who could keep his attention focused on a story of little consequence and less suspense?

In a sense, suspense grows naturally out of the writer's success in establishing and developing character and conflict—creating a problem, generating conflict over solving that problem, and building the protagonist and story through complication and reverse to the moment of crisis. Each complication makes us wonder how the protagonist will handle its consequences. Each reverse involves us in a challenge to and response by the protagonist. Crisis and climax generate the most suspense as we wonder whether or not the protagonist will fail and then whether he will carry his ultimate response through the climax to final failure or success. The final revelation of capacity on the protagonist's part must emerge in an atmosphere of great tension and suspense, or it will not matter to us.

The kind of suspense that relates directly to the protagonist's survival is *major suspense*. If some secondary problem comes up, we are dealing with *minor suspense*. Rocky's seduction of Adrian generates minor suspense; his fight with Apollo Creed, major. The ins and outs of Terry's relationship with Edie in *On the Waterfront* generate minor suspense; his confrontation with Johnny Friendly, major. When we use writers' lingo and speak of "the plot thickening," we are referring to major suspense.

This is not the place to go into techniques of artificially adding to suspense by breaking scenes up; cutting away from the action before the outcome of a scene is known; or deliberately inventing a complication, which may or may not be organic with the conflict, out of a sense the action is flagging. These are common practices and often common weaknesses. You should concentrate on the clarity and force of your premise for your story and on the primacy of the conflict you structure in your plot (BEGINNING, MIDDLE, END) for the generation of suspense, just as Schulberg does in *On the Waterfront* or Bergman so effectively in the scene taken from *Fanny and Alexander*.

Few scenes develop suspense with as much economy or feeling as does the love scene between Blanche and Mitch that we will turn to now from Tennessee Williams's *A Streetcar Named Desire*.

A Love Scene From A Streetcar Named Desire

Tennessee Williams's play *A Streetcar Named Desire* caused a sensation with its mix of raw vigor and symbolism in Elia Kazan's original Broadway production. The film production with the young Brando as the raw, abrasive Stanley Kowalski and Vivien Leigh as his wife's corrupted, fragile sister Blanche has become a film classic. Ann-Margret and Treat Williams took up its challenge in a 1980s adaptation for prime-time television on ABC.

Three areas concern us in the scene that follows: first, the use of dramatic elements like silence and symbol; second, the use of motivation and revelation at the crisis and climax; last, the way Williams dramatizes a protagonist whose efforts fail.

Typically, the protagonist succeeds in American screenwriting, though the most probing and moving dramas more often than not are stories in which the protagonist's supreme effort fails. One of the virtues of *Tootsie* and *Kramer vs. Kramer* is that their protagonists do not, at least, succeed easily. The happy ending in *Kramer vs. Kramer* comes as an unexpected gift from Joanna after she has won. Michael is at least chastened in *Tootsie*, even if he still gets the girl. Terry's success is one of the weaknesses of *On the Waterfront*, exciting as its climax is, because we suspect that in real life a punch-drunk, naive, immature, and drifting young man is unlikely to unseat a real Johnny Friendly. The best screenwriting does not leave us with an uneasy question in the back of our minds about how things might really have worked out: it has the force to replace reality because its vision seems truer.

Blanche is no longer a young woman in *A Streetcar Named Desire*, though she is not old, either. Her past is loaded: it includes Allan, a lover she drove to suicide when she discovered he was a homosexual, and a long period of promiscuity as she flung herself at men trying to forget. That finally cost her her job as a teacher. She had no one to turn to but Stella and so has come to live with her and make a new start. But she is losing her mental balance: she hears things from the past (Allan's gunshot, snatches of music). Neither her sister nor we know about her past as the scene begins.

Both Blanche and her sister belong to the dying culture of the old South—romantic, chivalrous, fantastic, and in its last manifestations exhausted and corrupt. Stella has made the transition to the new industrial world of the contemporary South through her marriage to Stanley Kowalski, a rough, uncultured, anti-intellectual factory worker, a proletarian. Blanche has clung to the mannerisms of the past and a lost affluence.

She and Stanley feel instant antipathy for each other. Blanche struggles with him for her sister's affections and starts to date one of his chums, Mitch, hoping to start her new life with him despite their vast differences. She is succeeding before Stanley investigates her past, discovers what it was, and reveals it to Mitch. Mitch stands Blanche up on a date. The scene that follows begins later the same night:

FADE IN:

INT.   BLANCHE'S BEDROOM   (EST) NIGHT

[A poor room with cheap furniture and only Blanche's superficial efforts to dress it up.] Blanche is seated in a tense hunched position in a bedroom chair she has re-covered with diagonal green and white stripes. She has on her scarlet satin robe. On the table beside chair is a bottle of liquor and a glass.

The rapid, feverish POLKA TUNE, the "Varsouviana," is HEARD [OVER]. The music is in her mind; she is drinking to escape it and the sense of disaster closing in on her, and she seems to whisper the words of the song. An electric fan is turning back and forth across her.

EXT.   STREET BEFORE KOWALSKI APARTMENT   NIGHT

Mitch comes around the corner in work clothes: blue denim shirt and pants. He is unshaven. He climbs the steps to the door and rings.

INT.   BLANCHE'S BEDROOM   NIGHT

> BLANCHE
> (Blanche is startled)
> Who is it, please?

> MITCH, OS
> (hoarsely)
> Me. Mitch.

The POLKA TUNE STOPS.

> BLANCHE
> Mitch! Just a minute!

She rushes about frantically, hiding the bottle in a closet, crouching at the mirror and dabbing her face with cologne and powder. She is so excited her breath is audible as she dashes about. At last she rushes to the door in the kitchen and lets him in.

BY DOOR

> BLANCHE
> Mitch!—Y'know, I really shouldn't let
> you in after the treatment I have re-
> ceived from you this evening! So
> utterly uncavalier. But hello,
> beautiful!

She offers him her lips. He ignores it and pushes past her into the flat. She looks fearfully after him as he stalks into her bedroom.

> BLANCHE
> My, my, what a cold shoulder! And
> such uncouth apparel! Why, you
> haven't even shaved! The unforgive-
> able insult to a lady! But I forgive you.
> I forgive you because it's such a relief
> to see you. You've stopped that polka
> tune I had caught in my head. Have
> you ever had anything caught in your
> head? No, of course you haven't, you
> dumb angel-puss, you'd never get any-
> thing awful caught in your head!

He stares at her while she FOLLOWS him [into the bedroom] while

CONTINUED

CONTINUED

she talks. It is obvious that he has had a few drinks on the way over.

TWO SHOT: MITCH & BLANCHE—BLANCHE'S BEDROOM

> MITCH
> Do we have to have that fan on?

> BLANCHE
> No!

> MITCH
> I don't like fans.

> BLANCHE
> Then let's turn it off, honey. I'm not
> partial to them!

She presses the switch and the fan nods slowly off. She clears her throat uneasily as Mitch plumps himself down on the bed in the bedroom and lights a cigarette.

> BLANCHE
> I don't know what there is to drink.
> I—haven't investigated.

> MITCH
> I don't want Stan's liquor.

> BLANCHE
> It isn't Stan's. Everything here isn't
> Stan's. Some things on the premises
> are actually mine! How is your
> mother? Isn't your mother well?

> MITCH
> Why?

> BLANCHE
> Something's the matter tonight, but
> never mind. I won't cross-examine the
> witness. I'll just—

She touches her forehead vaguely. The POLKA TUNE starts up again, [OVER].

CONTINUED

CONTINUED

> BLANCHE (CONT'D)
> Pretend I don't notice anything differ-
> ent about you! That—music again . . .

> MITCH
> What music?

> BLANCHE
> The Varsouviana! The polka tune
> they were playing when Allan—wait!

A distant REVOLVER SHOT IS HEARD. Blanche seems relieved.

> BLANCHE (CONT'D)
> There now, the shot! It always stops
> after that.

The POLKA MUSIC DIES OUT again.

> BLANCHE (CONT'D)
> Yes, now it's stopped.

> MITCH
> Are you boxed out of your mind?

> BLANCHE
> I'll go and see what I can find in the
> way of—. Oh, by the way, excuse me
> for not being dressed. But I'd prac-
> tically given you up! Had you forgot-
> ten your invitation to supper?

She crosses into the closet and pretends to search for the bottle.

CLOSEUP: MITCH

> MITCH
> I wasn't going to see you anymore.

BACK TO SHOT

> BLANCHE
> Wait a minute. I can't hear what you're
> saying and you talk so little that
> when you do say something, I don't
> (MORE)

CONTINUED

CONTINUED

> BLANCHE (CONT'D)
> want to miss a single syllable of it . . .
> What am I looking here for? Oh, yes—
> liquor! We've had so much excitement
> around here this evening that I *am*
> boxed out of my mind.

She pretends to find the bottle. Mitch draws his foot up on the bed
and stares at her contemptuously.

> BLANCHE
> Here's something. Southern Comfort!
> What is that, I wonder?

> MITCH
> If you don't know, it must belong
> to Stan.

> BLANCHE
> Take your foot off the bed. It has a
> light cover on it. Of course, you boys
> don't notice things like that. I've done
> so much with this place since I've
> been here.

> MITCH
> I bet you have.

> BLANCHE
> You saw it before I came. Well, look at
> it now! This room is almost—dainty!
> I want to keep it that way. I wonder if
> this stuff ought to be mixed with
> something?
> (trying some in a glass)
> Ummm, it's sweet, so sweet! It's terri-
> bly, terribly sweet! Why, it's a *liqueur*,
> I believe.
> (Mitch grunts)
> I'm afraid you won't like it, but try it,
> and maybe you will.

CLOSER ON MITCH & BLANCHE

> MITCH
> I told you already I don't want none of
> his liquor and I mean it. You ought to
> lay off his liquor. He says you been
> lapping it up all summer like a
> wildcat!

> BLANCHE
> What a fantastic statement! Fantastic
> of him to say it, fantastic of you to re-
> peat it! I won't descend to the level of
> such cheap accusations to answer
> them, even!

> MITCH
> Huh.

> BLANCHE
> What's on your mind? I see something
> in your eyes!

[DRAW BACK as Mitch gets up.]

> MITCH
> It's dark in here.

> BLANCHE
> I like it dark. The dark is comfort-
> ing to me.

> MITCH
> I don't think I ever seen you in the
> light.
> > (Blanche laughs
> > breathlessly)
> That's a fact.

> BLANCHE
> Is it?

> MITCH
> I've never seen you in the afternoon.

> BLANCHE
> Whose fault is that?

CONTINUED

CONTINUED

> MITCH
>
> You never want to go out in the afternoon.

> BLANCHE
>
> Why Mitch, you're at the plant in the afternoon!

> MITCH
>
> Not Sunday afternoon. I've asked you to go out with me sometimes on Sundays but you always make an excuse. You never want to go out till after six and then it's always some place that's not lighted much.

> BLANCHE
>
> There is some obscure meaning in all this but I fail to catch it.

> MITCH
>
> What it means is I've never had a real good look at you, Blanche. Let's turn the light on here.

> BLANCHE
> (fearfully)
> Light? Which light? What for?

> MITCH
>
> This one with the paper thing on it.

He tears the paper lantern off the light bulb. She utters a frightened gasp.

> BLANCHE
>
> What did you do that for?

> MITCH
>
> So I can take a look at you good and plain!

> BLANCHE
>
> Of course you don't really mean to be insulting!

CONTINUED

CONTINUED

> MITCH
> No, just realistic.

> BLANCHE
> I don't want realism. I want magic!
>   (Mitch laughs)
> Yes, yes, magic! I try to give that to
> people. I misrepresent things to them.
> I don't tell the truth, I tell what *ought*
> to be truth. And if that is sinful, then
> let me be damned for it!—*Don't turn
> the light on!*

NEW ANGLE

Mitch crosses to the switch. He turns the light on and stares at her.

CLOSEUP: BLANCHE

She cries out and covers her face.

BACK TO SHOT

He turns the light off again. Slowly and bitterly:

> MITCH
> I don't mind you being older than
> what I thought. But all the rest of it—
> Christ! That pitch about your ideals
> being so old-fashioned and all the ma-
> larkey that you've dished out all sum-
> mer. Oh, I knew you weren't sixteen
> any more. But I was fool enough to
> believe you was straight.

> BLANCHE
> Who told you I wasn't—"straight"?
> My loving brother-in-law. And you be-
> lieved him.

> MITCH
> I called him a liar at first. And then I
> checked on the story. First I asked our
> supply-man who travels through Lau-
>   (MORE)

CONTINUED

CONTINUED

> MITCH (CONT'D)
> rel. And then I talked directly over
> long distance to this merchant.

> BLANCHE
> Who is this merchant?

> MITCH
> Kiefaber.

> BLANCHE
> The merchant Kiefaber of Laurel! I
> know the man. He whistled at me. I
> put him in his place. So now for re-
> venge he makes up stories about me.

> MITCH
> Three people, Kiefaber, Stanley and
> Shaw, swore to them!

> BLANCHE
> Rub-a-dub-dub, three men in a tub!
> And such a filthy tub!

> MITCH
> Didn't you stay at a hotel called The
> Flamingo?

> BLANCHE
> Flamingo? No! Tarantula was the
> name of it! I stayed at a hotel called
> The Tarantula Arms!

> MITCH
> (stupidly)
> Tarantula?

FAVOR BLANCHE

> BLANCHE
> Yes, a big spider! That's where I
> brought my victims!
> (she pours herself another
> drink)

CONTINUED

CONTINUED

> BLANCHE (CONT'D)
> Yes, I had many intimacies with
> strangers. After the death of Allan—
> intimacies with strangers was all I
> seemed able to fill my empty heart
> with. . . . I think it was panic, just
> panic, that drove me from one to an-
> other, hunting for some protection—
> here and there, in the most—unlikely
> places—even at last, in a seventeen-
> year-old boy but—somebody wrote
> the superintendent about it—"This
> woman is morally unfit for her
> position!"

She throws back her head with convulsive, sobbing laughter. Then
she repeats the statement, gasps, and drinks.

> BLANCHE (CONT'D)
> True? Yes, I suppose—unfit some-
> how—anyway. . . . So I came here.
> There was nowhere else I could go. I
> was played out. You know what played
> out is?

ON MITCH

[as he stares at her.]

FAVOR BLANCHE

> BLANCHE (CONT'D)
> My youth was suddenly gone up the
> water-spout, and—I met you. You said
> you needed somebody. Well, I needed
> somebody, too. I thanked God for you,
> because you seemed to be gentle—a
> cleft in the rock of the world that I
> could hide in! But I guess I was ask-
> ing, hoping—too much! Kiefaber,
> Stanley and Shaw have tied an old tin
> (MORE)

CONTINUED

CONTINUED

> BLANCHE (CONT'D)
> can to the tail of the kite.

MITCH & BLANCHE

There is a pause. Mitch stares at her dumbly.

> MITCH
> You lied to me, Blanche.

> BLANCHE
> Don't say I lied to you.

> MITCH
> Lies, lies, inside and out, all lies.

> BLANCHE
> Never inside, I didn't lie in my
> heart . . .

EXT.   KOWALSKI APT.   NIGHT

A vendor comes around the corner. She is a MEXICAN WOMAN in a dark shawl, carrying bunches of those gaudy tin flowers that lower class Mexicans display at funerals and other festive occasions. She is calling barely audibly. Her figure is only faintly visible outside the building.

> MEXICAN WOMAN
> Flores. Flores. Flores para los muertos.
> Flores. Flores.

INT.   BEDROOM: BLANCHE & MITCH   NIGHT

> BLANCHE
> What? Oh! Somebody outside . . .

She goes to the door, opens it and stares at the Mexican woman.

BLANCHE'S POV

[of the Mexican woman at the door who offers Blanche some of her flowers.]

> MEXICAN WOMAN
> Flores? Flores para los muertos?

ON BLANCHE

> BLANCHE
> (frightened)
> No, no! Not now! Not now!

She darts back into the apartment slamming the door.

EXT.   KOWALSKI APT   NIGHT

[The Mexican woman] turns away and moves down the street.

> MEXICAN WOMAN
> Flores para los muertos . . .

INT.   BY DOOR: BLANCHE   NIGHT

The polka tune FADES IN, [OVER].

> BLANCHE
> (to herself)
> Crùmble and fade and —regrets—re-
> criminations . . . "If you'd done this,
> it wouldn't've cost me that!"

> MEXICAN WOMAN, OS
> Corones para los muertos.
> Corones . . .

> BLANCHE
> Legacies! Huh . . . And other things
> such as bloodstained pillow-slips—
> "Her linen needs changing"—"Yes,
> Mother. But couldn't we get a colored
> girl to do it?" No, we couldn't of
> course. Everything gone but the—

> MEXICAN WOMAN, OS
> Flores.

ANOTHER ANGLE

[SHOWING Mitch watching Blanche as she drifts back to him.]

MITCH & BLANCHE

> BLANCHE
> Death—I used to sit here and she
> (MORE)

CONTINUED

CONTINUED

> BLANCHE (CONT'D)
> used to sit over there and death was
> as close as you are. . . . We didn't even
> dare admit we had ever heard of it!
>
> MEXICAN WOMAN, OS
> Flores para los muertos, flores—
> flores.
>
> BLANCHE
> The opposite is desire.
>   (at Mitch)
> So do you wonder? How could you
> possibly wonder! Not far from Belle
> Reve, before we had lost Belle Reve,
> was a camp where they trained young
> soldiers. On Saturday nights they
> would go in town to get drunk—
>
> MEXICAN WOMAN, OS
>   (softly)
> Corones . . .
>
> BLANCHE
> and on the way back they would stag-
> ger onto my lawn and call—"Blanche!
> Blanche!"—The deaf old lady remain-
> ing suspected nothing. But sometimes
> I slipped outside to answer their calls.
> . . . Later the paddy-wagon would
> gather them up like daisies . . . the
> long way home . . .

. . . Blanche goes to her dresser and leans forward on it. After a moment, Mitch rises and follows her purposefully. The POLKA MUSIC
FADES AWAY. He places his hands on her waist and tries to turn her
about.

CLOSE TWO SHOT: MITCH & BLANCHE

> BLANCHE
> What do you want?

CONTINUED

CONTINUED

> MITCH
> (fumbling to embrace her)
> What I been missing all summer.

> BLANCHE
> Then marry me, Mitch!

> MITCH
> I don't think I want to marry you
> any more.

> BLANCHE
> No?

Dropping his hands from her waist.

> MITCH
> You're not clean enough to bring in
> the house with my mother.

> BLANCHE
> Go away, then.
> (he stares at her)
> Get out of here quick before I start
> screaming fire!
> (her throat is tightening
> with hysteria)
> Get out of here quick before I start
> screaming fire.

He still remains staring. She suddenly rushes to the big window
with its pale blue square of the soft summer light and cries wildly

> BLANCHE (CONT'D)
> Fire! Fire! Fire!

With a startled gasp, Mitch turns and goes out the outer door. [We
HEAR HIM CLATTER] down the steps and around the corner of the
building [OS]. Blanche staggers back from the window and falls to
her knees. The distant PIANO is slow and blue.

FADE OUT[4]

4. Tennessee Williams, *A Streetcar Named Desire*, Best American Plays, 3d
series (New York: Crown Publishers, 1952), pp. 83–86. Copyright © 1947 by
Tennessee Williams; reprinted by permission of New Directions Publishing Corporation and the Tennessee Williams Foundation. Please note that the screenplay
was not accessible to the authors; camera directions, screenplay format, and all
bracketed material have been added by the authors.

This scene has as individual a stamp as the one from Ingmar Bergman's *Fanny and Alexander*. Both are powerful confrontations rich in reverse and the unexpected ways in which their protagonists are challenged and respond. The past is a powerful element in both; a contest over the meaning of the past is the tool Williams uses to dramatize the irreconcilable differences between Blanche and Mitch and which Blanche daringly tries to use to gain her objective. Williams makes a particularly pointed use of symbol and invests the scene with a blend of gutter realism and lyricism that peaks in its crisis and climax. Jot down your notes on Williams's use of symbol, silence, and spectacle and on the scene's structure, and then compare them to ours.

Symbol, Spectacle, Silence—and Music

If symbol is to be effective, it must function within a clearly defined context: it is not a substitute for detail, but an amplification. Look how much is communicated to us as the scene opens. Blanche is seated, alone. She's hunched, tense. She's drinking. It's hot—the electric fan is working. Nothing is said, yet already we know she's a woman down on her luck and feeling bad about it.

Her re-covered chair emphasizes the odd blend of poor and elegant in her physical surroundings. It shows us a woman at odds with the setting in which she lives. And, at once casual and overtly symbolic, her red robe is specifically called a "scarlet" robe. A woman in red is a fallen woman. Her loneliness and robe plant a subliminal suggestion that she is abandoned because she is fallen: that is the fate of the fallen. We are amply prepared for Mitch's and Blanche's revelations, which confirm this feeling with an economy only symbol, used properly, can provide.

Now look at Mitch as he appears. He's in work denims and unshaven. At the time Williams wrote his play work denims were more sharply suggestive of a particular economic class than now. But we know Mitch is a buddy of Stanley Kowalski, a fellow factory worker. So his clothes are more than appropriate: they symbolize a life and outlook poles apart from Blanche's. Moreover, those clothes worn even now show us Mitch hasn't come to Blanche for a date, however late he is. He's come for something else.

Notice just two other details that take on a symbolic weight. First, the use of Southern Comfort. Blanche's "finding" it is a lie. Then she turns the drink into a symbol by asking, "Southern Comfort! What is that, I wonder?" That is like asking, What is *Southern*, Southern *comfort?* "If you don't know," responds Mitch, "it must belong to Stan." A thing is just a thing to Mitch: he neither thinks of the dying South of traditional comfort or aristocratic pretension nor senses her implication. He is mentally and culturally barren. The exchange about "Southern Comfort" characterizes both of them with great force, but in opposite ways.

That's a lot to get out of so simple an exchange, yet Williams doesn't blow it out of proportion by dwelling on it. He moves on swiftly. The power of the exchange adds its weight to that already operating on us from the scene's start. But notice how appropriate and unforced "Southern Comfort" is: we knew Blanche was drinking, and she could have been drinking Southern Comfort as logically as anything else. A symbol has to fit naturally into its surroundings.

Last, look at how Williams plays with light. Light is as old a symbol as there is. To shed light on something, to bring something into the light, or to turn on the light all mean getting at the truth. The scene itself is dimly lit: there is a lot in darkness or shadow, literally and suggestively. Mitch informs us Blanche avoids bright light, only seeing him in the evening or dim surroundings. When Mitch says, "Let's turn the light on here," he rips the covering off the light to see the truth about Blanche. Mitch looks. She cries out and turns her face away. Mitch turns the light off, embittered. Williams drives this symbolic usage home by Blanche's overt defiance of the light in her preference for magic, for what ought to be the truth. Even the covering Mitch rips off the light is one Blanche had made to give the light a little class.

These touches add weight to the scene; they help evoke the sense that great issues are at stake without the author's having to raise them overtly or discursively. We are made to feel these issues: we experience the scene on a highly personal level. We think about it later. For the most part Williams is careful to make symbols seem natural elements of the scene or character so that we don't think, Aha! Symbols! His touch falters with the use of the Mexican woman and her flowers for the dead. After the first time or two we hear her chant and see Blanche's reaction to it, we have the sense of being hit over the head with symbolic meaning. Never use a symbol that way! Only the strength of his prior writing carries Williams through this flaw.

Spectacle plays little role in this scene. We are familiar with the appearance of the neighborhood and apartment by this point in the story: nothing new is added by seeing them again. There are no great or sweeping effects. Hundreds of longshoremen don't hang on the action. What counts instead are the details of the setting that the camera can emphasize: details of clothing or appearance and the elements Blanche has contributed like the chair or the shade for the light. These are all small, but cumulatively revealing. They relate directly to place and character, just the sort of detail we mean for you to find for your own scenes.

This brings us to an interesting point. The stage production of *A Streetcar Named Desire* did involve elements of spectacle. There was a constant play of different light and sound effects to suggest mood or feeling or heighten the sense of lyricism. But the stage is a bare area naked to imagination and suggestion, while the camera *sees* the surface of things we call reality. The spectacle appropriate to the screen, as with screen symbols, must seem natural to the story, to the surface of reality, and gather its extra weight through the force of the story. In the case of fantasy or science fiction, an entirely new surface of reality has to be constructed in which spaceships, genies, or talking animals appear logically.

Silence is used three times in this scene crucially. First is the moment of silence as Mitch grabs and stares at Blanche in the light before she cries out and covers her face. It is a cruel and symbolic moment: he sees the truth. Blanche may once have been but is not now young or a lady.

Second, look at the sequence in which Mitch reveals what he knows from Kiefaber and Shaw. Blanche resists a moment, then reveals her past in order to assert that they are both people who need someone, and a second or a last chance. As Blanche makes her plea, the business indicates: "There is a pause. Mitch stares at her dumbly." Then he says: "You lied to me, Blanche." That silence dramatizes more effectively than a debate could Mitch's inability to cope with the idea that the past could mean many things and perhaps be overcome. The past can only be what it seems to be to Mitch, just as Southern Comfort can only be whiskey.

Last, there is a long moment as the Mexican Woman's cry becomes inaudible and Blanche leans on her dresser, lost in thought. Mitch ends it by reaching for her—as a whore. Not even her final revelation could touch him.

This is not a silent scene, however: music plays an important role and in a way that you as a writer can use in your own scenes. No one expects you to write a score; that is one of the collaborative elements of screenwriting that enter in the production phase. But you can use musical elements and insist on the function of any score. For instance, one of the characteristics of Ingmar Bergman's screenplays is the absence of any sort of "Hollywood" musical score. The natural sounds of the environment fill his films, and a moment of silence means real silence. A film like *The Emerald Forest* is flawed by the constant presence of a musical score that eliminates much of the feel of the jungle with its natural sounds. A much older Hollywood film, the popular *King Solomon's Mines*, was unusual and surprisingly effective, in part because so much of the sound in it was natural or native.

Some movies use their scores to give the film a coherency it would otherwise lack. A score may link scenes in an action-adventure film or serve as part of an epic effect, as it did in *Lawrence of Arabia*, which had the London Philharmonic seemingly behind every sand dune, or *Star Wars*. Scores can set a mood, prepare the audience for a moment of action, emphasize a dramatic moment: think of all the detective movies you have seen with foreboding scores.

Williams's scene does not begin with a silent shot like the CLOSE-UP of Joanna at the start of *Kramer vs. Kramer*, though something of the same sense of desperation is being communicated: instead, we hear the "Varsouviana Polka." It is present only in Blanche's mind. Moreover, she doesn't hear rock and roll or something from *Oklahoma*. What she hears is specific to her, triggered by something in the present: her unhappiness. She also hears it when it is inconvenient: its presence dramatizes her precarious grip on reality. She just barely controls herself with Mitch, who thinks she is "boxed." Events will eventually so loosen her grip on the present that she will be taken to an asylum. You can use musical elements also within your own scenes to set mood or characterize a moment or character or even, like Williams, as a symbol.

Crisis and Climax

The scene is also enriched by the way Williams varies the structure we have been emphasizing. Nonetheless, we can break this scene down in terms of BEGINNING, MIDDLE, and END.

> BEGINNING.   From the opening up to the point at which Mitch admits he wasn't going to see Blanche anymore is the first part.

> MIDDLE.   This sequence carries us from Blanche's fending off Mitch's attempts to leave or expose her to Mitch's revealing that he has discovered her past. She's not "straight," and he has Kiefaber, Shaw, and Kowalski to prove it. The relationship seems about to fail for good: crisis.

> END.   The final sequence is made up of Blanche's efforts to overcome the revelation about her past until his advance signals that she has failed and she drives Mitch away. Climax—and failure.

This is an accurate summary, but also deceptive. Actually, the scene approaches the crisis several times but is forced away each time by Blanche's ingenuity in confusing the linear, unimaginative Mitch. The crisis nearly arrives immediately when Mitch declares "I wasn't going to see you anymore," but Blanche deflects the moment by diving into the closet to search for drink, pretending not to hear him while insisting she wants to catch every word. An argument over liquor or even, next, over light is far more to her purpose than over his not wanting to see her and why. That initial deflection makes Mitch search for a way to deal with her, instead of moving straight to Kiefaber and Shaw as he might have if Blanche had asked him Why? instead of diving into her closet. Even the crisis of holding Blanche's face in the light is deflected in part by Blanche's tears, in part because the light he wants to shed isn't really on her lack of youth. But that at last leads him to the issue of whether she is "straight." This does lead to the crisis, yet even now with a twist as Blanche deflects Mitch from the issue by playing for pity and by being straight about what she did. She wants to underscore why she behaved as she did in the past. She hopes to change both the meaning of what she did and what Mitch should think about it. As in *On the Waterfront*, the truth of the past emerges as a critical issue in the crisis. But in Terry's case the argument is more over who did what (or who ratted); with Blanche, what was done is conceded but not its meaning. This makes motivation itself the issue, not some event, just as it ties suspense to meaning instead of overt action.

Suspense itself is heightened by this way of handling the crisis: nothing more is needed to involve us more deeply than the sense of imminent disaster Blanche fends off with increasing ineffectiveness. The heightened suspense and deferred crisis let Williams accomplish something more. We can imagine a scene in which Mitch tells Blanche much earlier that he isn't going to see her again because she lied and immediately reveals his information from Kiefaber and Shaw. This action would have taken almost all the suspense out of the scene and would have made her use of motivation seem like a desperate attempt to deny the truth rather than reach it. We would have been baffled as she told Mitch more than he knew, revealing her behavior with the soldiers, for instance. She would seem a dishonest woman who just couldn't say no, not one who never lied in her heart. But the author gives himself time to reveal more about Blanche through her immediate efforts to deflect the conflict from reaching crisis, most lightly with the liquor and then with increasing weight to the revelation that she is haunted by death. Blanche's reckless promiscuity appears as an attempt to bury death in life, namely, through desire: "The opposite is desire."

How is this compelling and suspenseful scene made possible? By making several reverses potentially the crisis. The need for ingenuity on the part of the protagonist to avert the crisis provides a constant challenge to the author through his character for ever more invention and insight. Characters cannot arbitrarily shy away from the crisis: they can only if they find an immediate ability to do so. What they have to find at such moments is something more substantial, however, if the weight of crisis is about to fall on them, as it is on Blanche.

Writing with a constant sense of crisis is writing on the edge and offers the most opportunity. Any meaning reached through this process will be at a profounder level than otherwise possible. Here Blanche's confrontation with death touches something fundamental in all experience. It transcends a tale of corruption and decay or of the replacement of the old South by the new, yet it fits easily into the other strands of meaning in the play. Mitch's reaction is painfully appropriate to him: all he can do is dumbly try to treat her like a whore and get chased out. Blanche wins, and loses.

Note the greater realism involved this way. Terry can march directly from discontent to resolve to the docks and overcome Johnny Friendly, but Blanche and Mitch create a more compelling reality because they have to search and struggle their way to their moment of truth. Reality isn't linear, except in our wishes. A playwright can dramatize reality through how he handles the pattern of reverses in a scene as well as through how he tries to simplify it (as Williams does with Mitch). Developing a character and conflict through complication and reverse means sustaining this back-and-forth struggle toward the truth between the characters. That is the movement Williams catches and that is the problem with which all the best writing wrestles. Why?

The idea that there is a division between pleasure and instruction in drama is profoundly false: few things give an audience a deeper thrill of delight than the sense they have arrived at the final truth about a man or a woman. The desire to know, to know truly, is deep in human nature. One of the roots of creativity is the urge to imagine a life and its problems so clearly that the audience is utterly convinced of the reality and meaning of those imagined lives. These are things a drama must face because it is centered on conflict, and conflict forces the audience to explore motivation, which hardly makes sense unless the past as well as the present is examined in the light of the immediate, urgent needs of the characters. You will succeed or fail as a screenwriter to the degree that that sense of knowledge and truth is evoked in the audience through empathy and identification with your characters.

The old cliché that runs to the effect that art lies and only reality is true consequently misses the truth. Truth is exactly what so often eludes us in our lives. The truth that the imagination finds by working on the substance of our experience is not less true for being visionary. It is often all we have and why certain dramas, as well as other works, hold a perennial interest. No one goes anywhere to be lied to. When we speak of the appearance of the past in drama, it is a way of emphasizing the way in which an entire life finally is envisioned through conflict. Blanche's struggle with Mitch involves the nature of her life: that is what is at stake in the argument over the past. Is there still room for life for her? Is there still hope? Or must the past swallow everything now?

What sort of issues should we write about other than those as central to our experience as we can reach? All our craft is nothing unless it brings us to ourselves.

A Word on What's at Stake

We use the phrase "what's at stake" often. We use it to draw attention to the importance of the immediate outcome of the conflict for a character, as we use "what's ultimately at stake" to draw attention to the importance of the final outcome to a character. *By now you may realize that what is at stake in strong writing is always the same thing, however different it appears in specific circumstances: the protagonist's survival,* either directly or through whatever it is he sees as most important. Michael in *The Godfather* intervenes in the family at the point its survival is called into question after promising his father he would be with him from now on. Ted is faced with the survival of his father-and-son family unit that has become all-important to him in *Kramer vs. Kramer.* Terry in *On the Waterfront* fights for survival on a literal level. Blanche struggles for survival in the new world of Mitch and Stanley. Michael in *Tootsie* fights for survival first as an actor and then as a man in love. Julie in *Private Benjamin* is faced with a choice of living a life of self-betrayal by marrying the philandering Henri or of defying everyone by standing up for herself. What the truth is; how to take, finally, a character's motivation; and what the past really was and means hang on the outcome of the protagonist's struggle for survival, whether in comedy or drama. An audience may laugh helplessly in a farce, but few characters take their situation as desperately.

If you can't conceive your story in terms of survival for your protagonist, then you will be left to write in the shallows. We as writers court suffering for our characters out of our sense that they will find truth in its rifts and upheavals. We drive our characters to the breaking point because it is only there that the Blanches and Terrys can show their ultimate nature in a moment suddenly luminescent with truth.

Your Fourth Assignment

Write a scene in which you bring your crisis—your moment of imminent failure—and your climax—your final, resolving effort—into sharp relief. See if you can conceive what's at stake in terms of survival. Use either Williams's technique of having your protagonist defer the crisis or Schulberg's technique of using a moment of real failure (Terry's beating) to heighten suspense and deepen the challenge to your protagonist's capacity. Make overcoming the crisis as hard as you can for your protagonist.

Don't turn any consideration of motivation, the past, or the truth into an abstraction. Ask yourself specific questions: Why does my character do this or that now? How does one action grow immediately out of the preceding? Actions must be in response to immediate needs. Ask yourself, Can my character avert this disaster staring him in the face? As long as he can, let him. The crisis doesn't arrive out of your convenience, but from unavoidable necessity. That tests your character and your imagination. If you have not put your character in a situation in which survival in some sense is at stake, your imagination is going to have little to respond to.

Be clear about the nature of the actual failure seeming to face your protagonist in the crisis. He or she does not face absolute failure, but this particular failure or that particular failure. You cannot dramatize survival either, only a particular threat at a particular moment in a particular context. What, specifically, does your character do to succeed, or try to, climactically?

Do a draft of your scene. Write that draft with complete freedom—don't hesitate to change your mind in its middle, follow sudden inspirations, reconceive your characters, or do whatever else may occur to you.

Then revise it. Pay attention to three areas: First, look at your structure. Have you made the march to crisis and climax too predictable and straightforward? Does it work the way you have it? Examine your reverses. Does each contribute to the development of your characters and conflict? Is more than one reverse capable of being the crisis your protagonist is trying to avoid? Are there any complications beyond the initial problem? What are they? Are they necessary or irrelevant?

Second, do your characters speak when silence would be more eloquent? Are there moments of action you cloud with dialogue? Have suggestive or symbolic elements appeared as part of the natural context of your action? Could you make more use of them? Can you use music or any other nonverbal element within the scene? Is spectacle involved? Could it be? Should it be removed?

Last, ask yourself how the past appears and what it means. How is not reality but the reality of your story finally defined by your characters', especially your protagonist's, response to your crisis and climax? What is revealed? Are these things clear, or have you failed to think through the consequences of your characters' ultimate responses?

We emphasize this immediate, layered process of revision. Remember that what cannot be dramatized is not believed or experienced and consequently diminishes your story's force. Only through your success with the immediate requirements of structure, conflict, and character can you reach any larger issue.

Sometimes we assign a murder scene to our students at this point. Someone must be killed in the scene. Survival is ultimately at stake, but as a consequence of some immediate needs. It's more fun if the murder is not premeditated but provoked by the action of the scene. What could lead a character to such behavior? What has made him resentful to begin with? What brings on the crisis? What does the turn toward murder reveal about the character in terms of the past and motivation? How does the murder resolve anything? What does it finally make clear?

Whether you use an idea of your own or the one we suggest, write this scene with gusto!

9. Handling Dialogue, Theme, Values, and Moral Urgency

We need to consider three final aspects of successful screenwriting: first, the proper handling of dialogue; second, the proper handling of thematic material, for a writer always writes from some point of view; and third, the related issues of values and moral urgency in good writing.

DIALOGUE

Once a drama had to be in verse, and sometimes that verse rose to poetry to express the depth of a character's suffering or joy. Some movie adaptations of such dramas still succeed with general audiences, whether *Romeo and Juliet* or Euripides' unsurpassed antiwar drama *The Trojan Women.* Even when verse died out as the received mode for dialogue, emphasis continued to be placed on how well characters spoke; it was believed that the urgency of a character's needs or passions should spill over into stirring, electrifying speech.

Even now that expectation exists for plays written for the legitimate stage and for theatrical release. Ingmar Bergman's screenplays are published without shots or screenplay format as literary works. Films like *Amadeus* or *A Man for All Seasons* possess obvious literary merit. *Romeo and Juliet* was adapted into *West Side Story,* an immensely popular stage and film musical, in which characters rise at critical moments not to Romeo or Juliet's speeches but to equally expressive songs. *Lolita* remains a classic American film, distinguished by Vladimir Nabokov's elegant and witty dialogue. Harold Pinter's dialogue has a great deal to do with his success as a writer for both stage and screen. Comedies have for a long time depended on their writers' invention of zany, unexpected lines. Contemporary dramas like *Ordinary People* or *Kramer vs. Kramer* are literate films that depend on their characters' ability to speak well and to the point at critical moments. *A Streetcar Named Desire* invests Blanche with rare power as a character in large part because of the poetic charge of her language. The greatest weakness of Eugene O'Neill, our most famous dramatist, is the inchoate dialogue he gave his characters at critical moments.

We stress this *literary* aspect of good dialogue because there is a current misconception that this kind of concern with language doesn't belong in film. That misconception is isolated from the evidence of our own good films. It is isolated from reality. Is quality in language really absent from the real world with which screenplays deal? Isn't a moment made memorable when someone of our own acquaintance or someone in public life is moved to speak with force, elegance, intelligence, and poetic sharpness? When your characters speak with as much force, wit, or elegance as possible in a film, that film is improved, both theoretically and, as our examples show, commercially. Don't let anyone tell you differently.

That said, three things must be emphasized about the proper nature of what a playwright does write:

1. *A playwright writes an action, not words.* Words are one of the primary tools, but only a tool, that help a writer create character and conflict and develop those through crisis and climax to their final revelation and resolution.

2. *How a character speaks must always be appropriate to that character and his immediate situation.*

3. *Dialogue used today is based on current conversational style.*

Appropriateness

You cannot have a character who is a redneck speak the same way as a neurosurgeon on the faculty of Harvard Medical School. A Southern belle does not speak like an Italian mother-in-law from New York City's Bronx. A starlet in Hollywood does not speak like an English teacher in a small midwestern town, nor does an Asian immigrant. You must fit the right kind of speech to your character. Take the following exchange between Blanche and Mitch from *A Streetcar Named Desire:*

> BLANCHE (CONT'D)
> True? Yes, I suppose—unfit some-
> how—anyway. . . . So I came here.
> There was nowhere else I could go. I
> was played out. You know what
> played out is?

ON MITCH

[as he stares at her.]

FAVOR BLANCHE

> BLANCHE (CONT'D)
> My youth was suddenly gone up the
> water-spout, and—I met you. You said
> you needed somebody. Well, I needed
> somebody, too. I thanked God for you,
> because you seemed to be gentle—a
> cleft in the rock of the world I could
> hide in! But I guess I was asking,
> hoping—too much! Kiefaber, Stanley
> and Shaw have tied an old tin can to
> the tail of the kite.

MITCH & BLANCHE

There is a pause. Mitch stares at her dumbly.

> MITCH
> You lied to me, Blanche.

> BLANCHE
> Don't say I lied to you.

> MITCH
> Lies, lies, inside and out, all lies.

> BLANCHE
> Never inside, I didn't lie in my
> heart. . . .[1]

Blanche's dialogue is charged with poetic phrases like "a cleft in the rock of the world." "I didn't lie in my heart" has a poetic resonance. Her language is immediate, spoken in response to Mitch, and also evokes a sensibility that transcends merely immediate needs. She is awash with words, too. We know that Blanche is educated and from a formerly prominent family and class and that she was a teacher. These lines fit and characterize her. Mitch, by contrast, is entirely down-to-earth. He makes simple declarative statements: "You lied to me, Blanche," he says, "Lies, lies, inside and out, all lies." He talks like the factory worker he is. If you go through their scene you will notice how characteristic their language remains. Look at Blanche's first lines to Mitch.

1. Williams, *A Streetcar Named Desire*, pp. 85–86.

BLANCHE

Mitch!—Y'know, I really shouldn't let
you in after the treatment I have received from you this evening! So
utterly uncavalier. But hello,
beautiful![2]

This is immediate—"I really shouldn't let you in"—and typically
charged with "uncavalier" and "But hello, beautiful!" The first thing
Mitch says is: "Do we have to have that fan on?" These lines fit and
characterize simultaneously. If the drama had just begun, you would
only need to be consistent with Blanche and Mitch, as indeed Williams
is, to develop the characterizations such lines suggest.

Look at the following exchange from the scene in the bar between Ted
and Shaunessy from *Kramer vs. Kramer:*

TED
(grim)
What if I fight it?

SHAUNESSY
(matter of factly)
We can appeal, but I can't guarantee
anything.

TED
(determined)
I'll take my chances.

SHAUNESSY
It's going to cost.

TED
(his mind made up)
Don't worry. I'll get the money.[3]

Their dialogue seems completely unremarkable. But think about it
for a moment. Both speak ordinarily and ordinarily well. They speak
like middle-class Americans. That's what both of them are. Their dialogue fits them as well as Blanche's and Mitch's. Imagine if Ted had said,
"Don't you worry, pardner. I'll git that thar money for ye." Same sense,
but an entirely different world of reference that has nothing to do with
Kramer vs. Kramer!

2. Ibid., p. 84.
3. Benton, *Kramer vs. Kramer*, p. 122.

Two additional facets of writing dialogue emerge from this:

1. Dialogue must be consistent with each character as well as appropriate to character and situation.

2. Dialogue characterizes the speaker.

Economy

Shakespeare's famous play *Richard III* begins in the following manner:

ACT I

Scene 1.   London.   A street.

Enter RICHARD, DUKE OF GLOUCESTER, solus.

RICHARD

Now is the winter of our discontent.[4]

We see immediately by virtue of the nature of the street and the fact that Richard is in some sort of historical costume that we're in for some sort of historical drama. We see also that Richard is well dressed: we don't have to know he's a duke to guess he has high status. Without a word being said, we guess he must be a man of influence. Moreover, we see immediately that one of his arms is shriveled and that he is a hunchback. Before he speaks we guess he is unhappy. We suspect his status gives him means of expressing his unhappiness. Now this is a lot to get from very little, and we get it all in silence through the detail we see on stage.

Then he speaks.

We get a fresh rush of detail. He speaks in blank verse. This only confirms our suspicion from his appearance that he's a figure of influence. But he also emphasizes "now." He's so unhappy he calls his present moment "the winter" of his discontent. But he doesn't use "my" discontent, but uses "our," which has the smack of royalty to it, like the royal "we." He is of royal lineage and will cut his way to the throne in this play. How he speaks fits how he looks, characterizes him further, adds the detail of how unhappy he is, and promises action. His first words are tremendously economic.

Turn back to the scene between Ted and Joanna in *Kramer vs. Kramer* in the restaurant as they meet for the first time since she abandoned Ted and Billy.

---

4. William Shakespeare, *Richard III*, act 1, sc. 1, line 1.

JOANNA
Hello Ted. You look well.

TED
So do you.

The WAITRESS appears, carrying a scotch and soda. She sets it down on the table in front of Ted.

WAITRESS
The usual, Mr. Kramer.

TED
(not taking his eyes off
Joanna)
Thanks.

The waitress promptly disappears.

JOANNA
How's the job?

TED
Fine.

There is a self-conscious pause.

TED
Look at us, Joanna. Just like any old
married couple having dinner. Who
would believe it.

JOANNA
Yes . . . How's Billy?[5]

How two people would greet each other who have not seen each other for a long time is a good challenge to a writer's imagination. Would they greet each other with a rush of words or with minutes of awkward silence? "Hello Ted. You look well," she says. He responds, "So do you." What could be more appropriate, simple, and economic? They move on to his job and then on to Billy. It's a natural sequence: there are no wasted words. The confrontation between them builds by such natural steps.

Examine Bonasera's long speech about what happened to his daughter from the opening of *The Godfather*. He doesn't call vengeance down

5. Benton, *Kramer vs. Kramer*, pp. 72–74.

from the heavens from his sense of outrage, he gives a straightforward account of the details. Then he succinctly expresses his indignation:

> BONASERA
> . . . Suspended sentence! They went
> free that very day. I stood in the court-
> room like a fool, and those bastards,
> they smiled at me. Then I said to my
> wife, for Justice, we must go to The
> Godfather.[6]

The Godfather replies directly to the point, reproaching him for coming for help only now, though they've been friends a long time.

The simple moral here is don't waste words. Don't use two words where one will do. Don't use any words where a silence or an action is more effective. *Effective dialogue is economic in giving a character's intention, response, or situation.* Equally important is the point we made about Richard III: *Effective dialogue leads to action.* Joanna will demand Billy, the Godfather will demand a price, Ted will pledge to get money and then give up his request rather than hurt Billy. Good dialogue is never static.

What Dialogue Communicates

We have seen that effective dialogue can communicate a character's intention, characterize that character, reveal a character's social or economic class; that if appropriate to a moment it can move us and give a poetic dimension to a character or scene; and that it works best when it is economic and leads to action. This is already a great deal, but just what is it that dialogue expresses?

This may seem an odd question, but a character can never express the writer's understanding, only his own. A character's understanding of his conflict or even of his objective, as we stressed in the last chapter, is very limited. He searches for understanding as he works through one immediate reverse and complication after another, constantly frustrated until his final triumph or failure. Most of the time, then, your character's response is going to be emotional.

Don Corleone tells Bonasera that the court gave him justice; Bonasera exclaims: "An eye for an eye!" Rocky, preventing Adrian from leaving in the scene we looked at from *Rocky*, tells Adrian, "I always knew you was pretty." She responds: "Don't tease me," which expresses

---

6. Puzo and Coppola, *The Godfather,* p. 1.

her fear of his taking advantage of her, her sense of herself as not pretty, and her wish for confirmation that she *is* pretty. Look at this dialogue from the climax of *On the Waterfront:*

> EDIE
>
> You think you've got to prove some-
> thing to them, don't you? That you
> are not afraid of them and—you won't
> be satisfied until you walk right into
> their trap, will you?

His silence maddens her. She seems on the verge of striking him out of frustration and impotent rage. Her voice is hysterical.

> EDIE (CONT'D)
>
> Then go ahead—go ahead! Go down
> to the shape-up and get yourself
> killed, you stupid, pigheaded, son
> of a—
> > (struggling to control
> > herself)
> What are you trying to prove?[7]

This economically and effectively expresses Edie's response to Terry's silent and growing decision to go down to the docks. The language itself expresses her struggle, first trying to be reasonable, if challenging, then breaking into anger, which she controls, finally coming to the point: "What are you trying to prove?" They don't know, yet. They're groping to find out. Everything is in immediate terms. When Terry says a moment later that he's going to get his rights, he doesn't know that to get those rights he will have to stage a revolution.

*Dialogue communicates feelings. Those feelings express a charac-
ter's immediate situation. Those feelings are what lead to action.*

Communicating Information through Dialogue

You may wonder how to communicate information necessary for understanding a character and situation if dialogue must always primarily reflect the feeling of a character at some immediate moment of conflict. Let's look at some examples where such information is given effectively.

First, look at Terry's outburst to his brother Charley in the scene from *On the Waterfront.*

7. Schulberg, *On the Waterfront*, pp. 127–128.

TERRY
It wasn't him!
(years of abuse crying out
in him)
It was you, Charley. You and Johnny.
Like the night the two of youse come
into the dressing room and says, "Kid,
this ain't your night—we're going for
the price on Wilson." *It ain't my
night.* I'd of taken Wilson apart that
night! I was ready—remember them
early rounds throwing them combinations. So what happens—This bum
Wilson he gets the title shot—out-
doors in the ball park!—and what do I
get—a couple of bucks and a one-way
ticket to Palookaville . . . [8]

This evokes the scene in the dressing room when Terry was asked to
take the dive and then recalls the fight; it shows how ready he was to
triumph and how the early rounds are the supporting evidence; and it
demonstrates the consequences of taking the dive. It makes us see that
he is better than his present situation, and lets us feel how bitterly he
resents that disparity. Last, he places the blame for this on Charley.
That's a lot of information. You must handle information with the same
economy as dialogue.

Why does Terry tell Charley this now? Because of the immediate conflict, namely, Terry's effort to persuade Charley to let him wrestle with
his conscience over testifying rather than, with the gun Charley is holding, take Terry to River Street and Gerry G. That is why the information
is not presented abstractly, but passionately, from Terry's point of view:
this happened, Charley, because you betrayed me. The implied demand
is, Don't betray me now.

*Information should appear in a scene only when a character needs to
bring it out in order to influence the immediate action.* Information in a
scene is always some character's information, never the author's, and is
presented from that character's point of view with appropriate feeling. Terry's outburst does influence the immediate action. Charley lets
Terry go.

Study again the scene between Bishop Vergérus and Alexander from
Fanny and Alexander:

8. Ibid., pp. 103–104.

EDVARD

In my childhood parents were not so
soft-hearted. Naughty boys were punished in an exemplary but loving
manner. With the cane. The motto
was: "Spare the rod spoil the child." I
have a cane too. It is there on the
table. Then we had another means
that was really efficacious, and that
was castor oil. There you see the
bottle, Alexander, and a glass. When
you've swallowed a few mouthfuls of
that you will be a little more docile.
And if castor oil didn't help there was
a dark and chilly bogey hole where
one had to sit for a few hours, until
the mice started sniffing at one's face.
You see, over there under the stairs,
Alexander, a nice big hole is waiting
for you. Then of course there were
other, more barbarous methods, but I
disapprove of them. They were humil-
iating and dangerous and are not applied, nowadays.

TWO SHOT: ALEXANDER & BISHOP VERGÉRUS

ALEXANDER

What punishment will I get if I
confess?[9]

The structure of the speech itself, as with Terry's, is active. Look, Alexander, here are the instruments of punishment—one, two, three, the
bishop says. Information isn't just thrown out or only used to affect another character's emotions: the dialogue that conveys information effectively is active.

This information functions in a very immediate context, too: the
bishop is trying to make Alexander give in to him. At the same time the
information gives us the sense that some of these methods, and perhaps
the more barbarous ones, were applied to the bishop. We need to know
that now because we are trying to understand the bishop's cruelty. Information should help us understand a character's motivation.

9. Bergman, *Fanny and Alexander*, pp. 136–137.

Now recall the scene between Blanche and Mitch as Mitch reveals what he knows about her past. We saw how Blanche resists him a moment and then reveals more information. This is information that we as an audience need to appreciate her fully and that she needs to tell to change Mitch's view so that she can hold on to him. Her revelation puts her motivation in a deeper context we wouldn't otherwise have guessed. A character must be motivated immediately to reveal information: and that information should reveal further motivation.

We have not spoken so far of exposition, information needed to understand the immediate situation in which characters find themselves. You might, for instance, need to communicate a lot of information about other characters that your protagonist doesn't know that he or she needs right away, as is often the case in a murder mystery. That is commonly done by arousing the protagonist's curiosity, by satisfying his often unspoken question: Why do I need to know this? Ideally, you should make such information *immediately* necessary for some character, as with any other kind of information.

Some Technical Aspects of Dialogue

Tag and Curtain Lines

You may encounter the terms *tag* or *curtain lines*. A *tag line* is simply a scene's final line or speech when either of those sums up what has come before and points toward the next scene. Not all scenes have such lines. A *curtain line* has the same function at the end of an act. Not all act breaks have curtain lines. Screenplays are not written with act breaks, though these are present structurally; however, teleplays often are so written for obvious reasons: they want to focus and hold your attention through commercial breaks. Teleplays are often written in four acts in order to fit the four standard commercial breaks. Those acts are more or less arbitrary and don't affect the three-act structure of the action that we have stressed here.

Dialects

Sometimes it is appropriate for a character to speak a particular dialect. You must familiarize yourself with that dialect, and then—there is no shortcut—you will have to write it accurately in the dialogue. But unless the dialect is completely unfamiliar, it may be enough to give a full sample of the dialect in your first lines, and thereafter simply evoke it. You must make that procedure clear in the business.

If your characters simply speak the more or less rough and ready kind of English spoken by rough or uneducated people, then you need to be consistent in the dialogue. *On the Waterfront* gives you a good example of that. Sometimes just the feel of a dialect is enough—Williams in *A Streetcar Named Desire* is content to give us the feel of Southern dialect and an older gentility in Blanche's vocabulary and through the structure of her lines.

Use phonetic spelling very sparingly in any attempt to render dialogue: it makes a script hard to read. The imitation of the structure of a dialect is more effective: write "'Tis a fine time we'll be havin' at the party" instead of "We'll sure hev a foin time at the pahrrty."

Common Errors

> CHARACTER
> (angrily)
> Dammit! I said stop that!

or

> CHARACTER
> (sadly)
> How could you say something so
> hurtful? . . . Oh dear, I can't stop cry-
> ing . . .

or

> CHARACTER
> (happily)
> I'm so happy to see you!

Nothing betrays the novice more than parenthetical directions to make sure we get what is obvious in a line. Don't put in "sadly," "happily," or "angrily" when a line is perfectly clear without that direction. Characterize a line only when there is legitimate doubt about how it should be understood. Always try to write with such economy and force that how a line should be taken is clear.

Another common error appears in dialogue written by the author who forgets to use contractions when characters speak. Language without contractions in the mouths of characters sounds precious and stilted. Don't have a character say "I will not," when ordinary speech would have him say, "I won't." Don't say, "I have not got it," when normal usage would be, "I haven't got it." Remember that we expect to hear characters use our everyday, conversational speech unless there is some special reason for modifying it.

Hone your dialogue as you work on your scenes. Make sure it expresses feeling and character appropriately and economically, reveals information under immediate necessity, and forwards the business of revealing motivation and driving the action forward. If you are spare, lean, economic, to the point, conversational, and immediate, you will be in good shape. If, beyond that, you can drive such language naturally or as part of a special character into a particularly forceful or even poetic mode, then your scene will be more effective. But do not lose the immediately realistic surface of speech.

THEME

Ideas in Dramatic Art

Art is not just an outpouring of feeling, nor is feeling the only content of drama. Characters without minds are morons. Ideas cause profound passions and are often at the center of effective drama. The ability to think is critical in a dramatist.

These may seem obvious statements, yet they are at odds with popular notions about drama, and make many American critics and dramatists uneasy. Hollywood is not famous for the play of mind in its films, nor has the American legitimate stage proved hospitable to dramas of ideas as frequently as the European. The result has been a tendency to underplay the thought involved in craft or in a given film and often to depend on plays and films from elsewhere to supply the gap of mind in American drama.

Any limited view of human nature is bound to fail, however. We know now that scientists pursue their research with passion and that some of the greatest scientific breakthroughs have been anticipated by intuition or dream, yet we are still less willing to admit how much thought and intellect go into the making of a drama.

The notion that an idea is of little dramatic interest is certainly an odd idea in itself. How could such an attitude ever have arisen in a century of revolution and war caused by ideas of social structure, economic practice, or political behavior? How could anyone even vaguely familiar with the history of religious ideas be ignorant of the convulsions those have caused? There are few things men and women become as passionate about as an idea whose time has come. Any dramatist who tries to deal with the conflicts around him today must be able to think about the ideas that so passionately divide us if he is to treat them adequately in his drama; otherwise, what will he be writing about? The streak of anti-intellectualism in American life has no room in the practice of playwriting with its attempt to deal with real characters confronting real issues.

By now you must find the idea that thought has no place in art a very odd one simply through your struggle to write effective scenes. You have discovered just how much disciplined and critical thought it takes, constantly reexamined and redefined rewrite by rewrite, to create an effective scene. Drama is not an easy art. The saying "Art is long but life is short" was not first said by a dilettante.

Similarly, you have seen how thought plays a considerable role in the content of many of the scenes at which we have looked. The question about the nature of justice is raised in the first scene of *The Godfather.* Ideas are deeply embedded in screenplays like *Tootsie, On the Waterfront,* or *Kramer vs. Kramer.* Part of their continuing interest as well as their initial impact was caused by their attempt to deal with issues that have meaning in the real world: sexual politics, labor corruption, the changing roles of men and women in the family. Robert Redford in *Brubaker* dealt with a reform-minded prison warden whose efforts to clean up a prison fail because prison cannot be made less corrupt than the world outside its walls.

Ingmar Bergman's *Fanny and Alexander* evokes a comparison of comfortable materialism with austere ideology to make a humanistic statement in favor of moderation and simple humanity. In the scene we quoted, Bishop Vergérus is incapable of outwardly giving up his faith, even though inwardly he has lost it. When confronted with Alexander, he goes through a form of doublethink: by "love" he really means hate; by "well-being," debasement. He is an ideologue in a century of ideologues, and he maintains his ideology in order to maintain his power. Bergman thus treats one of the oldest themes in a contemporary setting: power corrupts. Any look at the headlines will remind us how urgent an issue this is.

Even television cannot exclude ideas, though it suffers most from the Hollywood cliché of entertainment as mindless activity. Typically television reduces the scope of ideas so that a television drama might deal with the obvious drawbacks of alcoholism or drug addiction or wife beating without any attempt to deal with the larger issues of social structure, economic justice, or political theory that dominate and divide our society. Serious dramatic series constantly try to deal with real issues, though we have seen more than one such series canceled, even though it won an Emmy for its efforts. Miniseries often have minimal intellectual weight and so have fallen on lean times; some, like *Roots,* have dealt with issues central to our national experience.

The presence of real issues in a well-written drama can generate an unmatched level of involvement and excitement. Men are moved to great passions by their thoughts. It is not surprising, then, that so much of television has been preempted by reruns of theatrical release films: balance has to be found somewhere.

How to Handle Thematic Material

We have stressed thought and idea rather than theme to emphasize the intellectual involvement that is characteristic of good writing. Theme in drama is your, the writer's, point of view on your material. It involves your thought on the issues involved in your story: your ideas and reflections.

Writers cannot simply impose their thoughts on their material or use their characters to say what they think, however. Characters don't debate an issue at their creator's convenience, nor does a character speak the theme of a drama, even one simple enough to be reduced to an elementary statement. "There can be no doubt that all our knowledge begins with experience" was said not by a current critic but by Immanuel Kant at the beginning of his *Critique of Pure Reason,* one of the cornerstones of modern philosophy.[10] A dramatist creates that experience through the conflict: how he handles the conflict and how it turns out generate whatever thought he hopes to leave us with. Our involvement in drama is always immediate and emotional: *any theme, to be effective, must be embodied in the immediate action of the story.* As a screenwriter you must make us care by arousing our feelings for your characters through the conflict: then, because we care, we will think about what their story means.

Let's look at two examples to see how this works.

The Parting Scene from A Doll House

Reality is not a given; how it is experienced varies with time and culture. How reality appears to us is at least in part how we would like it to appear, a process that drama reflects with especial truthfulness with its emphasis on cause-and-effect connections. How often in reality do we find such connections so clearly rendered? We touched on how drama creates the truth often lacking in our lives; how modern drama does just that is primarily the nineteenth-century Norwegian playwright Henrik Ibsen's creation.

Ibsen created the realistic, conversational style we take for granted. He also wrote the first modern feminist, environmental, sociological, medical, and anti-ideological plays. His sense of structure underlies our own ideas about structure. A screenplay like *Kramer vs. Kramer* originates in form, tone, and attitude with Ibsen and would have been hardly conceivable without his revolution in dramatic practice. Ibsen's plays continue to be performed, adapted for television, or released as major films: *A Doll House,* repeatedly; *The Wild Duck,* recently, with Jeremy

---

10. Immanuel Kant, *Critique of Pure Reason,* trans. Norman K. Smith (New York: Modern Library, 1958), p. 25.

Irons and Liv Ullmann. So let's begin by looking at the climactic, final scene of *A Doll House*.

Both *Kramer vs. Kramer* and *A Doll House* start with a man at a peak of success who the story reveals is insensitive to his wife. Nora in *A Doll House* and Joanna in *Kramer vs. Kramer* leave their husbands and children to find themselves, resentful of the past and the way men have treated them. Joanna is forced to go to court to get her child back, where she is cross-examined and her behavior and motivations challenged; Nora is challenged immediately by her husband Helmer as she tries to leave. The women share identical attitudes about their rights.

Torvald Helmer has treated his wife Nora like a doll for the eight years of their marriage. That was the role that pleased him, and Nora began by wanting to please. But there was more to Nora. Early in their marriage Helmer became ill but, unwilling to borrow money and too poor otherwise, was unable to take the trip to a warmer climate necessary for his recuperation. Unknown to Helmer, Nora borrowed the necessary money by forging her dying father's signature on a loan she took from a moneylender. She tried to repay the loan out of her household allowance and by doing odd jobs like copying without Helmer's knowledge. She has lived in dread of being discovered. Helmer's "doll" has been a woman living year after year with anxiety, thrifty with the money Helmer thought she was casual about. Nora dreamed that if she was discovered, Helmer would stand up for her and take the blame. She had no intention of actually letting him do that: she fantasized committing suicide to take the shame off his shoulders.

Helmer discovers her loving deception through an attempt of the moneylender to blackmail him. His reaction reveals him as a pretentious hypocrite with no thought for Nora, only his own public image. He calls her a criminal, unfit to be a mother to his children. Then the blackmail attempt is withdrawn, and Helmer reverts to his former benign self in front of the shocked Nora. We pick up the action at that point.

FADE IN:

INT.   HELMER HOME: PARLOR   (EST) NIGHT

[HELMER, a successful banker, is alone by the parlor table. Nora, his wife, has just LEFT THE SHOT to change from her Christmas costume.] NORA ENTERS in her regular clothes.

TWO SHOT: HELMER & NORA

> **HELMER**
> What's this? Not in bed? You've
> changed your dress?

CONTINUED

CONTINUED

> NORA
> Yes, Torvald, I've changed my dress.

[She walks up to one side of the table, confronting him.]

> HELMER
> But why now, so late?

> NORA
> Tonight I'm not sleeping.

> HELMER
> But Nora dear—

Looking at her watch

> NORA
> It's still not so very late. Sit down,
> Torvald; we have a lot to talk over.

She sits at one side of the table.

> HELMER
> Nora—what is this? That hard
> expression—

> NORA
> Sit down. This'll take some time. I
> have a lot to say.

Helmer [sits] at the table directly opposite her. [CROSS-CUT between them.]

CLOSE ON NORA & HELMER AT THE TABLE

> HELMER
> You worry me, Nora. And I don't
> understand you.

> NORA
> No, that's exactly it. You don't under-
> stand me. And I've never understood
> you either—until tonight. No, don't
> interrupt. You can just listen to what
> I say. We're closing our accounts,
> Torvald.

CONTINUED

CONTINUED

                    HELMER
        How do you mean that?

After a short pause.

                    NORA
        Doesn't anything strike you about our
        sitting here like this?

                    HELMER
        What's that?

                    NORA
        We've been married now eight years.
        Doesn't it occur to you that this is the
        first time we two, you and I, man and
        wife, have ever talked seriously
        together?

                    HELMER
        What do you mean—seriously?

                    NORA
        In eight whole years—longer even—
        right from our first acquaintance,
        we've never exchanged a serious word
        on any serious thing.

                    HELMER
        You mean I should constantly go and
        involve you in problems you couldn't
        possibly help me with?

                    NORA
        I'm not talking of problems. I'm say-
        ing that we've never sat down seri-
        ously together and tried to get to the
        bottom of anything.

                    HELMER
        But dearest, what good would that
        ever do you?

                    NORA
        That's the point right there: you've
                (MORE)

                                CONTINUED

CONTINUED

NORA (CONT'D)
never understood me. I've been
wronged greatly, Torvald—first by
Papa, and then by you.

CLOSE-UP: HELMER

HELMER
What! By us—the two people who've
loved you more than anyone else?

BACK TO SHOT

NORA
(shaking her head)
You never loved me. You've thought it
fun to be in love with me, that's all.

HELMER
Nora, what a thing to say!

NORA
Yes, it's true now, Torvald. When I
lived at home with Papa, he told me
all his opinions, so I had the same
ones, too; or if they were different I
hid them, since he wouldn't have
cared for that. He used to call me his
doll-child, and he played with me the
way I played with my dolls. Then I
came into your house—

HELMER
How can you speak of our marriage
like that?

NORA
(unperturbed)
I mean, then I went from Papa's hands
into yours. You arranged everything
to your own taste, and so I got the
same taste as you—or I pretended to;
I can't remember. I guess a little of
both, first one, then the other. Now
(MORE)

CONTINUED

CONTINUED

NORA (CONT'D)
when I look back, it seems as if I'd
lived here like a beggar—just from
hand to mouth. I've lived by doing
tricks for you, Torvald. But that's the
way you wanted it. It's a great sin
what you and Papa did to me. You're
to blame that nothing's become of
me.

HELMER
Nora, how unfair and ungrateful you
are! Haven't you been happy here?

NORA
No, never. I thought so—but I never
have.

HELMER
Not—not happy!

NORA
No, only lighthearted. And you've always been so kind to me. But our
home's been nothing but a playpen.
I've been your doll-wife here, just as
at home I was Papa's doll-child. And
in turn the children have been my
dolls. I thought it was fun when you
played with me, just as they thought
it fun when I played with them.
That's been our marriage, Torvald.

HELMER
There's some truth in what you're
saying—under all the raving exag-
geration. But it'll all be different after
this. Playtime's over; now for the
schooling.

NORA
Whose schooling—mine or the
children's?

CONTINUED

CONTINUED

                              HELMER
              Both yours and the children's, dearest.

CLOSE-UP: NORA

                                NORA
              Oh, Torvald, you're not the man to
              teach me to be a good wife to you.

CLOSE-UP: HELMER

                              HELMER
              And you can say that?

BACK TO SHOT

                                NORA
              And I—how am I equipped to bring
              up children?

                              HELMER
              Nora!

                                NORA
              Didn't you say a moment ago that
              that was no job to trust me with?

                              HELMER
              In a flare of temper! Why fasten
              on that?

                                NORA
              Yes, but you were so very right. I'm
              not up to the job. There's another job
              I have to do first. I have to try to edu-
              cate myself. You can't help me with
              that. I've got to do it alone. And that's
              why I'm leaving you now.

NEW ANGLE

                              HELMER
                            (jumping up)
              What's that?

                                NORA
              I have to stand completely alone, if
                             (MORE)

                                                    CONTINUED

CONTINUED

NORA (CONT'D)
I'm ever going to discover myself and
the world out there. So I can't go on
living with you.

HELMER
Nora, Nora!

NORA
I want to leave right away. Kristine
should put me up for the night—

HELMER
You're insane! You've no right! I for-
bid you!

NORA
From here on, there's no use forbid-
ding me anything. I'll take with me
whatever is mine. I don't want a thing
from you, either now or later.

HELMER
What kind of madness is this?

NORA
Tomorrow I'm going home—I mean,
home where I came from. It'll be
easier up there to find something
to do.

HELMER
Oh, you blind, incompetent child!

NORA
I must learn to be competent,
Torvald.

HELMER
Abandon your home, your husband,
your children! And you're not even
thinking what people will say.

NORA
I can't be concerned about that. I only
know how essential this is.

CONTINUED

CONTINUED

>HELMER
>
>Oh, it's outrageous. So you'll run out like this on your most sacred vows.

>NORA
>
>What do you think are my most sacred vows?

>HELMER
>
>And I have to tell you that! Aren't they your duties to your husband and children?

>NORA
>
>I have other duties equally sacred.

>HELMER
>
>That isn't true. What duties are they?

>NORA
>
>Duties to myself.

>HELMER
>
>Before all else, you're a wife and a mother.

>NORA
>
>I don't believe in that anymore. I believe that, before all else, I'm a human being, no less than you—or anyway, I ought to try and become one. I know the majority thinks you're right, Torvald, and plenty of books agree with you, too. But I can't go on believing what the majority says, or what's written in books. I have to think over these things myself and try to understand them.

>HELMER
>
>Why can't you understand your place in your own home? On a point like that, isn't there one everlasting guide you can turn to? Where's your religion?

CONTINUED

CONTINUED

> NORA
>
> Oh, Torvald, I'm really not sure what religion is.

> HELMER
>
> What—?

> NORA
>
> I only know what the minister said when I was confirmed. He told me religion was this thing and that. When I get clear and away by myself, I'll go into that problem too. I'll see if what the minister said was right, or, in any case, if it's right for me.

> HELMER
>
> A young woman your age shouldn't talk like that. If religion can't move you, I can try to rouse your conscience. You do have some moral feeling? Or tell me—has that gone too?

> NORA
>
> It's not easy to answer that, Torvald. I simply don't know. I'm all confused about these things. I just know I see them so differently from you. I find out, for one thing, that the law's not at all what I'd thought—but I can't get it through my head that the law is fair. A woman hasn't a right to protect her dying father or save her husband's life! I can't believe that.

> HELMER
>
> You talk like a child. You don't know anything of the world you live in.

> NORA
>
> No, I don't. But now I'll begin to learn for myself. I'll try to discover who's right, the world or I.

CONTINUED

CONTINUED

>   HELMER
> Nora, you're sick; you've got a fever. I
> almost think you're out of your head.

>   NORA
> I've never felt more clearheaded and
> sure in my life.

>   HELMER
> And—clearheaded and sure—you're
> leaving your husband and children?

CLOSE-UP: NORA

>   NORA
> Yes.

BACK TO SHOT

>   HELMER
> Then there's only one possible reason.

>   NORA
> What?

>   HELMER
> You no longer love me.

ON HELMER

>   NORA, VO
> No, that's exactly it.

>   HELMER
> Nora! You can't be serious!

BACK TO TWO SHOT

>   NORA
> Oh, this is so hard, Torvald—you've
> been so kind to me always. But I can't
> help it. I don't love you anymore.

>   HELMER
> (struggling for composure)
> Are you also clearheaded and sure
> about that?

CONTINUED

CONTINUED

> **NORA**
> Yes, completely. That's why I can't go on staying here.

> **HELMER**
> Can you tell me what I did to lose your love?

> **NORA**
> Yes, I can tell you. It was this evening when the miraculous thing didn't come—then I knew you weren't the man I'd imagined.

> **HELMER**
> Be more explicit; I don't follow you.

> **NORA**
> I've waited now so patiently eight long years—for, my Lord, I know miracles don't come every day. Then this crisis broke over me, and such a certainty filled me: *now* the miraculous event would occur. While Krogstad's letter was lying out there, I never for an instant dreamed that you could give in to his terms. I was so utterly sure you'd say to him: go on, tell your tale to the whole wide world. And when he'd done that—

> **HELMER**
> Yes, what then? When I'd delivered my own wife into shame and disgrace—!

> **NORA**
> When he'd done that, I was so utterly sure that you'd step forward, take the blame on yourself and say: I am the guilty one.

> **HELMER**
> Nora—!

CONTINUED

CONTINUED

> NORA
>
> You're thinking I'd never accept such
> a sacrifice from you? No, of course
> not. But what good would my protests
> be against you? That was the miracle
> I was waiting for, in terror and hope.
> And to stave that off, I would have
> taken my own life.

> HELMER
>
> I'd gladly work for you day and night,
> Nora—and take on pain and depriva-
> tion. But there's no one who gives up
> honor for love.

CLOSE-UP: NORA

> NORA
>
> Millions of women have done just
> that.

BACK TO SHOT

> HELMER
>
> Oh, you think and talk like a silly
> child.

> NORA
>
> Perhaps. But you neither think nor
> talk like the man I could join myself
> to. When your big fright was over—
> and it wasn't from any threat against
> me, only for what might damage
> you—when all the danger was past,
> for you it was just as if nothing had
> happened. I was exactly the same,
> your little lark, your doll, that you'd
> have to handle with double care now
> that I'd turned out so brittle and frail.

[She] gets up.

> NORA (CONT'D)
> Torvald—in that instant it dawned on
> (MORE)

CONTINUED

CONTINUED

> NORA (CONT'D)
> me that for eight years I've been living
> here with a stranger, and that I'd even
> conceived three children—oh, I can't
> stand the thought of it! I could tear
> myself to bits.

> HELMER
> (heavily)
> I see. There's a gulf that's opened be-
> tween us—that's clear. Oh, but Nora,
> can't we bridge it somehow?

> NORA
> The way I am now, I'm no wife
> for you.

> HELMER
> I have the strength to make my-
> self over.

> NORA
> Maybe—if your doll gets taken away.

> HELMER
> But to part! To part from you! No,
> Nora, no—I can't imagine it.

[As she LEAVES THE SHOT.]

> NORA
> . . . All the more reason why it has
> to be.

ON HELMER

[A moment passes.] She REENTERS [THE SHOT] with her coat and a
small overnight bag, which she puts on a chair by the table.

TWO SHOT: NORA AND HELMER

> HELMER
> Nora, Nora, not now! Wait till
> tomorrow.

> NORA
> I can't spend the night in a strange
> man's room.

CONTINUED

CONTINUED

> HELMER
> But couldn't we live here like brother
> and sister—
>
> NORA
> You know very well how long that
> would last.
> (throws her shawl about
> her)
> Good-bye, Torvald. I won't look in on
> the children. I know they're in better
> hands than mine. The way I am now,
> I'm no use to them.
>
> HELMER
> But someday, Nora—someday—?
>
> NORA
> How can I tell? I haven't the least idea
> what'll become of me.
>
> HELMER
> But you're my wife, now and wher-
> ever you go.
>
> NORA
> Listen, Torvald—I've heard that when
> a wife deserts her husband's house
> just as I'm doing, then the law frees
> him from all responsibility. In any
> case, I'm freeing you from being re-
> sponsible. Don't feel yourself bound,
> any more than I will. There has to be
> absolute freedom for us both. Here,
> take your ring back. Give me mine.
>
> HELMER
> That too?
>
> NORA
> That too.
>
> HELMER
> There it is.

CONTINUED

CONTINUED

NORA

Good. Well, now it's all over. I'm putting the keys here. The maids know
all about keeping up the house—
better than I do. Tomorrow, after I've
left town, Kristine will stop by to
pack up everything that's mine from
home. I'd like those things shipped up
to me.

HELMER

Over! All over! Nora, won't you ever
think about me?

NORA

I'm sure I'll think of you often, and
about the children and the house
here.

HELMER

May I write you?

NORA

No—never. You're not to do that.

HELMER

Oh, but let me send you—

NORA

Nothing. Nothing.

HELMER

Or help you if you need it.

NORA

No. I accept nothing from strangers.

HELMER

Nora, can I never be more than a
stranger to you?

NORA

(picking up the overnight
bag)
Ah, Torvald—it would take the greatest miracle of all—

CONTINUED

CONTINUED

> HELMER
> Tell me the greatest miracle!

> NORA
> You and I both would have to trans-
> form ourselves to the point that—Oh,
> Torvald, I've stopped believing in
> miracles.

> HELMER
> But I'll believe. Tell me! Transform
> ourselves to the point that—?

> NORA
> That our living together could be a
> true marriage.

[Nora LEAVES THE SHOT as] she goes out down the hall. Helmer sinks down on a chair by the door, face buried in his hands.

ON HELMER

> HELMER
> Nora! Nora!
> (MORE)

Looking about and rising.

> HELMER (CONT'D)
> Empty. She's gone.
> (a sudden hope leaps in
> him)
> The greatest miracle—?

[OFF] the sound of a DOOR SLAMMING shut.

FADE OUT[11]

Ibsen caused a sensation with this scene when it was first performed in 1879. No characters had ever spoken before with such candor about their roles in marriage. No heroine had ever seemed so real or taken

11. Henrik Ibsen, *A Doll House,* from *Four Major Plays,* trans. Rolf Fjelde (New York: New American Library, 1978), pp. 190–196. Copyright © 1965 by Rolf Fjelde; reprinted by arrangement with NAL Penguin Inc., New York, NY. Please note that the screenplay was not accessible to the authors; camera directions, screenplay format, and all bracketed material have been added by the authors.

such action. Ibsen was vilified. His critics sensed an enemy, correctly: Ibsen wanted absolute freedom and purity with a total purge of existing life. If civilization could be likened to Noah's ark, then "with pleasure I will torpedo the Ark!" he wrote. He was called "an egotist and a bungler," "consistently dirty," and "ugly, nasty, discordant." His admirers were characterized as "lovers of prurience and dabblers in impropriety who are eager to gratify their illicit tastes under the pretence of art." According to one critic, "The unwomanly woman, the unsexed females . . . men and women alike—know that they are doing not only a nasty but an illegal thing." Much of this was written after the production of *Ghosts*, which dealt with syphilis: the same sort of response greeted all his realistic plays about social problems. *Kramer vs. Kramer* received many Oscars: Ibsen's Nora prepared the way.

Nora's departure is far more powerful than Joanna's in *Kramer vs. Kramer*. Nora's actions make no play on sentiment: she does not clutch a child in a final farewell. Instead, she tells Torvald to say good-bye to the children. Nora knows she has to leave, as does Joanna, but Joanna has no idea where she is going. Torvald knows where Nora is going and is refused any chance to write or help her. She leaves as Torvald contemplates self-transformation, but not before Nora invites a confrontation and gives Torvald a chance to martial every argument he can. His responses reveal both his shallowness and the shallowness of their relationship, immediate proof that they are indeed strangers. This lets Ibsen dramatize how little such arguments can mean until a woman is a true individual, fully realized as a human being in her own right.

Ibsen handles this thematic content artfully. He structures it in a series of reverses from the moment Nora declares her intent to leave, placing it within the context of the immediate confrontation between Nora and Torvald. First comes Nora's rejection of Torvald's traditional authority over her, and then follow her need to stand alone, her unwillingness to give in to what others might think, her more sacred duty to herself, her need to rethink what religion is, and her self-acknowledged ignorance of the world. Each reverse begins with Torvald sure he has raised a compelling reason to keep Nora from leaving: each ends as Nora proves the opposite is true. After Torvald forces her to reveal her ultimate disappointment at how he failed her during the blackmail attempt, his last thematic effort to hold her by claiming that men don't give up their honor is crushed by Nora's famous reply: "Millions of women have done just that."

This brings us to several important points about handling thematic material. First, *thematic material, handled properly, is never immediately at stake in a scene, only ultimately.* Every argument Torvald brings up is motivated by his immediate desire to stop Nora; every response by Nora is motivated by her immediate desire to leave. Nora's or Torvald's ideas matter only as they are relevant to immediate conflict. Ibsen doesn't cast his characters aside and have a character called "The Author" step on stage and deliver his points. A dramatist must embed his thematic material in an immediate personal conflict.

Second, nothing that Nora or Torvald says represents Ibsen's theme by itself: *theme emerges from the outcome of immediate, personal conflict.* That outcome represents a dramatist's point of view. Imagine how we would consider the thematic material Ibsen raises if Torvald persuades Nora to stay. The closest Ibsen lets Nora come to stating the theme is in her disillusioned hope for the kind of transformation that would make for a true marriage. Ibsen leaves us to sum up what has happened in the scene to figure out what a true marriage would mean. Clearly, it would involve both their personal transformation and the transformation of a society from one capable of using religion, mores, or the home as excuses for repression to one that valued self-realization.

Last, *the dramatist must succeed in arousing our empathy and sympathy for the characters, or the meaning of their struggle will not matter to us.* Throughout *A Doll House* Ibsen lets us watch Torvald treat Nora as his doll in a kindly but stifling way and Nora accept that role to please him while slowly letting us see the other side to her character that emerges so sharply at the climax.

Why, then, does this scene leave us uneasy? Part of the reason is structural. There is no crisis for Nora, the protagonist, only for Torvald, who moves from certainty to sadness and confusion and then, moved by love after all, to thoughts of changing himself. Nora moves from certainty to certainty. Another part of the reason is motivational. Is it credible that a wife who has been a doll, if one with a secret, could suddenly stand up with the iron displayed by Nora? That has a shock effect, but does anyone living in hope, as Nora has, think through the remorseless alternatives she reaches with such ease?

Unfortunately, it is also Ibsen's partial mishandling of characterization and conflict that makes us uneasy. Where is Nora's immediate struggle? Where is the discovery a character needs to go through to piece together a sense of direction? Even Nora's lack of sentimentality is suspicious: could someone who has lived a life that was itself a cliché of sentimentality emerge, suddenly, completely free of that? Despite the scene's artfulness, there is too strong a sense of the author's direct hand in Nora. She is dangerously close to being that supposed character, "The Author," despite the immediacy of her conflict.

Even Ibsen's artfulness is a problem. It is refreshing to see two characters settle down to a confrontation with the real issues between them. Human beings are not always inchoate models of confusion. But the pattern of reverses is very schematic—sacred vows, home, religion, moral feeling, ignorance of the world, failure of love. They are natural things to deal with in such a situation, but, oh, how neatly laid out by Ibsen. It has little of the feel of reality between Blanche and Mitch in *A Streetcar Named Desire.*

Ideas can appear directly in a scene if there is a real excitement about them, a sense of their discovery and delight or terror by characters, with sudden jabs of illumination. Even then, however, the situation between characters must be immediate and what is at stake personal, whether marriage as in George Bernard Shaw's *Man and Superman* or the well-being of a patient as in Peter Schaffer's stage and screenplay *Equus.* The efficacy of psychotherapy is important in *Ordinary People,* but experienced through the protagonist's need for help and the presence of a warm professional. *All the President's Men* deals with Watergate through the immediate efforts of two reporters who piece together the truth. That sense of discovery is absent from Nora in *A Doll House.* It is a scene to admire that has faults to avoid.

Let's compare it with Joanna's cross-examination from *Kramer vs. Kramer.*

A Courtroom Scene from Kramer vs. Kramer

Joanna has returned after abandoning Ted and Billy and demanded Billy from Ted. As we saw, he refuses her and storms away. Both get lawyers and find themselves in court involved in a custody battle. In the following scene, Joanna is put on the stand by her lawyer, Gressen, and then cross-examined by Ted's lawyer, Shaunessy.

FADE IN:

INT.   COURTROOM   (EST) DAY

ON THE DOOR

as Ted enters, looks around [PULL BACK.]

[COURTROOM]

Mrs. Willewska sits in one of the back rows, wearing her best Easter hat. Ted pauses by her, thanks her for coming.

Several rows in front of her is Margaret. Ted crosses to her, they talk quietly between themselves for a few moments. Then Ted moves on to a table at the front of the room where John Shaunessy waits.

ON THE DOORS AT BACK OF COURTROOM

as they swing open and Joanna, along with her lawyer, A MR.

CONTINUED

CONTINUED

GRESSEN, [ENTERS THE SHOT]. THE CAMERA PANS WITH THEM as they walk to the front of the room and take their seats at the table opposite Ted and his lawyer.

>   CLERK
> Oyez, oyez . . . The Supreme Court of
> the State of New York, New York
> County, Judge Atkins presiding, is
> now in session. All rise.

WIDE SHOT

as the JUDGE enters and takes her seat.

Opening business of the court . . . Gressen (Joanna's lawyer) gets to his feet.

>   GRESSEN
> Your honor. As our first witness I
> would like to call Joanna Kramer.

TWO SHOT: TED & SHAUNESSY

The lawyer leans across to Ted.

>   SHAUNESSY
>   (stage whisper)
> Real direct. Motherhood . . . They're
> going right for the throat.

WIDE SHOT

as Joanna gets to her feet, crosses to the witness stand and is sworn in.

Note: Throughout the following we continually CROSSCUT to Ted Kramer, leaning forward, listening intently. It becomes evident that, in spite of himself, there are moments he feels great compassion for Joanna.

>   GRESSEN
> Now then, Mrs. Kramer, would you
> tell the court how long you were
> married?

>   JOANNA
> Six years.

CONTINUED

CONTINUED

> GRESSEN
> And would you describe those years
> as happy?
>
> JOANNA
> The first couple, yes, but after that it
> became increasingly difficult.
>
> GRESSEN
> Mrs. Kramer, did you ever work in a
> job while you were married to your
> ex-husband?
>
> JOANNA
> No, I did not.
>
> GRESSEN
> Did you wish to?
>
> JOANNA
> Yes. I tried to talk to Ted—my ex-
> husband—about it, but he wouldn't
> listen. He refused to discuss it in any
> serious way. I remember one time he
> said I probably couldn't get a job that
> would pay enough to hire a baby-sitter
> for Billy.
>
> GRESSEN
> Tell me, Mrs. Kramer, are you em-
> ployed at the present time?
>
> JOANNA
> Yes, I work for Jantzen as a sportswear
> designer.
>
> GRESSEN
> And what is your present salary?
>
> JOANNA
> I make thirty-one thousand dollars a
> year.

TED   REACTION

stunned.

[BACK TO SCENE]

GRESSEN
(switching tactics)
Mrs. Kramer, do you love your child?

JOANNA
(emphatically)
Yes. Very much.

GRESSEN
And yet you chose to leave him?

There is a long pause, then, speaking carefully, with great thought:

JOANNA
Yes . . . Look, during the last five
years we were married, I had . . . I was
getting more and more . . . unhappy,
more and more frustrated. I needed to
talk to somebody. I needed to find out
if it was me, if I was going crazy, or
what. But every time I turned to Ted—
my ex-husband—he couldn't handle
it. He became very . . . I don't know,
very threatened. I mean, whenever I
would bring up anything he would act
like it was some kind of personal attack. Anyway, we became more and
more separate . . . more and more isolated from one another. Finally, I had
no other choice, I had to leave. And
because of my ex-husband's attitude—
his unwillingness to deal with my
feelings, I had come to have almost no
self-esteem . . .
(with feeling)
At the time I left, I sincerely believed
that there was something wrong with
me—that my son would be better off
without me. It was only when I got to
California and started into therapy I
began to realize I wasn't a terrible per-
(MORE)

CONTINUED

> JOANNA (CONT'D)
> son. And that just because I needed
> some creative and emotional outlet
> other than my child, that didn't make
> me unfit to be a mother.

> GRESSEN
> (to the judge)
> Your honor, I would like to place in
> evidence a report on Mrs. Kramer's
> therapy by her therapist, Dr. Elinore
> Freedman of La Jolla, California.

And with that he hands both the judge and Shaunessy a thick sheaf
of papers. Then, turning his attention back to Joanna:

> GRESSEN
> Mrs. Kramer, why did you set up resi-
> dence in New York?

> JOANNA
> Because my son is here. And his fa-
> ther is here. As a mother, I don't want
> my child to be separated from his
> father.

> GRESSEN
> Mrs. Kramer, can you tell the court
> why you are asking for custody?

There is a pause, then:

> JOANNA
> Because he's my child . . . Because I
> love him. I know I left my son, I know
> that's a terrible thing to do. Believe
> me, I have to live with that every day
> of my life. But just because I'm a
> woman, don't I have a right to the
> same hopes and dreams as a man?
> Don't I have a right to a life of my
> own? Is that so awful? Is my pain any
> less because I'm a woman? Are my
> (MORE)

CONTINUED

230

CONTINUED

> JOANNA (CONT'D)
> feelings any cheaper? I left my child—
> I know there is no excuse for that. But
> since then, I have gotten help. I have
> worked hard to become a whole hu-
> man being. I don't think my son
> should be punished for that. Billy's
> only six. He needs me. I'm not saying
> he doesn't need his father, but he
> needs me more. I'm his mother.

There is a beat of silence, then:

> GRESSEN
> Thank you, Mrs. Kramer. I have no
> further questions.

ON SHAUNESSY

as he stands, collects his papers from the table and, taking his own
sweet time, crosses to Joanna.

[COURTROOM]

> SHAUNESSY
> Now then, Mrs. Kramer, you said you
> were married six years. Is that correct?

> JOANNA
> Yes.

> SHAUNESSY
> In all that time did your husband ever
> strike you or abuse you physically in
> any way.

> JOANNA
> No.

> SHAUNESSY
> Did your husband strike or physically
> abuse his child in any way?

> JOANNA
> No.

CONTINUED

CONTINUED

> SHAUNESSY
> Would you describe your husband as
> an alcoholic?

>> JOANNA
> No.

> SHAUNESSY
> A heavy drinker?

>> JOANNA
> No.

> SHAUNESSY
> Was he unfaithful?

>> JOANNA
> No.

> SHAUNESSY
> Did he ever fail to provide for you?

>> JOANNA
> No.

> SHAUNESSY
> (wry smile)
> Well, I can certainly understand why
> you left him.

>> GRESSEN
> Objection.

> SHAUNESSY
> (switching his line of
> questioning)
> How long do you plan to live in New
> York, Mrs. Kramer?

>> JOANNA
> Permanently.

Note: During the early part of Shaunessy's cross-examination,
Joanna has been very forthright, very sure of herself. Now, as he starts
getting tougher, she begins to falter.

CONTINUED

CONTINUED

> SHAUNESSY
> Permanently?
> (smiles, like a shark smiles)
> Mrs. Kramer, how many boyfriends
> have you had—permanently?

ON JOANNA

Her head snaps back as though she'd been hit.

[BACK TO SCENE]

> GRESSEN
> Objection, your honor, on the grounds
> of vagueness.

> JUDGE
> I'll allow it.

> JOANNA
> I don't recall.

> SHAUNESSY
> (boring in)
> How many lovers have you had—
> *permanently?*

> JOANNA
> (looks toward Gressen for
> help)
> I don't recall.

> SHAUNESSY
> More than three, less than thirty-
> three—*permanently?*

Gressen is again on his feet, outraged.

> GRESSEN
> *Objection!*

> JUDGE
> The witness will answer, please.

> JOANNA
> (almost a whisper)
> Somewhere in-between.

CONTINUED

CONTINUED

> SHAUNESSY
> Do you have a lover now?

Joanna is silent.

> SHAUNESSY (CONT'D)
> (to the judge)
> Your honor, I would request a direct
> answer to a direct question. Does she
> have a lover?

> JUDGE
> I'll allow that. The witness will an-
> swer, please.

> JOANNA
> (in a whisper)
> Yes.

> SHAUNESSY
> Is that . . . *permanent?*

By now Joanna is becoming thoroughly rattled.

> JOANNA
> I . . . I don't know . . .

> SHAUNESSY
> Then, we don't really know, do we,
> when you say "permanently," if
> you're planning to remain in New
> York, or even to keep the child, for
> that matter, since you've never really
> done anything in your life that was
> continuing, stable, that could be re-
> garded as permanent.

ON PETITIONER'S TABLE

Gressen jumps to his feet.

> GRESSEN
> Objection! I must ask that the coun-
> sel be prevented from harassing the
> witness.

[BACK TO SCENE]

> JUDGE
> Sustained.

> SHAUNESSY
> (a new attack)
> Mrs. Kramer, how can you consider
> yourself a fit mother when you have
> been a failure at virtually every re-
> lationship you have taken on as an
> adult?

> GRESSEN
> (red in the face)
> *Objection!*

> JUDGE
> Sustained.

> SHAUNESSY
> I'll ask it in another way. What was
> the longest personal relationship you
> have had in your life—other than par-
> ents and girlfriends?

> JOANNA
> (rattled)
> Ah . . . I guess I'd have to say . . . with
> my child.

> SHAUNESSY
> (wonder, irony)
> Whom you've seen twice in a year?
> Mrs. Kramer, your ex-husband, wasn't
> he the longest personal relationship
> in your life?

> JOANNA
> (reluctantly)
> I suppose . . .

> SHAUNESSY
> Would you speak up, Mrs. Kramer? I
> couldn't hear you.

CONTINUED

CONTINUED

>JOANNA
>(louder)

Yes.

>SHAUNESSY

How long was that?

>JOANNA

We were married two years before the
baby. And then four very difficult
years.

>SHAUNESSY

So, you were a failure at the longest,
most important relationship in your
life.

>GRESSEN

Objection!

>JUDGE

Overruled. The witness's opinion on
this is relevant.

>JOANNA

I was *not* a failure.

>SHAUNESSY
>(sarcastic)

Oh? What do you call it then—a success? The marriage ended in a divorce.

So angry she forgets her cool:

>JOANNA

I consider it less my failure than his.

>SHAUNESSY
>(seizes on this)

Congratulations, Mrs. Kramer. You
have just rewritten matrimonial law.
You were *both* divorced, Mrs. Kramer.

>GRESSEN
>(on his feet)

Objection!

CONTINUED

CONTINUED

> SHAUNESSY
> (to the judge)
> Your honor, I'd like to ask what this
> model of stability and respectability
> has ever succeeded at?
> (to Joanna)
> Mrs. Kramer, were you a failure at the
> longest, most important personal rela-
> tionship in your life?

CLOSE ON JOANNA

who sits silently.

[BACK TO SCENE]

> JUDGE
> This is cross-examination so I'll allow
> it, Mr. Gressen. Please answer the
> question, Mrs. Kramer.

> JOANNA
> (whisper)
> *It* did not succeed.

> SHAUNESSY
> (suddenly fierce)
> *Not it* . . . Not it, Mrs. Kramer—*you.*
> Were *you* a failure at the most impor-
> tant personal relationship of your life?

CLOSER IN ON JOANNA

Silence.

> SHAUNESSY VO (CONT'D)
> *Were you?*

EXTREME CLOSE-UP: JOANNA

> JOANNA
> (barely audible)
> Yes.

WIDE SHOT

Shaunessy smiles, turns his back on Joanna and walks towards the

CONTINUED

CONTINUED

respondent's table.

>   SHAUNESSY
>   No further questions.

CLOSER IN ON THE TABLE

as Shaunessy sits down next to Ted.

>   TED
>   (leaning over, in a whisper)
>   Jesus Christ. Did you have to be so
>   rough on her?

>   SHAUNESSY
>   (tough)
>   Do you want the kid, or don't you?

ON JOANNA

Shaken, she gets down from the witness stand, crosses to the petitioner's table without looking at Ted. She sits, leans across to her
lawyer and whispers something in his ear. As he nods

ON THE JUDGE

>   JUDGE
>   If the petitioner has no further wit-
>   nesses, we will hear the respondent
>   tomorrow morning at 9:30.

>   FADE OUT[12]

The drama of the wholly realized woman coming home to a reunited
family remains to be written: there have been no successful sequels to
A Doll House or *Kramer vs. Kramer*. That diminishes neither the
achievement nor popularity of these two dramas. Both underscore what
an on-going process the attempt to achieve sexual equality is in Western
society: we can imagine the problem, but not yet see its solution.

We raise this point about social process to confront the weaknesses in
Kramer vs. Kramer. At no point do religion, conventional mores, con-
formity, and society play the same role as in Torvald's desperate attempt
to hold onto Nora. Shaunessy asperses Joanna's character in a way that
has become a cliché when he asks about the number of her lovers, and

12. Benton, *Kramer vs. Kramer*, pp. 101–111.

Joanna herself admits how wrong it was to leave her child. In both cases
a conventional moral outlook is taken for granted. Nora, on the other
hand, is overtly defiant. What have morals to do with me? is, in effect,
her response to Torvald's conventional use of them. Nora recoils from
taking a lover earlier in the play, but at the end she clearly tells Torvald
to forget her and look to others and implies she will do the same as a
right of self-exploration.

Religion doesn't come up at all in *Kramer vs. Kramer,* though its connection with the family in conventional thinking is apparent. Similarly,
what society thinks and expects is unexamined: *Kramer vs. Kramer* as-
sumes conventional attitudes toward both, which is made apparent by
Joanna's conventional sense of guilt. There is no guilty tone in Nora
when she takes her stand.

If we had only these dramas to deduce their societies from, Ibsen's
would evoke a sense of individuals in a complex of issues, Benton's a
picture of individuals almost isolated in egocentric concerns. As a consequence, Joanna is a less important character than Nora. Nora refuses
to accept *any* preconceptions about proper behavior—we can imagine
her shocking Shaunessy on the stand, instead of the reverse. Nora is a
revolutionary; Joanna, a confused woman operating within the prevalent attitudes of existing middle-class society. Ibsen is after a profound
social transformation, ready to "torpedo the Ark," but not Benton in
Kramer vs. Kramer. If you're going to tackle the remaking of woman,
why pull your punches as *Kramer vs. Kramer* ultimately does? *Kramer
vs. Kramer* is a popular film and will have a long afterlife in reruns and
video rentals; *A Doll House* will be given new productions repeatedly.

This said, what Benton does choose to handle comes across with
greater credibility than what Ibsen achieves at the end of *A Doll House.*
A Doll House prepares us to accept a defiant Nora, but not the revolutionary. *Kramer vs. Kramer* establishes characters who accept their society in general, but wish to change their roles within their affluent,
middle-class world. At no point do Joanna and Ted, pursuing their own
interests, imply Ibsen's kind of revolt. They remain consistent.

Nora, once she drops her disguise as a doll, is remorseless and without conflict. Joanna is fallible. She begins in confidence and is nearly
shattered by Shaunessy. His first attack makes her leaving Ted seem an
exercise in whimsy. His next attack undermines her character: lovers, a
lack of permanence, failure in her most important relationship. She
tries to maintain that their *marriage* ("it") failed and that Ted was at
fault for his insensitivity, but she is driven to see and admit that *she*
failed, too. She grows as a character in this scene as the action works on
her. She reacts; she changes. She moves Ted and us. We feel for her, and
we must feel for a character if thematic material is to matter to us. Nora

can shock us, but her certainty keeps her at a distance.

We said the audience must care about your characters' immediate situation for thematic material to be effective, too. Ted's situation dominates the story before Joanna reappears, and so this scene is our first chance to develop feelings about her. The earlier part of the scene with Gressen disposes us favorably to her, not because she is now making $31,000 a year, but because she has struggled to change herself. When she reveals the nature of that struggle, we are made to feel it is an on-going thing. She does not march relentlessly to conclusions like Nora, but struggles to make clear as much to herself as to Shaunessy what has happened to her. Look at her language.

> I was getting more and more . . . unhappy. . . . He became very . . . I don't know, very threatened. . . . Anyway, we became more and more separate . . . more and more isolated . . .

Joanna searches and discovers here; she doesn't make a speech. Nora speaks as if she knows everything already. Look at Joanna's language where her dialogue becomes overtly thematic:

> Don't I have a right to a life of my own? . . . Is my pain any less because I'm a woman?

Earlier in this same speech she asks:

> But just because I'm a woman, don't I have a right to the same hopes and dreams as a man?

Joanna asks questions; Nora delivers certainties. Joanna lets us come up with the answers. When Shaunessy turns on Joanna and forces the admission of failure out of her, we sense his victory is Pyrrhic. She wins the moral victory. Just how should a woman struggling to find herself behave? Why shouldn't there be lovers? Why wouldn't there be failures? Of course she went into therapy. How natural to come back for her child when she realized she was normal to want a life and occupation of her own! Her effort to blame the marriage—"it"—rather than herself for failure is only too human.

We already care about Ted; now both Ted and Joanna seem right to us. How are we to put them together? What would be the ideal marriage, that real transformation of male and female roles and conceptions of self that Nora alludes to at the end of *A Doll House?* We might wish Benton had Ibsen's breadth or that he had not chosen to speak about "wholeness" or indicated Joanna had gone to California and gone into therapy. One is a cliché; the other, now a stock laugh. Although Benton and Ibsen raise similar issues, we live them with Joanna; we listen to them with Nora. It is a crucial difference.

VALUES AND MORAL URGENCY

A dramatist creates, affirms or denies, values. He can't help himself. Creating, affirming, or denying values is built into the art form. A scene and story always affirm some values and deny others.

Look at the two scenes we've just evaluated. Torvald and Nora struggle over values. He offers her the values of religion, propriety, morals, or just caution before the world when ignorant. He interprets them in particular ways; each time Nora reinterprets them or asserts a counter value. Joanna asks if a woman doesn't have a right to a life of her own. Never mind how we would ordinarily, unthinkingly answer such a question: the scene makes us agree—Yes, of course!—enough to forgive at least a temporary abandonment of her child, both creating and affirming through the conflict the value of self-realization. Suppose Shaunessy had proved the opposite? Then self-realization for a woman would be experienced in the scene as having little or no value.

Values are often what are ultimately at stake in a scene. Bonasera in *The Godfather* forsakes one set of values for another motivated by vengeance. His change lends credibility to the Godfather's values: we feel that in some circumstances there is more justice in them than in conventional justice. Bishop Vergérus in *Fanny and Alexander* makes us feel the hollowness of conventional belief and of the attempt to maintain the form of a belief in order to maintain power. There is no doubt Bishop Vergérus revolts us with his treatment of Alexander. Through that, the value of what he stands for is both revealed and spurned by the author.

Although values and theme obviously overlap, values emerge primarily from the outcome of the conflict, and theme is embodied in the on-going action. There are no techniques for handling values—they are the natural outcome of your story.

Here is the core of the final exchange between Michael and Julie in *Tootsie* after he has given up his female impersonation as Dorothy in a spectacular public unveiling. Julie is the girl he fell in love with while disguised as Dorothy. They have not seen each other since his unveiling.

JULIE
I read your reviews from Syracuse.
Surprised you went up there—you
were pretty hot after your "unveiling." You didn't have to go up there to
work.

CONTINUED

CONTINUED

> MICHAEL
> I didn't *have* to . . . but I *wanted* to.
> (then)
> It's a good play. It deserves to be seen.
> (beat)
> Besides, I made a promise.

Julie slows, stops, and then turns to him.

> JULIE
> (soberly)
> I miss Dorothy.

> MICHAEL
> You don't have to. She's right here.
> *I'm* Dorothy.

He takes her hands in his.

> MICHAEL (CONT'D)
> Listen . . . The hard part's over—we
> were already best friends. Don't hold
> it against me that I wear pants.[13]

This is very simple but value and theme rich. First, Michael, despite being a hot ticket after revealing his brilliant performance as Dorothy, hasn't capitalized on it, but gone to Syracuse to do a friend's play. Friendship and a promise are affirmed as higher values than grabbing fame and fortune, which was available to him and what he thought he wanted at first. Second, Julie frankly admits she misses the woman Michael played, who had become—impossibly, for Michael—Julie's best friend. His assertion that "she's right here" carries layers of meaning. She is right there: Michael was Dorothy. But Dorothy *is* there, too: Michael is *still* Dorothy in the sense that what we are able to create remains a part of us. Third, it is possible for a man to develop a "feminine" empathy. Julie's choice to stay with Michael affirms the value of that transformation in Michael.

There is more to values than this. We said survival is what is often ultimately at stake in a scene or story. That survival is always an attempt to survive in some particular way at some particular time in some particular place by some particular character. His or her survival—or

13. Gelbart, *Tootsie*, pp. 143–144.

failure—affirms some values, denies others, and creates perhaps yet others. Alexander tries to protect his individuality, Nora and Terry to gain their rights, Blanche to affirm her right to a new chance. Their success or failure comes as the final outcome of struggle—urgent, desperate, deeply felt. We are made to feel those values, their rightness or wrongness, passionately. Every writer worth his salt communicates a sense of moral urgency about the values involved in his story. Values emerge through the story's outcome, but that outcome emerges in the white heat of the characters' passionate, ultimate efforts in the crisis and climax.

Moral urgency is the opposite of a writer's pushing some conventional set of morals. A writer may give little attention to any abstract presentation of whatever moral system might be implicit in his treatment of conflict: he is a playwright, not a minister. What a dramatist does communicate, if he is successful, is the truth of the conflict in each story. Something is true and right in this particular instance; something else, perhaps, in another. A dramatist must be free of preconceived ideas about the possibilities of human behavior and meaning: he must remain free to see the truth of any imagined conflict, however conservative or liberal he may be as a man. This, too, is not a technique to be mastered, but a fundamental observation: any belief that appears in any drama must be tested through the conflict in some particular character. We come full circle here: we stress that a writer creates truth more than finds it and that such a creation is a matter of vision—craft and vision. What is a vision without a sense of urgency and rightness?

Your Fifth Assignment

Review the last three assignments. Any scene you write for this assignment must fulfill their requirements successfully. Next, develop some simply stated theme like crime doesn't pay, the truth sets us free, alcoholism is a bad thing, or abortion can never be (or can be) justified. Don't just grab at anything: what has aroused *your* passions recently? What ideas have triggered the most thought? Then write a scene in which no one speaks the theme but the action embodies it. Have the theme emerge from how your conflict develops and turns out. Consider what value you want us to feel about your theme. Suppose you write a psychological study of a character suffering from some personal misconception and the action of your scene is the gradual revelation of the truth. If that truth resolves your protagonist's conflict we will think: the truth sets us free. If not, we will think: truth does not set us free.

Remember we must care about your characters—they must arouse our feelings—or we will not think about their situation. Remember what is immediately at stake must be something immediate and personal, not your theme. Remember to let your characters struggle, discover, and reveal themselves. Let them grow because what they must do to resolve their conflict changes them. Let them care passionately about solving their immediate problem.

Don't hesitate to use Ibsen's technique of using reverses to dramatize particular aspects of your theme. Don't let that technique lure you into becoming too schematic. Feel free to use the courtroom procedure of *Kramer vs. Kramer* if it fits your story naturally. Don't let that lure you into a mere recitation of information.

Pay attention to how your characters speak, too: is their speech appropriate to them? Can you define them further through how they talk? Does their speech reflect their process of discovery as they grope for the solution to their conflict? Or do they speak with such certainty that they lose credibility? Is there an immediate need for any information they divulge? Does that information influence the immediate action?

Give yourself the freedom of a first draft to explore your characters, conflict, and particular thematic material, and then go back and examine it as we suggested in your last assignment. Make sure you haven't missed the point, that your characters don't debate, that the thought you want to leave us with is triggered by the action. Just what values are you communicating to us with moral urgency? Are they what you intended?

Then rewrite your scene, the more passionately felt by your characters and the more thoroughly thought out by you, the more entertaining and exciting for your audience.

10. Writing the Miniscreenplay

It is time to undertake a longer project, a miniscreenplay of 15–25 pages. Although all writers have individual ways of working, a very specific story development process is expected of a writer professionally when he attempts to sell a story to a studio or network. Such potential buyers first expect to see some brief statement of a story, variously referred to as an "idea" or a "premise." If the writer succeeds in making a sale, he will be asked to write a treatment before being allowed to write the script. You should prepare both a premise and treatment for your miniscreenplay as a way of developing your own dramatic thinking for a story and of familiarizing yourself with forms expected from you professionally.

A Word on Superstructure

We stressed that the same dramatic structure applies to both individual scenes and entire screenplays. Both scenes and screenplays must establish character and conflict, develop these to some point of crisis, and reach a climax and resolution. A story contained within a scene accomplishes all of these within that concentrated space; a story told in a screenplay places such scenes within a larger application of the same structure.

Thus the same dramatic structure exists on two levels:

1. The dramatic structure within each scene.

2. The dramatic structure of the entire screenplay, which is in turn primarily made up of scenes. The plot is the dramatic structure of such scenes developed to tell your story.

We also stressed that structural terms are not abstractions but reflections of particular sequences of action. A reverse is one moment of action-reaction within a scene; a complication is a scene-causing additional problem that leads to action on the part of your protagonist. Now, for a screenplay, you must think of acts. Acts reflect particular sequences of action already familiar to you through our association of BEGINNING with establishing character and conflict, MIDDLE with developing character and conflict to the crisis, END with climax and resolution. Let's look at how these apply to acts in a little more detail.

Act 1 (BEGINNING): Establishing Character and Conflict

Typically, Act 1 introduces your characters, their initial situation, the problem that will disrupt their lives, and their first efforts to deal with that problem. Because their efforts are opposed, an antagonist or obstacle also is introduced and conflict generated. Your protagonist may try several ways of dealing with the conflict, without, at first, having any clear focus for achieving a solution.

Kramer vs. Kramer begins with Joanna's abandonment of Ted. But Act 1 does not end there: it continues through a series of scenes as Ted and Billy struggle to survive as a family unit. Ted and Billy succeed, growing together and changing their values. Then Joanna reappears and demands Billy back. The threat to the family takes on a new and more serious form. Ted decides to resist. We saw the scene in which he storms out on Joanna after meeting her in the restaurant. That is the end of the first act.

The effort that the protagonist must make to succeed in ending the conflict is defined at the end of Act 1. In Ted's case, he must fight and win a custody battle. In *Places in the Heart,* the wife must plant and harvest a cotton crop. Another way of putting it is that the type of conflict (man versus man, Joanna versus Ted in *Kramer vs. Kramer*) joins with the immediate problem (defending the family unit of Ted and Billy).

Act 2 (MIDDLE): Developing Character and Conflict to Crisis

Act 2 develops the action that the protagonist realizes he must take at the end of Act 1 to the crisis where it seems his or her effort is going to fail. In *Kramer vs. Kramer* Act 2 centers around the vivid courtroom struggle for Billy, which reaches the crisis when Ted loses. In *On the Waterfront* Terry tries to find a reasonable way to deal with his situation until his brother is killed.

Typically, Act 2 takes less time than Act 1 because of the greater focus of the action. There may be many twists and turns to the action in Act 2, yet they are all generally related to the *particular* effort on the part of the protagonist now the focus of the action. But the crisis provokes a sharper focus, for at the end of Act 2 the protagonist discovers the final form the obstacle to ending the conflict takes: Ted faces the loss of Billy; Terry knows he must personally confront Johnny Friendly.

Act 3 (END): Handling the Climax and Resolution

We saw earlier how the dramatic obstacle changes constantly in effective writing, whether in Mrs. Robinson's artful manipulations of Ben in *The Graduate* or in the bishop's moral terrorism with Alexander in *Fanny and Alexander*. The final form of that obstacle appears at the end of Act 2 and is acted on decisively in Act 3. Terry strikes against Johnny Friendly. Ted accommodates himself and Billy to the court's decree. Michael "destroys" Dorothy in *Tootsie*. Michael, in *The Godfather*, assassinates all his enemies after Don Corleone's death.

Just as crisis and climax lead to revelation and resolution in a scene, they do in a screenplay. Ted rises to the challenge of losing Billy (the final obstacle) with deep feeling and humanity, while Joanna discovers she can't take Billy away from Ted (revelation and resolution). Terry discovers testifying against Johnny Friendly (the final obstacle) isn't enough and finds it in himself to confront and overcome him directly (revelation and resolution).

Don't write your screenplay with act breaks: acts are a way of organizing your dramatic thinking about particular sequences of the necessary, dramatic action your protagonist takes to overcome the problem facing him in order to end the conflict. Teleplays for series are often written with act breaks, however. If the miniscreenplay you undertake is conceived as a teleplay, then you should include actual act breaks. Those breaks are not the ones a viewer sees, however: those are determined by commercial breaks. You might want to anticipate those (there are, minimally, four for an hour, two for a half-hour show). Try to use curtain lines in the appropriate scenes.

Remember two simple points. First, though every scene is dramatically structured, not every scene has equal weight. Some are more obviously transitional than others, as the scene in which Terry struggles with Edie to decide his next step in *On the Waterfront* or the earlier scene in which Johnny Friendly sends Charley to get Terry under control. The scene between Alexander and Bishop Vergérus is obviously one of the major moments of the story's conflict, as is the scene between Terry and Charley in the cab in *On the Waterfront*. Length and importance aren't always linked. Important as the scene between Ted and Shaunessy is when Ted learns the court's verdict, it is not a long scene.

Second, remember the camera offers you great fluidity and economy in moving from place to place, setting mood, or conveying information. Use individual shots or miniscenes to give information, establish mood, or help link and develop your scenes. *Kramer vs. Kramer* begins with alternating shots of Joanna and Ted at home and at work. In *On the Waterfront* we saw the simple shot of the cab driving Charley into the River Street garage where Gerry G. is waiting. *Tootsie* starts with alternating highly compressed miniscenes and insert shots of Michael's scrapbook. Some scenes take place in one setting; others are more fluid, as is the climax from *On the Waterfront*. Even the simple scene between Michael-as-Dorothy and Les in *Tootsie* moves back and forth from a restaurant table and a dance floor.

The Premise

The premise is the brief initial statement of your story and its dramatic structure. It shouldn't run more than two typewritten pages double-spaced. A premise starts with an indication of your main characters, the kind of conflict, the theme or themes that may be involved, and the point of departure—what problem sets off the conflict. This is written in clear summary statements, act by act, in three paragraphs.

Because the form is so brief, mention only the most significant actions, not the many details or transitions that would appear in an actual script. Done properly, a premise gives you a first opportunity to define the nature of your story and to test yourself for a cohesive view of the development of the conflict.

Before you write your premise, write a brief overview of the story like the following sample overview for *Kramer vs. Kramer:*

> *Kramer vs. Kramer* is a contemporary marital and family drama about the changing roles of men and women in the American family. It is centered around Ted, a hard-working but initially insensitive husband; his wife Joanna, an attractive but confused woman; and their young son, Billy. Joanna, suffering from years of neglect and insensitivity, with a deep need to find herself as an individual, abandons both Ted and Billy. Ted and his values are transformed as he becomes a devoted father. He struggles to keep Billy with him when Joanna reappears and demands Billy for herself after she and Ted have been divorced. A tough custody battle is fought, with a surprise ending from its victor, Joanna, who is unable to take Billy from Ted.

This gives you a useful perspective with its thumbnail description of character, situation, and necessary elements of back story—Ted's insensitivity and Joanna's long-suffering confusion. We see what the story will be about, what sets the action in motion, how the characters change, and what some of the key complications are. The conflict is man versus man. Ted must learn to cope with Billy and enters into a major confrontation with Joanna. Ted's relationship with Billy is immediately at stake. The obstacle to its success changes from Joanna's disappearance to her threat when she reappears. From the overview we get a sense of the story's dramatic changes and an idea of what the crisis and climax are. The theme is apparent.

Write your actual premise with your overview in mind. Clearly mark each act, as in the following example of Act 1 from *Kramer vs. Kramer:*

PREMISE: *Kramer vs. Kramer*

Act 1. Joanna leaves Ted after he has had an especially successful day at the office. Dumbfounded, unbelieving, Ted tries to hold onto her, but after telling Ted she must find herself and no longer loves him, she abandons him and Billy. Several scenes show how Ted and Billy grow close as Ted learns to put Billy ahead of his work, which had been all-important before. They overcome memories of Joanna, which haunt them at first. A sympathetic neighbor helps Ted, while he learns that placing Billy first undercuts his position at work. His and Billy's relationship is succeeding when Joanna reappears, self-supporting and self-confident after two years of therapy. Ted and Joanna are now divorced. Joanna demands Billy from Ted: he refuses. He will fight to preserve his new, hard-won family.

A particularly important scene, such as the one in which Joanna leaves Ted or the later one in which she returns, should get individual attention, though in a very summary way. For the rest, indicate the thrust of the action clearly so that, without actually listing them in detail, a reader would know what sort of scenes to expect. Keep in view the thematic slant and importance of the action. Mention elements like Ted's compromising his position at work in order to be closer to Billy because it underscores how his character changes and because he will lose his job at a critical moment in Act 2 during the custody battle. Only critical details appear in a premise.

The premise makes clear how our emotions will be roused in a story. We're told about characters involved in a conflict who have urgent reasons for acting from eminently understandable motivations. In *Kramer vs. Kramer* we see that a child is involved and that the characters change in critical ways because of their immediate impact on each other. Ted does this, which makes Joanna do this, because . . . which results in . . . A premise makes clear the primary action-reaction collisions of your main characters.

Think of a story you want to develop. Review the various sources or techniques for finding or developing stories we touched on earlier, or take a scene written for an earlier assignment that you want to treat in greater depth. What theme does your story embody? Who are the major characters? What urgent problem must they solve? How does it first appear? How does their attempt to solve the problem develop? Who or what opposes their effort to end the conflict?

Boil your reveries and notes down to a premise. Write a clear introductory paragraph giving an overview of theme, situation, character, conflict, and story development. Then treat each act in a paragraph in the style we have just shown. If you're dissatisfied, revise your premise. Change your characters. Rethink your acts, the main thrust of the action, or theme. Write a new premise. Don't go on until you feel your work is coherent and interesting and you have a clear delineation of the primary action-reaction collisions of your protagonist and antagonist.

The Treatment

A successful premise can excite interest but cannot give more than a bare overview. The real test in preparing to write a long script comes with the treatment, *a full narration of the dramatic action of your story scene by scene.*

Narrate your treatment in the style of an omniscient author who knows what each step of the action will be and what the motivations of his characters are at any moment. Take a page instead of paragraph to give an overview of your characters, conflict, and theme. Tell us how your characters look and what their ages are. If it was for *Kramer vs. Kramer,* you would expand on Joanna's discontent or on Ted's insensitivity. Any elements from back story necessary to understand the present situation should be mentioned. Give a broader statement of the theme and what it means when Joanna doesn't take Billy away from Ted after having won the right to do so.

Then narrate the action of your story as it will take place scene by scene, within each clearly marked act, from your protagonist's point of view. Double-space and write in the present tense. Terry does this because . . . Michael does this, which leads to . . . Use your premise as your starting point. Do not include shots or dialogue. Do not depend on novelistic statements like "Several scenes show Ted and Billy grow close." That's only appropriate for the premise. In a treatment you narrate the actual scenes of your story and show their connection with each other.

Act 1 should clearly establish and develop character and conflict and show what your protagonist first tries to do to overcome the obstacle or antagonist confronting him. Show how your protagonist's attempts to end the conflict reach a point of clarity when he or she settles on some single course of action, like planting cotton in *Places in the Heart* or fighting a custody battle in *Kramer vs. Kramer.* That point will come quickly for you in your short piece.

Acts 2 and 3 should be narrated with similar immediacy and clarity, making it apparent how your protagonist's effort, scene by scene, reaches the crisis and then develops into the intensely focused final push shown in Act 3's climax. Since you are writing a treatment and not a script, bring out the thematic implications of your critical scenes that would in a script emerge in our reflections through our emotional involvement. Bring out the nature of any critical revelations in the climax and the process of change and discovery in the earlier action. Conclude with a statement that ties the outcome of the action with meaning.

Give more space to important scenes, such as the confrontations between Ted and Joanna in *Kramer vs. Kramer,* Charley and Terry in *On the Waterfront,* or Alexander and the bishop in *Fanny and Alexander. Narrate the critical reverses in such scenes.* We need these to understand how Blanche in *A Streetcar Named Desire* attempts to hold onto Mitch or is able to plumb motivation to the depth that she does. We need to have some specific idea about the content and manner of Nora's confrontation with Torvald in *A Doll's House.* A treatment tests your understanding of those critical moments as well as how well you communicate them to others.

Your characters should be coherent and interesting. Your narration must show that their motivations are credible and that they act in immediate cause-and-effect ways on each other. Make clear the immediate cause of the action and motivation of your story—your point of departure. Make clear the immediate causes for action in succeeding scenes. *A clear immediate cause-and-effect development between your scenes should be apparent.*

Be economical. A treatment for a full-length screenplay runs 20–25 pages; for an hour's script, 12–15; for a half-hour story, 7–10. Such scripts are approximately 120, 60–70, and 30–35 pages, respectively. Do not write more than 5 pages for your 20-page script. Professionally, economy and clarity are prized: stay within these limits. Remember you are giving an immediate description of the actual story, but not yet writing that story fully.

Bear in mind that a writer and reader look for two essential things in a treatment: first, for a clear sense of the immediate development of the story and characters in a series of culminating actions rising to climax and resolution; second, for the meaning of the action. The immediate cause-and-effect level must exist or we cannot be involved in the story.

But if we are to accept the immediate choices your characters face and the decisions they make in response to the conflict, then you must satisfy our primal desire for truth. Do we understand what is ultimately at stake? Do we know what that means? Do we believe that a man or a woman can be the particular way your story shows? Do we believe a story can culminate in the manner you show? We are interested at first in passion, but ultimately in reason.

The Stepsheet

Many writers go directly from the treatment to their script. Others prefer to chart their action in more detail. Some use a note card for each scene and leave the linking shots or miniscenes to the actual script. We suggest you use a stepsheet initially. Organize your stepsheet scene by actual scene as you structure these in acts. If a major scene has multiple locations, indicate those. Be clear; be brief. Use the following form:

WHERE? Set the scene.

WHEN? Establish the time (DAY or NIGHT).

WHO? Name the characters involved.

WHAT? State what action takes place.
  What is the complication?
  What choices does the protagonist have?
  What decision does the protagonist make?
  What change occurs?

WHY? Give the motivation of the characters.

HOW? Describe how this scene motivates the next.

Here is a sample stepsheet for the climactic sequence excerpted from *On the Waterfront:*

1. WHERE? INT. Terry's room.

   WHEN? DAY. A moment after Edie and Terry have been on the roof arguing.

   WHO? Terry, and his girlfriend, Edie.

   WHAT? Edie wants Terry to leave: he remains silent. Then he picks up a cargo hook and declares, to her despair, that he is going down to the docks.

WHY? She is afraid for his life. Terry realizes he must earn his rights where he lives.

HOW? Terry goes down to the docks.

2. WHERE? EXT. Pier.

WHEN? DAY. A few minutes later.

WHO? Terry, Big Mac, dockworkers.

WHAT? Terry wants to be chosen to work, but is left standing alone. Sonny is sent to find someone other than Terry as the last man.

WHY? Terry wants his rights. Johnny Friendly has obviously told Big Mac not to give him work.

HOW? Terry stands and decides to act.

3. WHERE? INT. Johnny Friendly's office nearby on the pier.

WHEN? DAY. Later.

WHO? Johnny Friendly, Truck, Sonny, and Specs.

WHAT? They see Terry. Johnny wants him—after the scandal is off the front page.

4. WHERE? EXT. Pier.

WHEN? DAY. Later.

WHO? Terry, Big Mac, Sonny, Mutt, dockworkers.

WHAT? Mutt is revealed as the last man to be chosen by Big Mac. Terry must choose whether or not to accept that.

HOW? Terry decides to go to Johnny Friendly's office.

5. WHERE? INT. Johnny Friendly's office.

WHEN? DAY.

WHAT? Johnny Friendly's thugs want to shoot Terry as they see him approach. Friendly takes their guns away.

WHY? They have to stay within the law for the time being.

HOW? They decide to meet Terry.

6. WHERE? EXT. Pier by Johnny Friendly's office.

   WHEN? DAY. A few moments later.

   WHO? Terry and all the dockworkers, who follow him; Johnny
   Friendly and his thugs, who come out to meet Terry; Boss Stevedore, Father Barry, and Edie.

   WHAT? Terry challenges Johnny. They fight: Terry is beaten. Father Barry and Edie run to help him. Johnny Friendly exults in
   his victory and is thrown into the water by Pop. Edie and Father
   Barry try to get Terry up.

   WHY? To challenge Johnny Friendly and win Terry's rights.

   HOW? If Terry can get up, the dockworkers will follow him.

7. WHERE? EXT. Pier

   WHEN? DAY.

   WHO? Continuing from previous.

   WHAT? Terry staggers to his feet, up the ramp, and down the dock,
   now followed by the longshoremen, to work. Johnny Friendly
   futilely tries to stop them. The End.

A stepsheet, then, is simply a methodical way of laying out the required ingredients for every scene of your dramatic action. A particular
category can be left out if it is unnecessary: the length devoted to any
where-when-who-what-why-how sequence can vary. There is no particular length requirement for a stepsheet, but be brief.

Once you have finished your stepsheet begin your screenplay.

11. A Last Word

There is a tendency to think that filmmaking has no history before the motion picture camera made its appearance in 1895 and that screenwriters have no dramatic heritage or are in an artistic sense poor cousins to real dramatists. Arthur Knight begins his popular *The Liveliest Art:*

> For more than half a century, people all over the world have been going to the movies, drawn by the mysterious fascination of lifelike images appearing on a screen in a darkened room. . . . There is something so casual about seeing a film. Somehow it is too entertaining, too popular to be identified with the arts. And so it has taken root not because of its original masterpieces, but because its way of telling a story, of showing life, stirs both the heart and imagination of the viewer. . . . Through eighty years of trial and error, of box-office hits and box-office failures, the novelty of 1895 has been slowly transformed into the art of the 20th century.[1]

This is of course true in terms of the technology of the camera, but in terms of drama, completely false. Drama has had a very long history and many masterpieces; nonetheless, the stage's primary appeal to audiences has almost always been the same as that Knight indicates for movies. Movies only took over the broad appeal typical of the legitimate theatres of the day and brought such comedies and melodramas to ever-wider audiences through filmmaking's far greater ability to create an appearance of reality. But this flow and freedom of image and story offered by the camera simply brings drama far closer to the dreams always held by dramatists—Aeschylus would have delighted in cinematic resources. Bergman might have written Greek tragedies if he had lived in fifth-century Athens. Some theatres, like Shakespeare's, even emulated a cine-

---

1. Arthur Knight, *The Liveliest Art* (New York: New American Library, 1979), p. 1.

matic freedom of movement. The camera has not transformed the nature of drama so much as it has opened up powerful new dramatic media for its realization. Its essential structure and impact remain unchanged. That is why we have emphasized the screenwriter's heritage of a wealth of dramatic experiment and achievement going back to the Greeks.

But we don't think drama as movies has existed only since 1895, either. Twenty to thirty thousand years ago our ancestors in Europe gathered in caves having difficult access and covered the walls with brilliant evocative images of the animals around them. Those images are well known to us through reproductions; some caves became such tourist centers they had to be closed to avoid damage. You may wonder what the static animals on those undulating cave walls have to do with films. Here is how one cave expert describes a proper visit:

> Ideally one should spend an hour or two in complete darkness before looking at the paintings. Modern eyes are not accustomed to viewing things with just a little bit of light, so you must first prepare yourself, and get in the mood for what you are about to see. Then you can light your lamp, preferably the sort of lamp the artists used. . . .
> After you light your lamp, it takes a while for the experience to build up, perhaps as much as fifteen to thirty minutes, certainly much sooner for prehistoric people. The animals become animated in a flickering, yellow light which plays on the hollows and projections of the cave walls. Sometimes they seem to be moving deeper into the cave.[2]

No one knows what religious rites the caves were used for, but drama has twice grown out of religion's effort to bind us together by celebrating some mystery. Drama preserves that communal power, recreating through its presentation a transient flicker of community in the audience. Even older than that communal heritage is the cinematic flood of images that sweeps across our minds each night, not once, but several times, remembered or not. Film, the most commercial of the arts, is rooted in our inherent sense of the free-flow meaningfulness of images. The dramatist still holds us in our darkened rooms with a flicker of images disciplined through the conflict toward a central point of final cohesion and revelation. Then the lights go on, and we leave the auditorium with our friends and go out into the social night.

2. John E. Pfeiffer, *The Creative Explosion* (New York: Harper & Row, 1982), pp. 113–114.

Appendix: The Market

After This Book

You are ready to move on to more ambitious efforts if you've done the assignments suggested here and familiarized yourself with the essentials. Other texts may have additional scripts within them. A number of filmscripts have been published, also. You should read these. Above all, see films or watch the kind of television that interests you. There is no substitute for knowledge of the prevailing practice and taste. If you want to write for a particular television series you must be familiar with its format.

A great many films are adaptations from other media. Essentially, the information about dramatic structure would apply to an adaptation; however, you may care to sample a text on adaptation. Be sure to get permission from the copyright holder (usually the publisher) of the original work before you make an adaptation, or you will not be able to market your screenplay legally.

Making a Connection

Publications like *Variety*, the *Hollywood Reporter*, or *Writer's Digest* give the names of various production companies looking for writers or material, but you will need an agent to sell a particular script or idea.

Finding an agent poses problems. Most agencies are not interested in writers without credits, and most networks or studios won't buy from a writer without an agent. The Writers Guild of America periodically publishes a list of bonded literary agencies that subscribe to the Guild's Basic Agreement and indicates those agents willing to look at material from a novice writer. The Writers Guild will send that list to a nonmember. Each fall the Writers Guild publishes a market list of every television production open to submission by an agent. The list includes a précis of the plot lines for new series together with the kind of material they are looking for. The Writers Guild's address is Writers Guild of America West, 8955 Beverly Boulevard, Los Angeles, California 90048, or Writers Guild of America East, 22 West 48th Street, New York, New York 10036. You will eventually need to belong to the Writers Guild in order to work with most production companies. It is $300 to join plus quarterly dues of $10 or 1 percent of your gross income over $1,000.

The film industry is litigious. Production companies have to protect themselves against potential plagiarizers. They are happy to have agents weed out unsuitable material or inept writers because they are normally inundated with scripts from already established writers. If you don't live in New York or Los Angeles you will have additional trouble finding an agent or dealing with producers: a great deal of such contact has to be personal, and any script sold invariably goes through a revision process that demands your presence.

Whether you try to submit material in person or through the mail, be sure to protect it. Dramas for stage, screen, or television can be registered for copyright before publication by writing for the appropriate application form to Register of Copyrights, Library of Congress, Washington, D.C. 20540. You can register ideas, treatments, or formats with the Writers Guild for $10.

A beginner has to face the fact that his ideas and treatments are not going to arouse instant and profound interest. If your interest is in a particular television series, your best bet is to study several episodes carefully and send for any available guidelines from the production company. Ask through an agent or producer (a friend can work wonders) for permission to submit a brief statement of your idea for a story if the series is open for submissions. If your interest is in screenplays, submit a finished script in the same way. Send a premise with the script, but don't expect to succeed with a premise alone. An established writer can begin the process with an idea or premise because a producer knows his credits. Exceptions always occur to these rules, but that's what they are— exceptions!

Once you are functioning within the industry, you can then arrange to have your agent set up meetings for you with various companies interested in buying material or can facilitate such meetings through your own contacts. Your agent may submit material for you. In either case, you will present, often verbally, several potential projects. If any of these interest a prospective buyer, you leave a premise or idea behind. If a sale is then made, a very specific sequence takes you through writing a treatment, first draft, and then a revised final draft of a script. What you submit as a first draft may really be your fifth. The same is true of your final draft, which may well be preceded by many earlier versions. Most contracts have a clause reserving the right to cut you off at any point in the process if your story doesn't develop as expected. Story editors, directors, producers, actors in a production, and other writers are likely to rewrite your script to varying degrees. The Writers Guild regulates these practices and makes sure you get appropriate credit and remuneration according to a negotiated schedule of fees.

Why There Is So Much Weak Writing

You are probably aware of the great number of television shows that fail each year and of the poor quality of many others. Many movies must have made you think afterward, "I could do better than that!" Many may have held you immediately, but left you with a feeling of being had later. Each season is full of technically and directorially excellent films that are dramatically inane.

There are many reasons for this. It is not a problem unique to movies alone: many a best-selling novel has left a reader with the same perception of technically adept inanity, too. Not all writers are good. Some discover particular markets that pay and then write for them regardless of quality. It is not a perfect world.

But there are institutional problems that face the screenwriter and go some distance in explaining the poor quality of much screenwriting. You cannot work in film or television with any assurance that the final script produced will represent your best craft and your vision. Almost invariably it will be rewritten, often extensively. Your interest is protected financially by the Writers Guild, and this "team" effort is taken for granted within approved guidelines. All through this text we have stressed the unity of craft and vision, however, and emphasized again and again that both are inherent and central in drama and are offspring of one particular dramatist. But there is no way such unity can survive a team effort: the vision becomes a blur of visions or is lost altogether in an artificial reworking of the conflict without attention to its inherent inner values. The result is usually the poor quality that we see.

On the other hand, if you write for the legitimate stage you will not make as much as a screenwriter, but you will retain sole legal responsibility for your play, thanks to the Basic Agreements of the Dramatists Guild in New York. The moral of this difference is that the stage continues to produce outstanding playwrights, and most in our century who have written for the legitimate stage, not movies, have done so to avoid compromising their work. Many of the most prominent screenwriters are drawn from the stage; for example, the three outstanding English screenwriters, Robert Bolt, Peter Schaffer, and Harold Pinter, either began as playwrights for the stage or continue to consider that their primary interest. This will go on until the Writers Guild matures into a fully responsible guild for writers. That won't happen until its writers pay themselves enough respect to demand proper control over their creations. Artistic control and professional competence simply are not commercially separable unless all that is desired is a well-paid mediocrity.

Sometimes particular writers are in vogue and are able to have their scripts filmed with a minimum of meddling. We have a way of remembering those films—their vision hasn't been blurred nor the point of their craft been lost. This is as true of a script like Robert Towne's *Shampoo* as it is of Robert Benton's *Kramer vs. Kramer.* It is true of Bergman's films and films by a number of other prominent European and American directors. Many films attain a high quality of craft and storytelling because their director is also their writer. Director-writers tend to be the equivalent in film of the legitimate stage's playwright, because both exercise similar control over their scripts.

We don't intend to discourage you, but it would be wrong to leave a prospective screenwriter unacquainted with the actual working conditions. It is not impossible to have a script go to production without others' meddling. It is possible to develop into an industry "hyphenate" and control directing and writing, or producing and directing, or some other combination of talents. And it is true that many producers place a premium on high-quality writing. If you want to go on, good! Do it realistically, in hope, with your eyes open.

Glossary of Film Terms

ACTION—1. The development of conflict in a scene and screenplay; 2. the function of movement that takes place in the camera's view; 3. the emotional content of a line reading, usually found in parentheses under the character's name.

ANIMATION—The movement of inanimate objects, such as cutouts or puppets, photographed one frame at a time in order to create the impression of action; also used to describe action that is drawn by an artist instead of live.

ANSWER PRINT—The first print of a finished film that combines audio, sound effects, optical effects, and music in a form that is ready to be released.

ART DIRECTOR—The set designer; frequently relied on for choosing locations.

AUDIO—The sound portion of a motion picture.

BACKGROUND (BG)—Sound or properties that are distant from the camera in any given shot.

BACK LIGHT—A light thrown from the rear of the set to give an impression of depth.

BACK LOT—Exterior portion of a studio that contains streets and the façades of buildings commonly used in motion pictures.

BEAT—A significant pause; a momentary increment of time.

BLIMP—Housing in which a camera is placed to muffle the sound of its motor.

BLOWUP—An enlarged film image produced by a laboratory optical process.

BOOM—A mount used to project a microphone or camera over a set. *See also* DOLLY.

BUSINESS—Description of the movements of the actors in a scene; usually contained in paragraphs written below shots.

CAPER—An adventure film in which characters plot to achieve a goal, as in planning a robbery.

CLOSE SHOT (CS)—This is not to be confused with a close-up. It is a close angle of two or more elements close to the viewer.

CLOSE-UP (CU)—This shot focuses clearly on a single object in a scene, either a person or an object. *See also* EXTREME CLOSE-UP.

COMPOSITE—A single piece of film with corresponding sound and images.

COMPOSITION—The balance of the artistic elements of a picture.

CONFRONTATION—A moment of conflict in which one force or character tries to reach an immediate goal and the opposing force or character poses an obstacle to it.

CONTINUITY—A comprehensive description of the complete action, scenes, dialogue, and other screenplay elements in the order in which they are to be shown on the screen.

CONTRAST—Creating a comparison of explicit difference in lighting objects or areas for dramatic effect.

CRANE—A type of camera boom.

CREDIT—Any title that acknowledges the contribution of a person to a film.

CURTAIN LINE—The closing speech in an act.

CUT—An instantaneous transition from one shot to the next by splicing the two shots to each other.

CUTAWAY—A form of continuity cutting most discernible in a point of view shot: for example, a character opens a desk drawer and looks in; the following shot shows a gun in the drawer.

CUTBACK—The shot that follows the cutaway.

CUTTER—*See* EDITOR.

CUTTING—An edited film version of a script designed to maintain a continuous flow of action.

CYCLORAMA—A semicircular backdrop behind a set.

DAY FOR NIGHT—Shooting exterior shots in the daytime with a filter to achieve the appearance of night; when a nighttime shot is actually shot at night, it is called "night for night."

DENOUEMENT—Another word for the resolution of the plot.

DEUS EX MACHINA—A contrived device used to resolve a problem; a condition that arises when a writer tries to play God and bring something to pass in the play that defies all logic or naturalness and for which the audience has not been prepared.

DISSOLVE—An optical effect of bringing a picture in while collaterally fading the previous picture out.

DOLLY—A wheeled mount upon which a camera is placed for ensuring the smooth movement of the camera within the area of the shot. *See also* BOOM.

DOLLYING—The movement of the camera on its dolly toward or away from its subject.

DOWN—Reducing the volume of sound (decibel level).

DUB—The application of sounds to the film that were not recorded at the same time the film was shot.

EDITOR—The individual who brings together all the film that has been shot into one composition by selecting, arranging, cutting, and splicing and whose aim is to make the best picture.

EFFECTS—1. Sound effects: separately recorded sounds applied to the film as needed; 2. special effects: visual effects created in the laboratory through animation or other processes.

ESTABLISH (EST)—Shot made to communicate the total atmosphere of a scene or sequence; usually indicated when the settings are complex and contain a number of points of interest.

EXPOSITION—*See* Chapter 6.

EXTREME CLOSE-UP (ECU)—This is simply a tighter close-up in which a specific object or feature, such as the eyes or mouth of an individual or a ring on someone's finger, is the subject.

FADE—An optical effect in which the light dims: FADE OUT is dimming to complete darkness; FADE IN goes from a blank screen to a full picture.

FAVORING—Selects the character to be favored in the shot.

FLASHBACK—A shot or sequence that reveals something that occurred in the past.

FOCUS—Achieving sharpness or fuzziness of an image.

FOLLOW—A shot in which the camera follows an individual or specific action as requested.

FOREGROUND (FG)—Voices or properties that appear nearest the camera in a given shot.

FRAME—To arrange the composition of a single picture on a strip of motion picture film; a *frame* is a single picture.

FREEZE FRAME—To hold one image on a strip of motion picture film by repeating the single frame.

FULL SHOT—This angle is taken at a considerable distance and is used to establish the entire scene for the purpose of orientation.

GAFFER—The chief electrician, whose job is to light the sets as the first cameraman designates.

GAG—A stunt set up by professional stuntmen.

GIMMICK—A device that is uniquely employed to help solve a problem situation.

GRIP—A stagehand who moves and repairs the properties that are used in the shooting of a picture.

GROUP SHOT—A shot that includes four or more characters in the action.

HAND HELD—An effect in which the camera is physically held and moved by the cameraman; the resulting jerky motion, similar to that in newsreel footage, is often used to create an on-the-spot sense of reality.

HEAD-ON SHOT—Straight into the camera.

HIGH ANGLE—When the camera shoots down from above the subject.

HIGH-KEY LIGHTING—When the main light isolates an area that is contrasted sharply and brilliantly with the rest of the set.

HOOK—An incident in the opening of a picture that is used to capture audience attention.

INKY-DINK—A small incandescent lamp that is used to spotlight something.

INSERT—A shot, usually close, of an item, done separately and later inserted into the picture.

JEOPARDY—When the complexion of circumstances is threatening to a character.

JUMP CUT—An effect of jerkiness achieved when a film is spliced so as to leave a gap in what should be continuous movement; sometimes it is the result of negligence or, sometimes, by design because of too little film; it generally occurs when there is a cut in the film that interrupts the action without a corresponding change of camera angle.

KEY LIGHT—The main source of light in a shot.

LAP DISSOLVE—A laboratory process in which one shot fades out as the next fades in.

LEAD—The protagonist or central character.

LIGHTING SETUP—The gaffer's layout or plan to supply all the necessary setups of shots with the needed light; a major shooting expense.

LIMBO—A shot that has no physical connection with a set or appears to be in space.

LIP SYNC—Dialogue synchronization in which an actor, separately from the shooting of the film, utters the speech by matching it to the filmed lip movements; usually required when the original scene was shot under conditions that made the audio unusable and the lip sync sound is subsequently dubbed in.

LOCATION—A real exterior or interior setting rather than a staged set or the back lot; off the studio lot.

LONG SHOT (LS)—This angle differs from a full shot: though taken from the same long distance of the viewer from the subject, the LS shows only the portion of the scene that the audience is specifically meant to see.

LOOP—A strip of film that is so spliced it can be projected continuously; a loop is frequently used in dubbing (looping) sessions in which actors may be required to repeat their lines over and over in order to lip sync them properly.

LOW ANGLE—When the camera shoots up from below.

MACRO SHOT—An extreme close-up that outlines a small, critical detail in the action.

MAIN TITLE—The listing at the opening of a picture that includes the title and the main contributors to the production.

MATCHING—The necessity that all the elements of a scene remain constant from shot to shot: for example, if an actor is wearing a tie in one shot, it must be there in the next unless we see him remove it; customarily the duty of the script supervisor.

MATCHING SHOT—A transition in which a shot is dissolved to a successive shot that has the same character of composition (e.g., a shot of a running faucet dissolves to a shot of a waterfall).

MATTE—1. A shot in which a background is painted in; 2. the term *mask* is also used when an optical printer is used to simulate the kind of view that is effected, such as through a keyhole or binoculars.

MEDIUM SHOT (MS or MED. SHOT)—This angle is neither long nor close; a middle distance from the subject.

MINIATURE—A small-scale rendition of the physical elements that would normally be involved in an actual happening; a cost-saving device prepared by those in charge of special effects.

MISE-EN-SCÈNE—The surroundings or environment of a stage setting.

MIX—Rerecording on one track a balanced combination of the three separate tracks of voices, effects, and music and giving each the desired level of volume.

MIXER—A person who mixes sound.

MONTAGE—A juxtaposition of abbreviated shots, optical effects, or both that produce an effect, such as a sense of the passage of time, the distorted mind of a drug addict, etc.

M.O.S.—"Mit out sound": the actual utterance of a well-known German cinematographer that took root; silent shots or sequences (filmed without synchronized sound).

MOVIEOLA—A machine used by editors for viewing the picture with sound; can be run forward or backward by foot pressure (*Movieola* is a brand name).

MUSIC TRACK—A track on which music alone is recorded.

OBLIGATORY SCENE—A confrontation at some point in the play—in many cases, the climax—which has been promised or indicated as a necessary conclusion to the earlier behavior of the parties involved.

OFF SCREEN (O.S.)—The designation for any element or character present in the action but visually excluded by the camera angle.

OVERHEAD SHOT—Looking down at a subject, for instance, at a pool table.

OVER THE SHOULDER—Shooting from behind one person over his shoulder to see the face of another when two characters face one another.

PAN—The movement of the camera, on a pivot, from side to side on a horizontal plane.

PAYOFF—An inevitable result for which the audience has been prepared.

POINT OF VIEW (POV)—A shot in which the camera becomes the eyes of a particular character, seeing what the character sees.

PROCESS—A shot in which the foreground (FG) action is played on a stage while the background (BG) action is rear-projected on a translucent screen from behind.

PROPERTIES (PROPS)—The decorations and furnishings on a set.

REVERSE ANGLE—An angle the opposite of the one that precedes it.

RUSHES—The uncut film, as it was shot, which is printed for viewing by the filmmakers; also called "the dailies" because the film is usually viewed the day after it was shot; the object is to check for errors before the set is taken down.

SCENARIO—The general outline or form of a script; rarely used in TV or film today.

SECOND UNIT—A minimal camera crew that photographs parts of a film that do not require the use of the main cast; usually a cost-saving device.

SEGUE—The transition from one sound or scene to another (pronounced sā'gwā).

SEQUENCE—A series of related shots that together constitute a dramatic step in the development of the plot.

SETUP—A new setup occurs any time the camera angle changes.

SHOOTING SCHEDULE—The day-out-of-days assignment board constructed by the production manager for the sequential shooting of the screenplay or teleplay.

SHOOTING SCRIPT—The final script used for principal photography and commonly considered to be the production blueprint.

SMASH CUT—An abrupt cut in the action from one critical moment to the next used by a screenwriter to communicate a sense of pressure or urgency to an editor or reader.

SOUND STAGE—The area of a building in which sound film is shot.

SPINE—The backbone of a play, the basic plot.

SPLICE—Sealing two pieces of film together.

SPLIT SCREEN—The effect of wiping half the picture off the screen and replacing that half with another picture.

STOCK SHOT—Footage that is general in nature and may be used to supply mood, atmosphere, or details of imagery; collected and stored in libraries, such film may be rented for a fee in order to avoid the necessity of shooting it.

STORY ANALYST—A specialist who synopsizes, analyzes, criticizes, and assesses the value of teleplays and screenplays.

STORYBOARD—A series of sketches of key incidents in a film's proposed action that is arranged on a board with captions to indicate the visual development.

STORYLINE—The play's story development.

STRUCTURE—The organized blocks of dramatic action of a plot.

SUBPLOT—A separate story involving collateral characters that is parallel to the main plot; although it progresses with the story, one could as easily dispense with it and still have the full story.

SUPERIMPOSE (SUPER)—A laboratory process in which one image on film is printed on another.

SWISH PAN—A panning shot that is so rapid it creates a blurred effect; usually used for transitions from one shot to the next.

SYNCHRONIZATION (SYNC)—Matching the audio to the video so that dialogue or sounds occur at the same moment as their visual counterparts.

TAG LINE—The closing speech in a scene.

TAKE—A filming of a shot, from the time the camera rolls (begins filming) until it stops.

THREE SHOT—A camera angle including three characters in the action.

TILT (UP or DOWN)—The movement of the camera up or down on its axis vertically.

TRANSITION—Any effect—music, sound, or optical—that links the sequential elements of a film.

TRUCKING SHOT—Moving the camera on its dolly to follow the action on a lateral plane.

TWO SHOT—A camera angle including two characters in the action.

UP—Increase of volume of sound.

VIDEO—The video portion of a motion picture.

VIEWER—An enlarging unit by which film can be more closely examined.

VOICE OVER (VO)—When the one who is speaking is not on the screen (not seen).

WIDE SHOT—A "wide-angle" shot including the maximum of scenery or action for scenic or dramatic impact.

WILD SHOT—Similar to a stock shot, but photographed by the film's own production unit.

WILD SOUND—Sound recorded nonsynchronously with the picture (e.g., sound effects or random voices).

WIPE—An optical effect with two succeeding shots by which the second wipes the first off the screen.

WORK PRINT—A print of the picture used for cutting and editing so that the original negative is not marred in the process of making corrections.

WRAP—The end of a day's shooting.

ZOOMAR—A lens that achieves the effect of moving toward (ZOOM IN) or away (ZOOM OUT) from a subject without the camera physically moving.

Note: The Glossary was revised and expanded from Brady, *The Keys to Writing for Television and Film,* pp. 291–294.

Index